On Foot
Through Europe
A TRAIL GUIDE TO
AUSTRIA, SWITZERLAND &
LIECHTENSTEIN

Here's What Europe's Walking Organizations Say About this Book

"The most complete reference for the hiker in Germany." —LUDWIG LENZ, 3rd Direktor, Deutscher Alpenverein (German Alpine Club), Munich.

"Extraordinarily comprehensive." —JOHN NEWNHAM, assistant secretary, The Ramblers' Association, London.

"Excellent. Many more or less experienced alpinists could learn quite a lot on how to prepare a tour and on what to do in cases of emergency."—LUCETTE DUVOISIN, general secretary, Schweizerische Arbeitsgemeinschaft für Wanderwege (Swiss Footpath Protection Association), Basel.

"A very comprehensive and most valuable book." —DR. SONJA JORDAN, Österreichische Fremdenverkehrswerbung (Austrian National Tourist Office), Vienna.

"I was very impressed. This book will be of great value to all hikers who want to go to other countries." —FINN HAGEN, Den Norske Turistforening (Norwegian Mountain Touring Association), Oslo.

"By far and away, the chapter from ON FOOT— 'Trail Emergencies' —is excellent. Your information is timely and accurate, and the writing is explicit." —LOUIS A. PEREZ, M.D., chief, Section of Nuclear Medicine, Norwalk Hospital, Norwalk, Connecticut.

"You've done a helluva good job assembling and organizing a truly awesome amount of data. You seem to have thought of every contingency—and then some—so the prospective walker will be able to plan his vacation well in advance of departure. . . . This guide should become something of a classic in its field—a backpacker's Baedeker." —STEPHEN R. WHITNEY, former managing editor, Sierra Club Books, and author of *A Sierra Club Naturalist's Guide: The Sierra Nevada.*

"Your work is very complete and accurate (something we find seldom, even in our own country)." —FREDDY TUERLINCKX, general secretary, Grote Routepaden (Long-Distance Footpath Association), Antwerp.

"I am really impressed with the enormous work that you have been able to do in a short time—and by the amount of knowledge and experience that you show!" —INGEMUND HÄGG, Svenska turistföreningen (Swedish Touring Club), Stockholm.

"A Bible of European hiking opportunities." —EDWARD B. GARVEY, member of the Appalachian Trail Council Board of Managers and author of *Appalachian Hiker: Adventure of a Lifetime.*

On Foot Through Europe

A TRAIL GUIDE TO AUSTRIA, SWITZERLAND & LIECHTENSTEIN

by Craig Evans

Walking, Backpacking, Ski Touring,
Climbing—Everything You Can Do On Foot

QUILL
New York   1982

Library of Congress Catalog Card Number: 82-600

ISBN: 0-688-01159-4 (pbk)

Printed in the United States of America

First Quill Edition

1 2 3 4 5 6 7 8 9 10

Behind the Scenes

M ANY PEOPLE HAVE contributed to this book—people in tourist offices, weather bureaus, forestry services, sport shops, guide offices and tour organizations. In addition, the members of the ski clubs, alpine clubs and walking organizations in Austria, Switzerland and Liechtenstein have been especially helpful. Without the assistance of these people—and the time and effort they devoted to answering questions, researching information and reviewing the final manuscript—this book would not have been possible.

To all who helped prepare the manuscript—typists, translators, proofreaders, friends—I also owe my sincere gratitude.

And to those who helped the most, a special thanks:

For reviewing the entire manuscript, helping offset my American bias and providing otherwise hard-to-get information:

Arthur Howcroft, president of the European Ramblers' Association's Walking Committee and a tour leader for England's Country-Wide Holidays Assocation.

Ingemund Hägg, secretary of the European Ramblers' Assocation's Walking Committee, consultant to the Svenska turistföringen (Swedish Touring Club) and author of *Walking in Europe,* a 40-page booklet on where to get information to go walking in 25 countries, published in English by the Swedish touring Club, 1978 (a handy booklet, incidentally, that is well worth owning).

For providing information on walking and ski touring in their areas, and for reviewing the accuracy of the chapters on their countries:

AUSTRIA

Dr. Sonja Jordan, responsible for checking foreign-language guidebooks, Österreichische Fremdenverkehrswerbung (Austrian National Tourist Office), Vienna.

Günter Auferbauer, director of the Österreichischer Alpenverein—Sektion Graz (Austrian Alpine Club section in Graz).

Sieghard Baier and *Helmut Herbert,* of the Landesfremdenverkehrsverband Vorarlberg, Bregenz.

Franz Groissböck, Wegreferent for the Österreichischer Alpenverein—Sektionenverband Niederösterreich, St. Pölten.

Hansjörg Köchler, director of the Österreichischer Alpenverein Bergsteigerschule (Austrian Alpine Club Climbing School), Innsbruck.

Wolfgang Nair, Österreichischer Alpenverein, Innsbruck.

Dr. Klaus Listner, director of the Österreichischer Skiverband, Innsbruck.

Helmut Reisch, information officer of the Osterreichische Fremdenverkehrswerbung, Vienna.

Adolf Wieser, of the Pinzgauer Saalachtal, Saalfelden.

Dr. Robert Wurst, Sonderbeauftragter für Weitwanderwege, Österreichischen Alpenverein (minister with special responsibilities for Austria's long-distance footpaths), Perchtoldsdorf bei Wien.

Dr. Ingo Zlamal, director of the Landesfremdenverkehrsamt Kärnten, Klagenfurt.

LIECHTENSTEIN

Xaver Frick, president, Liechtensteiner Alpenverein, Balzers.

Berthold Konrad, director, Liechtensteinische Fremdenverkehrszentrale (Liechtenstein National Tourist Office), Vaduz.

SWITZERLAND

Fred Birmann, a public relations director, Schweizerische Verkehrszentral (Swiss National Tourist Office), Zürich.

Lucette Duvoisin, general secretary, Schweizerische Arbeitsgemeinschaft für Wanderwege (Swiss Ramblers' Association), Riehen.

Martin Gurtner, Eidgenössische Landestopographie (Topographical Survey of Switzerland), Wabern.

Numa Perrier, administrative secretary, Schweizer Alpen-Club (Swiss Alpine Club), Bern.

Edi Thomann, head mountain guide, Schweizer Alpen-Club, Spiez.

Bernard Truffer, president, Schweizerische Bergführerverband (Mountain Guides Association of Switzerland), Sion.

There was also the enormous dedication of the people who made the trail guide series come to physical reality. The basic team was: Ed Meehan who drew the maps, Brian Sheridan who did the illustrations, Vincent Torre who designed the cover and Elisabeth Kofler Shuman, my research and editorial assistant.

There was also Stephen R. Whitney, my editor, whose involvement in this book escalated far beyond that of simply an editor, and whose commitment to its completion became much more than he—or his wife—ever bargained for. As deadlines approached and the size of each chapter swelled, he evolved from copy editor and devil's advocate to co-author, writing first short sections of unfinished chapters from my notes, then whole chapters. And I, in turn became his rewriter and editor. Together, we were able to complete seven books, ensure their accuracy and oversee every detail of their production, a job I could never have accomplished alone and still have met the final deadline.

In this book, he co-authored the chapters on Switzerland and Liechtenstein.

Finally, there was William Kemsley, Jr., president of Foot Trails Publications, Inc., whose own passion for detail sustained his unfaltering belief in this trail guide series through all of its growing pains, despite the advice of his accountants. Few publishers would have put up with so much when lesser books could have been produced more economically. Yet he rarely asked that compromises be made. He only asked that it be done. And done well.

Thank you, each of you. You've been great friends.

Craig Evans
Washington, D.C., 1981

How to Use this Book

THIS BOOK IS PACKED with information. It describes every aspect of walking, backpacking, climbing and ski touring in Austria, Switzerand and Liechtenstein: all the places you can go, the maps and guidebooks you need, where you can get information on trail lodgings and camping, the weather conditions you can expect and the telephone numbers to call for weather forecasts. There's even a list of special train and bus fares that can save you money in each country. And more: the clothing and equipment you will need, walking tours and mountaineering courses you might like to take advantage of, what you should know about property rights, even some tidbits of history and folklore.

There are also hundreds of addresses—places you can write for maps and guidebooks, obtain train and bus schedule information and get specific answers to questions on walking, ski touring and traveling in particular areas. And you get a lot more than just an address. Everything is spelled out: the information and services available, the languages in which inquiries can be made and, if useful publications are available, what their titles are and what information they contain.

The result is a complete sourcebook to all the information available on walking, backpacking, ski touring and climbing in Austria, Switzerland and Liechtenstein.

This book has been designed to make finding the specific information you need as easy as possible. The table of contents lists the major divisions in each chapter, plus some minor divisions, so you can turn right to the page where, say, the services provided by the walking organizations or the emergency telephone numbers for search and rescue are given. The name of each organization has been set off from the rest of the text by means of a darker type face and additional spacing so it can be found easily—again and again. And all the addresses and telephone numbers are listed in an alphabetical *Address Directory* at the back of each chapter so you only have on place to look when you need to use one. There is even a section entitled *A Quick Reference* at the end of the chapters on each country, which gives you the page numbers where the most important information is located on walking in that country.

Another help: this book was bound so you can remove pages—and thus save lugging the entire book along—when you just want one chapter on the trail for easy reference. To remove pages: 1) open the book to the first page you wish to remove; 2) bend the book open as far as it will go; 3) turn to the end of the section you wish to remove; 4) again, bend the book open as far as it will go; 5) with one hand, hold down the pages on either side of the section you wish to remove; 6) with the thumb and index finger of the other hand, grasp the top part of the section at the point where it attaches to the spine, and 7) slowly pull the section away from the spine. The pages should come out in a complete section, with all the pages attached to one another.

When you wish to return a chapter you have removed to the book, simply slip it back into the space where it belongs. Then put a rubber band around the book so the loose sections don't fall out.

Finally, one last note: every attempt has been made to ensure the information in this book is both complete and accurate. Nonetheless, those who worked on the book—myself, the reviewers in each country, copy editors and typesetters—are not perfect. An occasional mistake might have slipped past. Two numerals in a telephone number might have been transposed and never caught. A name may have been misspelled or a valuable guidebook overlooked. If so, it was not intentional.

There are the inevitable changes to consider, too. All addresses, telephone numbers and prices were verified prior to publication. But people and organizations move, telephone numbers change and prices go up. Hence, I cannot accept responsibility or liability for any inaccuracies or omissions.

Prices, of course, change constantly. *Those quoted are meant only as guides.* For each year after 1981, expect a yearly increase of *at least 15 percent.* Maybe more.

This book describes the opportunities in the many different regions of Austria, Switzerland & Liechtenstein. Six other books cover the rest of Europe:

- *On Foot Through Europe: A Trail Guide to West Germany*
- *On Foot Through Europe: A Trail Guide to the British Isles*
- *On Foot Through Europe: A Trail Guide to Scandinavia*
- *On Foot Through Europe: A Trail Guide to Spain & Portugal*
- *On Foot Through Europe: A Trail Guide to France & the Benelux Nations*

Use this or any of the area guides in conjunction with *On Foot Through Europe: A Trail Guide to Europe's Long-Distance Footpaths,* which gives you an overview of walking in Europe and tips on how to plan your hikes. All the background information available—and the places where you can get it—is here. It includes how to get information by mail, how to get to and stay along the trails, how to follow the paths safely, what to do in an emergency, and what equipment to bring, and many other facts to get you started hiking through Europe.

I welcome your comments. If you find an address or telephone number has changed, or you think some additional information should have been included in the book and was not, please let me know. Write to me at: Foot Trails Publications, Inc., Bedford Road, Greenwich, Connecticut 06830, U.S.A.

Contents

Where & How to Go Hiking
in Austria, Switzerland & Liechtenstein

Where & How
to Go Hiking in
Austria & Switzerland

Difficulty:
What the Footpath Gradings Mean

The footpaths described in this book have been graded according to their difficulty. These gradings are based upon the *Schwierigkeitsgrade*—or difficulty gradings—developed for walkers in Austria. They are:

Easy (Schwierigkeitsgrad A & B). A path across either level or gently undulating terrain. Differences in altitude are small—less than 250 meters. The path requires minimal effort. It can be walked in any weather. Suitable for families with young children.

Easy to Moderately Difficult (Schwierigkeitsgrad C). A path across hilly terrain or mountains of medium height (up to 1,800 meters in altitude). The path presents few complications: climbs and descents are rarely steep, altitude differences are less than 600 meters and route finding is generally not difficult. Except in extremely bad weather, the path can be walked without great effort.

Moderately Difficult (Schwierigkeitsgrad D). A path with regular climbs and descents. Sections of the path may cross steep, rocky or marshy terrain. Some sections may also be above treeline or partially obstructed with undergrowth. The path generally can be walked without difficulty in good weather—providing you are physically fit, have the proper equipment and know how to use a map and compass. In bad weather use caution. Check with local authorities before you set out to be sure you are aware of any peculiarities in the local weather and path conditions.

Difficult (Schwierigkeitsgrad E). A strenuous route across rough terrain. Climbs and descents are steep and difficult. Precipices, swiftly flowing streams, thick undergrowth or snowfields may be encountered. In some places use of a map and compass may be essential to follow the route. On particularly exposed or dangerous sections safety devices—such as fixed cables and ladders—may be installed along the path. No climbing skills nor climbing equipment are required. Sections of some routes, however, will require that you are sure footed and are not subject to acrophobia. Novices and families with young children should not attempt such a route. In bad weather, *all* walkers should avoid it.

For Experienced Mountain Walkers Only (Schwierigkeitsgrad F). An extremely difficult route—across glaciers, on routes with exposed or dangerous sections (and no fixed cables or other safety devices), or cross-country through rough terrain where accurate route-finding with a map and compass is essential. Climbs and descents are steep and treacherous and may require rock climbing (up to Class II). Stream crossings are tricky and may require use of a rope. Severe, quick-changing weather conditions also may be encountered. To follow this route mountaineering experience is imperative, as is specialized equipment—crampons, ice axe or rope—and knowledge of its use.

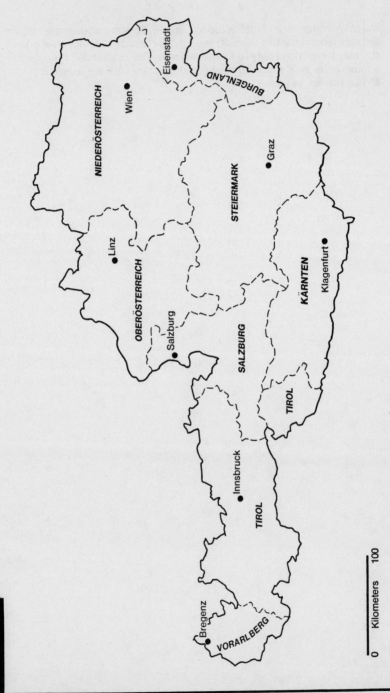

AUSTRIA

NIEDERÖSTERREICH

Wien ●

Eisenstadt ●

BURGENLAND

STEIERMARK

Graz ●

Linz ●

OBERÖSTERREICH

Salzburg ●

KÄRNTEN

Klagenfurt ●

SALZBURG

TIROL

Innsbruck ●

TIROL

Bregenz ●

VORARLBERG

0   Kilometers   100

Austria

FOR MOUNTAIN WALKING, few countries excel Austria.

From Austria's border with Switzerland, the Alps stretch east for more than 450 kilometers (280 miles). Altogether, the alpine peaks and foothills cover 70 percent of the country—nearly 58,000 square kilometers. No other country encompasses as much of the Alps. And only one—Switzerland—has as many kilometers of mountain paths.

Of Austria's trails, 40,000 kilometers are marked by the Öster-reichischer Alpenverein (Austrian Alpine Club). More than half of these trails cross hanging valleys and vast mountain-ringed amphitheaters carved out of the rock by Pleistocene glaciers, zigzag across alpine pastures bursting with wildflowers and follow knife-edge ridges that plunge precipitously into deep green valleys dotted with villages. Occasionally, cables are bolted into the rock on steep sections of a trail as insurance against a fall. Trails generally are not difficult, although they aren't terribly easy either. It is helpful if you are sure-footed and not prone to acrophobia, the fear of heights. The steep terrain also makes physical fitness a necessary prerequisite. A few trails, such as some of the *Höhenwege*—the high alpine routes—require mountaineering experience and the use of crampons, an ice axe and, occasionally, a rope. But unless you are an experienced mountaineer you should not attempt these routes without a guide (and then he will provide most of the specialized equipment). Valley paths, on the other hand, are usually gentle, winding through fields strewn with haystacks, alongside streams and past ancient castles perched on promontories above the valleys.

In addition, Austria has numerous woodland paths, which wind in and out of the rolling foothills of the Alps, pass through forests and meander up broad river valleys dotted with thatched cottages, forests and farms.

Ten long-distance footpaths are also being established across Austria. Of these, eight have already been completed. Sections of the other two are now being marked. When finished—early in the 1980s—four of these *Weitwanderwege* will traverse the country from east to west, and six will go from north to south. Their combined distance is more than 9,000 kilometers.

Overnight accommodation can be found in more than 700 mountain huts. And even in the most remote regions of the Alps, you are rarely more than a two-day walk from the nearest village, where you can find food and

5

lodging—or hear a brass band marching up the street playing polkas and marches.

For cross-country skiers, there are more than 7,000 kilometers of marked ski touring tracks. And for climbers, more than 300 peaks in excess of 3,000 meters (9,865 feet).

Austria also includes the 400-meter (1,283-foot)-high Krimml Waterfalls—the highest in Europe—and the 42-kilometer (26-mile)-long Eisriesenwelt, the world's largest ice cave. Both are located in the province of Salzburg.

The best-known walking areas in Austria are the western provinces of Vorarlberg, Tirol (Tyrol) and Salzburg. Here, the Northern Limestone Alps rise to sharp summits above dark green forests and rocky mountain basins, and waterfalls plunge in white plumes down the gray limestone cliffs. Three major river valleys—the Inn, Salzach and Enns—cut from east to west across the provinces, separating the Northern Limestone Alps from the Central Alps, a formidable barrier composed mostly of granitic rocks. This range is made up of a succession of ridges capped with glaciers and includes the highest peaks in Austria, topped by the 3,797-meter (12,485-foot)-high Grossglockner. For more than 240 kilometers (150 miles), the line of crests hardly drops below 2,000 meters, and is only rarely broken by a pass.

Next in popularity is the province of Kärnten (Carinthia), to the south of the Central Alps, with its dry, sunny climate, warm lakes and the peaks of the Southern Limestone Alps, which form Austria's southern border with Italy and Yugoslavia.

Less well-known—and hence, less crowded—are the mountains of Steiermark (Styria), with their flower-strewn pastures and orchards, Renaissance cities and network of paths, which pass below numerous peaks in excess of 2,100 meters (7,000 feet).

For gentle walks, there is the rolling countryside of the Danube Plateau, which stretches across the provinces of Oberösterreich (Upper Austria) and Niederösterreich (Lower Austria). Or, you can stroll across the narrow plain of Burgenland, the only flat region of Austria.

Trails are inconspicuously but adequately marked by occasional multi-colored paint stripes on rocks and trees, except in meadows, where metal stakes are sometimes driven into the ground along the path to mark its route. Color of the markings varies according to the path. Some paths are marked with blue, green or yellow paint, but most are indicated by red-white-red diagonal bars, which are usually numbered according to the mountain group in which the path is located. Path number 411, for instance, is located in the Berchtesgadener Alpen, while path number 511 is located in the Zillertaler Alpen, and path number 711 is in the Glocknergruppe. This number is written on the trail markings as well as on many hiking maps.

Despite the good markings, the paths are not always clear-cut where they cross scree and talus, meadows or areas thick with undergrowth. Bad weather can also make even the most conscientiously marked path difficult to follow. For this reason, it is necessary to always carry the appropriate maps and guidebooks on the trail with you.

Before you begin a walk, you should also check with local residents, who can give you valuable advice on the routes you intend to follow. And when hiking alone, always be sure to inform someone of your next destination.

Flora & Fauna

Because of its highly varied topography Austria has a rich variety of plant and animal life. Virtually every species of alpine plant can be found in the country. Above timberline alone, more than two-thirds of Europe's mammals—about 260 species—are found in Austria, among them the chamois, roe deer, stag, moufflon, wild boar, marmot, fox and weasel. Birds include the golden eagle, heron, griffon vulture, falcon, heathcock, capercaillie, partridge, and—in Burgenland—the stork. There are also more than 20,000 species of insects. Fortunately, those pesky to humans are not common. Poisonous snakes are also rare, but there are a few adders and vipers. These are dangerous and medical assistance should be sought immediately if you are bitten.

Although 44 percent of Austria is forested, the general impression of the Alpine regions is one of openness. Rarely do you walk through large stretches of dense forest, except in the Alpine foothills. As a result, you can almost always see where you are going, and from where you came on the trails.

The characteristic timberline trees are crippled conifers—primarily Arolla pine, mountain pine and larch. Below this zone, Norway spruce is dominant. Larch, silver fir and Scots pine are also found between 1,100 meters (3,600 feet) and timberline. Mixed conifers and deciduous trees extend down to about 500 meters (1,600 feet), where the conifers give way to mixed hardwoods dominated by beech, oak, ash and sycamore.

Many plants and animals are protected throughout Austria. The protected species are well-publicized by color posters, which are found on the walls of many train stations and alpine huts. Some plants, such as the edelweiss, gentian, tiger-lily, lady's slipper and Turk's cap are completely protected. Picking one is strictly forbidden and will result in a stiff fine. Protected animals include the brown bear (which occasionally crosses into Austria from other countries), ibex, otter and marmot, as well as birds such as the heron, golden eagle and other birds of prey.

Austria has nine nature parks, three nature reserves with rare plants, 12 wildlife refuges and four bird sanctuaries. Most have a network of paths and can be explored on foot. A booklet published by the Austrian National Tourist Office entitled *The Experience of Nature in Austria* briefly describes the reserves and shows their locations. It also indicates the locations of 17 alpine gardens and 40 notable waterfalls and gorges in the country. The

booklet is published in German, English and Dutch. It is free on request
from any branch of the Austrian National Tourist Office (for their
locations, see the section on *Useful Addresses & Telephone Numbers* later
in this chapter).

Excursions for nature lovers are arranged every year by the provincial
sections of the *Österreichischer Naturschutzbund* (Austrian Nature Preser-
vation Society). Further information on the excursions can be obtained by
writing:

> **Österreichischer Naturschutzbund** (Gesellschaft für Naturkunde und
> Naturschutz). For its address and telephone number, see the *Address
> Directory* at the back of this chapter. You may write to the
> organization in English, French or German.

Climate

As with any mountain region, Austria's climate is diverse and changeable.
Vast differences in temperature, rainfall and the occurrence of storms exist
between valley floors and mountain summits. In the mountains, freezing
temperatures, heavy winds, rain, snow, hail and fog can occur at any
time. During the early summer, lightning and thunderstorms are frequent.

Generally, precipitation is heaviest during the months of June, July and
August, tapers off during the autumn months and reaches a low point in
February. Amounts, however, vary widely. On the ridges of the Hohe
Tauern Massif, between Salzburg and Kärnten, as much as 2450 mm (98
inches) of precipitation may fall during the year, much of it in the form of
snow. Precipitation also is high around the Salzkammergut Lakes in
Salzburg and Oberösterreich. In contrast, the city of Vienna receives an
average of only 683 mm (26.9 inches) of precipitation per year. The
provinces with the most precipitation are Tyrol and Salzburg; the province
with the least is Kärnten.

Temperatures at low elevations in Austria are moderate. During January,
the coldest month, daytime averages usually hover around freezing, while
summer temperatures rarely exceed 27°C. (80°F.), even in southern
Steiermark and Kärnten, the warmest regions in Austria. Altitude,
however, greatly affects temperature. For every 300 meter rise in elevation, average temperatures drop by about 1.4°C. (3°F.). Thus, while the
average yearly temperature at Innsbruck is 8.5°C. (47.3°F.), on the summit
of the Zugspitze, 32 kilometers away and 2,500 meters higher in
elevation, the yearly average is *minus* 5°C. (23°F.). Add a wind, and the
chill factor makes the conditions at high altitudes even more severe.

Snow generally covers the entire country by mid-December, lasting
until the end of March in the mountain areas and, on higher slopes, up
until the end of April, or even later. The permanent snow line occurs at
about 2,600 meters (8,500 feet). Snow may fall at any time at high

elevations. The first heavy snows, however, do not usually come to the mountains until the beginning of November.

Spring brings the legendary *Föhn,* a warm, dry wind that is most strongly felt in the Inn, Salzach and Ötz valleys. It is rumored that the wind causes nervousness and increases in hospital admissions. Although there is argument on this point, the effects of the *Föhn* are taken seriously. Streams swell into raging torrents, avalanches rumble down mountainsides and the risk of fires escalates. At schools in Innsbruck examinations are sometimes suspended. And in criminal trials, the *Föhn* still can be adduced as a defense.

On the positive side, the *Föhn* melts the snow and enables flocks to be sent up to the alpine pastures early. Also, it enables some valleys that would otherwise be too cool to grow fruit trees and wheat.

The walking season at low elevations, and in areas such as the Wienerwald and southern Steiermark, generally extends from about mid-April until November. For high-altitude walks, the best months are from mid-July until the end of September, with September being favored because then the trails are less crowded, mountain huts are still open and the weather is traditionally clearer.

For skiing, the best months are from mid-December until the end of March.

Weather Forecasts

To obtain weather forecasts in Austria, look on the first page of the phone book for the number listed under *Wettervorhersage* or *Wetterauskunft.* In Vienna, this number is:

Wetterauskunft: Tel. (0222) 15 66.

The local number for general forecasts in the larger places of all other federal provinces is: Tel. 16. In small places in **Niederösterreich,** call Vienna. All forecasts are in German.

Also, the ÖRF (Österreichischer Rundfunk & Fernsehen—Austrian Radio & TV) broadcasts the news and a weather forecast each morning in English at 8:05 a.m. and in French at 8:10 a.m.

Where to Get Walking Information

A good starting place for planning a walking trip in Austria is *Mountain Rambles in Austria,* published by the Austrian National Tourist Office. The 92-page booklet describes 60 spectacular six-day hikes of varying diffi-culty in all the provinces of Austria. In addition, the booklet lists the maps and guidebooks needed for each hike, gives the names and altitudes of the mountain huts in which you can stay along the routes, provides information on where to hire mountain guides, lists the addresses of mountaineering schools in the country and gives the locations of the cable cars, mountain railways and chair lifts that can be used to reach many trails. For the most part, the hikes described in the booklet do not require mountaineering experience (sections of 11 hikes do, but in all cases you are advised to hire a guide). As defined in the booklet, *mountain rambles* refer to walks just below dangerous cliffs and ice, *mountaineering* includes cliffs and climbs, and *Alpinism* demands technical climbing skills.

No maps are included in the booklet, so a map such as the Austrian Alpine Club's *Alpenvereinshütten in den Ostalpen* (see the section on *Maps*) is useful in helping you plan your trips. Or if you read German, you can obtain an expanded edition of the booklet (entitled *100x Wanderbares Österreich*) that describes 100 hikes, includes sketch maps of each and provides additional information for planning hiking trips in Austria, including a description of the trail wear and equipment required for hikes in various parts of the country.

100x Wanderbares Österreich is currently published only in German and can be obtained only from the head office of the Austrian National Tourist Office in Vienna, ÖSTERREICH-INFORMATION (see *Address Directory*). *Mountain Rambles in Austria* is published in English and Dutch and is free on request from any branch of the Austrian National Tourist Office.

General information on walking in Austria can be obtained from the head office of the:

Österreichischer Alpenverein (Austrian Alpine Club), Innsbruck (see *Address Directory*).

English-speaking readers will be able to obtain more information from the club's English section. Mimeographed information provided by the section will also be written in English, rather than in German.

Austrian Alpine Club, U.K. Branch (see *Address Directory*).

Sections of the club are also maintained in Belgium, Denmark and Holland (see *Address Directory):*

Vlaamse Bergsportvereniging, Belgium.

Österreichischer Alpenverein—Sektion Dänemark, Denmark.

Nederlandse Bergsport Vereniging, The Netherlands.

For specific information on the areas in which you intend to walk, you should contact the regional sections of the Österreichischer Alpenverein. Many local tourist offices—known as *Fremdenverkehrsverband*—can also provide valuable assistance in helping you plan walks. Their addresses are also listed in the *Address Directory*.

Walking Clubs in Austria

For all addresses, see the *Address Directory* at the back of this chapter.

Österreichischer Alpenverein (ÖAV). This is one of the largest mountaineering clubs in Europe. It has nearly 160 sections located in Austria and four foreign countries with more than 205,000 members. The various sections of the club maintain the majority of Austria's trails and operate 258 mountain huts. The club runs a climbing school based in Innsbruck, which also organizes tours, both in Austria and abroad, and has groups for skiing, nature photography, canoeing and the exploration of subterranean caves. It also publishes a high-quality series of 1:25,000 maps as well as instruction books and pamphlets on mountain climbing, rescue, getting bearings, first aid and a series of scientific publications.

Members of the club benefit from discounts in the club huts, on club publications and on train and bus fares in the country. Section members also receive discounts on equipment from sport shops located in the town where the section is based.

In addition, members are covered by the club's search-and-rescue and liability insurance. Members can also purchase supplemental insurance through the club that provides hospitalization coverage as well as additional coverage for rescue costs.

As if this weren't enough, members benefit from the club's reciprocal membership agreements with the alpine clubs in Germany, Greece, France, Italy, Liechtenstein, Spain, Switzerland and Yugoslavia. These agreements allow members to stay in the mountain huts in these countries at reduced rates.

Virtually anyone can join the club. You must, however, join one of the club's sections since direct membership in the main club does not exist.

Non-Austrians may wish to join one of the club's foreign sections so they can receive translations of the club publications. The larger sections of the club also accept applications for membership from non-Austrians. One of these is:

Österreichischer Alpenverein—Sektion Innsbruck.

Applications should be accompanied by two passport-size photographs, plus the appropriate membership fee (check on this in advance).

To save the club time, please make your money order payable in Austrian Schillings to Konto Nummer 100-260-182 *Bank für Tirol und Vorarlberg* when joining the Innsbruck section.

Additional information on membership can be obtained from the section you wish to join.

Österreichischer Touristenklub (ÖTK). The ÖTK operates 58 mountain huts, has a mountaineering school and maintains 39 sections throughout

Austria. The club also organizes walking and climbing tours for its 20,000 members. Members benefit from reductions in the club huts and on train and bus fares in Austria.

Touristenverein "Die Naturfreunde" (TVN). The TVN is affiliated with the international Friends of Nature Society with branches in 13 other countries. The club operates 170 mountain huts and seven climbing schools in Austria, and organizes walking, climbing, canoeing and skiing tours for its members, both in Austria and abroad. In addition to receiving discounts in the TVN's huts in Austria, members receive discounts when staying in any of the 592 *Die Naturfreunde* huts in Belgium, Germany, France, Holland and Switzerland.

Members of the Österreichischer Alpenverein may stay in the ÖTK and TVN huts. To qualify for discounts in the ÖTK huts however, ÖAV members must purchase a stamp from their club section that is affixed to their membership card.

Österreichischer Alpenklub. A club devoted solely to climbing. Operates one mountain hut on the Grossglockner. It has slightly more than 650 members.

Österreichischer Gebirgsverein. Another club devoted to climbing. Has affiliate membership with the ÖAV. Operates three mountain huts.

Maps

Five different series of maps are available to hikers:

1. The most popular maps for walking are those published by **Freytag & Berndt.** Of the company's 70 different maps, 49 are published in a scale of 1:100,000 and cover the entire country. In addition, 21 maps are published in a scale of 1:50,000. These cover the more well-known mountain regions. On the back, many of the maps have a description—in German—of the area covered by the map. This gives the bus connections to trailheads, lists the facilities in the various mountain huts and gives the walking times between the huts. Trail numbers are also indicated on the maps.

2. The most detailed maps are those published by the Österreichischer Alpenverein—the **Alpenvereinskarten.** These maps are drawn in a scale of 1:25,000 and cover the most important mountain massifs in the country. The alpine club also publishes the *Alpenvereinshütten in den Ostalpen,* a map in a scale of 1:500,000 on which the locations of all the alpine club huts in Austria are indicated. Alpine club members can buy these maps from the club at a discount. You can also buy them from many bookstores.

3. Another high-quality series of maps are the 1:50,000 **Öster-reichische Karte,** published by the *Bundesamt für Eich- und Vermessungswesen* (Austrian Bureau of Standards and Survey). When buying these maps, be sure to get the ones *mit Weg-markierung*—with trails marked. These maps cover the entire country. Unfortunately, they are laid out in quadrants. Hence, you must sometimes buy three maps to hike a 10-kilometer-long trail. Also, trail numbers are not indicated on the maps as they are on the *Freytag & Berndt* maps and the *Alpenvereinskarten.*

4. For the regions they cover, the **BV Tourenblätter** published by Bergverlag Rudolf Rother are an excellent route-finding aid. Footpaths and, in some cases, ski touring and climbing routes are shown on the maps. Each *Tourenblatt* also includes photos and route descriptions and comes in a plastic binder so individual pages and map sections can be taken out to be carried on the trail. Of the 13 *Tourenblätter,* six cover mountain groups in Tyrol, Salzburg and Vorarlberg.

5. Finally, there are the 1:50,000 **Kompass Wanderkarten** which cover the provinces of Vorarlberg, Tyrol, Salzburg, Kärnten and parts of Steiermark and Niederösterreich. Some of these maps are accompanied by a brief explanation of the trails and huts in the region covered by the map. Path numbers are not indicated on the maps.

Where to Buy Maps

Maps to local areas can be purchased in bookstores throughout Austria. All maps, plus a free index, are available by mail from:

Freytag-Berndt & Artaria KG, Vienna.

Freytag-Berndt & Artaria KG, Innsbruck.

(See *Address Directory.*)

You may write to the outlets in English, French or German.

Guidebooks

German-language guidebooks are published to virtually every mountain massif in Austria. By far the largest publisher of guidebooks is:

Bergverlag Rudolf Rother GmbH (see *Address Directory*). The company publishes nearly 80 guidebooks to Austria, as well as a series of ski guides and maps. The pocket-size guides include full-color map sections, thorough route descriptions, information on lodgings along the trails, and color photographs of protected plants in the regions covered by the guides.

Other major publishers of guidebooks to Austria include:

Fink-Kümmerly + Frey.
Verlag Styria.
Tyrolia Verlag.
Verlag Niederösterreich Pressehaus (Verlag Nö. Pressehaus).
Verlag Karl Thiemig.
Verlag F. Bruckmann KG.
(See *Address Directory*.)

In addition, many sections of the ÖAV and other local groups publish guides. The result is that no matter where you want to walk in Austria, you can find at least one—and sometimes four or five—guides that describe the area's trails.

Several guidebooks worth mention are:

- *Wandern in Österreich* by Helfried Knoll, Verlag Kremayr & Scheriau, Vienna.
- *Freizeitland Österreich* by Dieter Maier, Ringier-Verlag, Zürich.
- *Berg Heil* and *Von Hütte zu Hütte*, both by Walter Pause, BLV Verlagsgesellschaft, Munich, Germany. *Berg Heil* describes 100 one- to five-day mountain tours in the Alps, many of them in Austria. *Von Hütte zu Hütte* describes 100 two- to eight-day hut-hopping trips on some of the most spectacular high alpine trails.

Other books by Walter Pause describe 100 day hikes in the Alps, 100 ski tours in the Alps, 100 classic rock and ice climbs in the Alps, 100 easy climbs in the Alps, 100 moderately difficult climbs in the Alps, 100 difficult climbs in the Alps and the 100 best ski runs in the Alps.

Another book worth mention is:

- *Schlag nach!*, Bibliographisches Institut, Zürich, Switzerland. A comprehensive lexicon for walkers and climbers. Includes more than 2,500 terms covering virtually all subjects of interest to walkers and climbers. Among the information included is: 1) a brief description and history of each of Europe's alpine clubs and major walking, climbing and cave-exploring associations (addresses are included); 2) a brief description of the major hiking regions in the

Alps; 3) address lists of European climbing schools, mountain-rescue organizations and numerous other kinds of organizations, such as those that offer walking tours without packs; 4) explanations of first aid techniques, knot tying, use of a map and compass, understanding contour lines on a map, and predicting mountain weather; and 5) information on mineralogy, geology, flora and fauna, plus much, much more. The book is generously illustrated throughout and includes 30 color plates. And it's compact. At the back is an extensive bibliography that includes, among other publications, the guidebooks covering the major hiking regions in the Alps with—in each case—the name of their publishers. Packed with information. One of the best sourcebooks available anywhere.

English-Language Guidebooks

- *Salute to the Mountains: The hundred best walks in the Alps* by Walter Pause, translated into English by Ruth Michaels-Jena and Arthur Ratcliff, George G. Harrap & Company Ltd., London, England.

- *Hut Hopping in the Austrian Alps* by William E. Reifsnyder, Sierra Club Totebook, 1973. Describes three week-long tours in the Schladminger Tauern, Lechtaler Alpen and Stubaier Alpen. Available by mail from Sierra Club Books, San Francisco, U.S.A.

- *Wandering: A Walker's Guide to the Mountain Trails of Europe* by Ruth Rudner, Dial Press, 1972. Describes one two-week long trip in the Karwendelgebirge above Innsbruck.

- *100 Hikes in the Alps* by Ira Spring and Harvey Edwards, The Mountaineers Books, 1979. Describes 21 one- and two-day hikes throughout Austria. Available by mail from Mountaineers Books, Seattle, U.S.A.

- *Ötztal Alps, Glockner Range, Kaisergebirge, Stubai Alps, Karwendel* and *Zillertal Alps,* all from West Col Productions. Highly recommended. Available by mail from West Col Productions, Reading, England.

Where to Buy Guidebooks

Guidebooks to local trails can be purchased in bookstores throughout Austria. They can also be ordered by mail directly from the publishers (see the *Address Directory*), or from the *Freytag-Berndt und Artaria* bookstores in Innsbruck and Vienna.

The two Freytag-Berndt bookstores stock most of the mountain guides to Austria—including many of the guides to Austria's long-distance footpaths. The stores will order any guide they do not have in stock. They also will send you on request their catalog, *Bücher für den Bergfreund,* which lists all the guidebooks and maps they sell.

Trailside Lodgings

A variety of alpine clubs and societies own and operate more than 700 mountain huts in Austria. The majority of the huts—nearly 670—are operated by the *Österreichischer Alpenverein, Deutscher Alpenverein* (German Alpine Club), *Touristenverein "Die Naturfreunde"* and the *Österreichischer Touristenklub.*

In addition, there are numerous privately owned lodgings located on trails throughout Austria.

Most of the huts—or *Schutzhütten* as they are known—are staffed with a warden and are open from mid-June until the end of September. A few are open all year. And many have unstaffed winter rooms that are stocked with mattresses, blankets and cooking equipment. Club members may also obtain keys from the alpine clubs and societies to use the huts off-season. Anyone, however, can stay in the huts and use the unstaffed winter rooms.

Accommodation in the huts is usually in dorms. In addition, many huts have individual rooms with from one to six bunks made up with sheets. In the dorms—or *Matratzenlager*—there are no sheets. You must either bring your own sack sheet or roll up in the blankets provided.

Most huts provide hot meals. Many also sell sack lunches that you can take on the trail with you. A few huts are self-service, usually providing cooking facilities and dishes, but no food. In the huts that provide meals, cooking facilities for do-it-yourselfers are rarely available.

In many huts there is a nominal charge for hot water to make tea or coffee. You might also be charged if you eat your own food or drink your own wine or beer in the huts—sometimes as much as it costs to buy it in the huts. In cold weather, there may also be an additional charge for heat. Nonetheless, prices are very reasonable, especially if you are a club member. Then you only pay half-price.

No reductions are given in privately owned lodgings, but they are usually cheap and friendly.

Opening and closing dates for the huts vary widely. Also, not all huts have winter rooms. Before you begin your walk, you should check with the club or society that runs the huts, or with local people, to ensure the huts in which you intend to stay are open and provide meals.

Hut Guides

You can also obtain this information from the hut guides published by the clubs (see the *Address Directory* for their addresses):

- *Taschenbuch der Alpenvereins-Mitglieder* (in German). The Alpine Club Members' Handbook. Lists the alpine club huts in the Eastern

Alps, which cover Austria and parts of Germany, Italy and Yugoslavia. The type face is in a Gothic script, which is difficult to read for those who are not fluent in German. Available from any section of the Österreichischer Alpenverein or Deutscher Alpenverein.

• *Alpenvereinshütten in den Ostalpen.* A map in a scale of 1:500,000 published by the Österreichischer Alpenverein. Shows the locations of all the mountain regions and alpine club huts in the Eastern Alps. Available from any section of the ÖAV and DAV. (Recommended)

• *Die Alpenvereinshütten* (co-published by the ÖAV and DAV). Lists the alpine club huts in Austria and Germany. Includes photographs and sketch maps to help you locate each hut. A series of symbols is used to give the essential information on each hut—its location, facilities, approach routes, telephone number (if it has one), and so on. The key to the symbols is in German, but even if you do not understand German, the symbols are easily understood—as are the descriptions of the huts. Comes with the ÖAV's 1:500,000 map, *Alpenvereinshütten in den Ostalpen.* Available from any section of the ÖAV and DAV. Also can be ordered by mail from the Deutscher Alpenverein.

• *Naturfreunde Österreich: Schutzhütten und Unterkünfte* (in German). Gives full details on all the Naturfreundehäuser operated by the Touristenverein "Die Naturfreunde" (TVN) in Austria. Includes a map of Austria on which the locations of the TVN huts are shown. Also gives the names, locations and altitudes of Naturfreundehäuser in Belgium, France, Germany, Holland and Switzerland. Available by mail from the club's headquarters in Vienna.

• The *Österreichischer Touristenklub* publishes a one-page list of its huts with a sketch map, available by mail from the club's headquarters.

Another book is the:

• *Internationaler Hütten-Atlas,* published by Geo-Buch Verlag in Munich. This covers Austria, Bavaria, Südtirol (Italy) and part of Yugoslavia. Gives full details on all the alpine club huts—plus more than 300 privately owned trailside lodgings. A series of symbols are used in the book so that language is not a barrier. A key to the symbols—in English, French, Italian and German—is printed on a fold-out flap inside the back cover. The book also includes 36 pages of maps on which the locations of the alpine club huts and trailside inns are shown. Available from most bookstores in Austria as well as by mail from Freytag-Berndt und Artaria.

All of the booklets list approach routes to the huts, give their opening and closing dates, note which have winter rooms, tell you where keys can be obtained off-season and list the facilities and services provided.

Many of Austria's youth hostels also make good starting places for a walk. A list of the hostels, plus a map with their locations, is available from:

Österreichisches Jugendherbergswerk (see *Address Directory*).

Despite Austria's comprehensive network of trail lodgings, a sleeping bag may be required on some tours. Check before you set out.

Camping

It is forbidden to camp near many huts and in all nature preserves. Also, most trails cross private property—some even go right through a farmer's backyard. Before you camp on private property, you must ask the landowner's permission. If you don't, trespassing and vagrancy laws apply. Restrictions on building campfires are also strict; they are forbidden in all forest areas and nature preserves.

A list of commercial campgrounds, with a map, is available from all branches of the Austrian National Tourist Office (see *Address Directory*).

Water

Water can safely be taken from springs and most high alpine brooks. Water troughs and fountains are also safe sources of water, unless posted with a sign that says: *Kein Trinkwasser*. Tap water is very good throughout Austria. But caution should be exercised when drinking from streams at low altitudes. The best rule of thumb is: if you can't see a stream's source, don't drink from it.

Equipment Notes

Warm clothing, a windbreaker, raingear and solid, full-grain leather hiking boots are *essential* on all mountain trails—even if you only plan to stroll around one of the upper terminals of Austria's 400 or so cable cars and chair lifts. (Last summer there were several incidents in which people died because they rode up to the mountaintops for an afternoon hike with improper clothing and were caught unprepared by bad weather. If you don't have the proper clothing and footwear, don't go.) On some mountain trails, it is advisable to carry a sleeping bag. Check on this before you set out. Also, be sure your boots are *well* broken in before you attempt a long hike.

Crowded Trails

Some trails near the upper terminals of cable cars and chair lifts become crowded in July and August. Trails in the Vienna Woods are crowded on weekends. A few of the *Hauptwanderwege* (described under the section on *Austria's Long–Distance Footpaths*) can also have a lot of hikers on them during the summer months. Mountain refuges sometimes reach their capacity—especially on weekends—and must pull out their stock of extra mattresses for makeshift beds on the floor.

There are no trails in Austria where you will be completely alone in the summer. But the crowds do thin out once you get away from the cable car and chair lift terminals. And you can always find paths to walk where you can go for as long as an hour or two without seeing another hiker.

If that is still too crowded for you, hike the trails in September. The weather is nice, most mountain huts are still open and, during the week, you can have many trails almost to yourself.

Walking & Climbing Tours

Numerous walking and climbing tours are offered in Austria. Many organizations in other countries also organize walking, climbing and skiing tours to Austria.

Lists of walking tours are available from the provincial tourist boards in Austria (see the sections in this chapter describing each province). These tours span all grades of difficulty, and some, such as those offered by many hotels, include complimentary maps and route descriptions, your food and lodging and a pick-up service when you arrive at the train station.

The climbing school of the *Österreichischer Alpenverein* has an extensive program of tours that are open to its members, as well as to the members of affiliated alpine clubs. Altogether, it offers more than 400 tours each year. These include high alpine ski tours, mountain-climbing weeks, ice-climbing weeks, glacier tours and tours specifically for people over 50 years of age. Most are one-week tours. In addition, the ÖAV offers tours to the French and Swiss Alps, the Dolomites, Corsica, Scandinavia, Alaska, Mexico, Greenland, South America, Africa, New Zealand and Nepal. A complete list of the tours is available on request from:

Bergsteigerschule des Österreichischen Alpenvereins (see *Address Directory*).

The *Österreichischer Touristenklub* and the *Touristenverein "Die Naturfreunde"* also organize tours for members. A list is available from the clubs (see the *Address Directory*).

In addition, many of Austria's climbing schools offer week-long tours with qualified mountain guides. They are listed in the section on *Mountaineering Schools.*

Finally, there is the international three-day walk in the Vienna Woods, held each year in August. Information is available from:

Organisation der Internationalen Wienerwald-Wanderung (see *Address Directory).*

Mountain Guides

Officially authorized mountain guides are available through the tourist offices in mountain villages throughout Austria. To hire a guide, you should contact the tourist office in the village closest to the area in which you wish to climb. The guides are usually available on short notice.

Guides can also be hired through many of Austria's climbing schools.

Fees for fairly easy climbing expeditions—up to the IIIrd grade of difficulty—and glacier tours are usually standard per day for one person. Each additional person on a glacier tour is charged 10 percent of the basic fee. The maximum number of people a guide will take on a rock climb is two. The charge for the second person is 25 percent of the basic fee. For tours of more than the IIIrd grade of difficulty, prices are reached by agreement. The guide provides his own provisions.

Enquiries about mountain guides should be directed to the *Verband der Österreichischen Berg- und Skiführer* (Association of Austrian Mountain and Ski Guides), to which more than 700 authorized mountain guides belong.

Verband der Österreichischen Berg- und Skiführer (see *Address Directory).*

Mountaineering Schools

Mountaineering schools in Austria teach basic and advanced techniques in rock and ice climbing, ski mountaineering and ski touring. There are special courses both for young people and for people over 50 years of age. At least one school offers instruction in mountain rescue and tour guiding as well. In addition, many schools conduct tours. All courses and tours are carried out under the direction of authorized mountain and ski guides.

Requests for information on the specific courses offered and the dates they are available should be directed to the mountaineering schools (see *Address Directory):*

Austrian Alpine Club, U.K. Branch. Organizes mountaineering courses and tours for English-speaking participants.

Bergsteigerschule des Österreichischen Alpenvereins. Basic and advanced alpine instruction in rock and ice. Junior and senior courses. June to September. Ski touring and long-distance ski courses until May. **Tours:** Mountain rambles, high-alpine tours, climbing weeks, glacier tours, high-alpine ski tours. *Open to Austrian and foreign members of the alpine club only.*

Bergsteigerschule des Österreichischen Touristenklubs. Basic alpine instruction in rock and ice. February to October. Ski touring courses. **Tours:** Touring weeks, mountain rambles. *Open to ÖTK members only.*

Bergsteigerschulen des Touristenvereins "Die Naturfreunde" (TVN). The TVN operates five mountaineering schools in Kärnten, Saltzburger Land, Steiermark and Tirol offering alpine instruction and rock climbing, glacier- and ice-technique courses for beginning, advanced and expert mountaineer's; courses for youths (10 to 15 years); touring weeks and senior touring weeks. *Courses are open to TVN members only.* Further information is available from the individual schools: **Bergsteigerschule Karawanken,** located in Kärnten; **Hochgebirgsschule Glockner-Kaprun,** located in Salzburger Land; **Hochgebirgsschule Sonnblick,** also located in Salzburger Land; **Bergsteigerschule Schladminger Tauern,** located in Steiermark; and **Bergsteigerschule Wilder Kaiser,** located in Tirol.

Kärnten (Carinthia)

Alpine Ski- und Bergsteigerschule Reisseck. Courses in rock and ice. June to end of September. **Tours:** Alpine rambles and guided tours in all mountain districts of Carinthia. Guided ski tours.

Alpinschule Glockner-Heiligenblut. One- to three-day climbing courses in the Grossglockner region. End of June to October 1. Ski touring courses. **Tours:** Throughout the Grossglockner region. Equipment for hire.

Klettergarten Kanzianiberg, Information: Verkehrsamt (Tourist Office), Faak am See.

Niederösterreich (Lower Austria)

Bergsteigerschule Schneeberg. Mountaineering and rock and ice climbing courses. Walking and climbing tours. Rambling weeks for youths. May to October.

Wander- und Bergsteigerschule Schwarzatal. Basic alpine instruction, climbing courses for advanced climbers. February to October. **Tours:** Mountain rambles, touring weeks. Ski tours from December to the beginning of April.

Oberösterreich (Upper Austria)

Alpinschule Oberösterreich. Beginning and advanced alpine instruction and rock-climbing. Courses for youths and people over 50 years of age. Mid-June to mid-September. **Tours:** High-alpine mountain rambles and rock climbs in the Dachstein and Totes Gebirge.

Salzburg

Bergsteigerschule Filzmoos. Basic alpine instruction, mountaineering courses. Mid-June to end of October. **Tours:** Guided climbing tours, one- and several-day mountain rambles, summer glacier skiing.

Bergsteigerschule Hohe Tauern. Basic alpine instruction, courses for tours in rock and ice. Spring courses until June. Summer courses July to October. Touring weeks, geological excursions, ski tours.

Bergsteigerschule Leogang. Climbing courses in rock, ice and snow for beginners and advanced mountaineers. End of May to end of October. **Tours:** Touring weeks, youth weeks.

Bergsteigerschule Oberpinzgau. Two-day basic alpine instruction. June to September. **Tours:** Mountain rambles, geological excursions, mountain photography, glacier tours, mountain and climbing tours.

Hochgebirgsschule Sonnblick, Touristenverein "Die Naturfreunde," Vienna. Glacier- and ice-technique courses for beginners and advanced mountaineers. Mid-July to mid-August. *Open to TVN members only.*

Pongauer Wander- und Alpinschule. Basic alpine instruction. June to August. **Tours:** Rambles and climbing tours.

Salzburger Bergsteiger- und Wanderschule. Basic alpine instruction (four to seven days); mountain rambles for beginners; junior courses. March to the end of September. **Tours:** Guided one-day excursions, touring weeks.

Steiermark (Styria)

Alpinschule Dachstein. Basic alpine instruction. Junior courses. June to mid-October. **Tours:** Touring weeks in rock and ice, high-alpine rambles. High-alpine ski tours and winter mountaineering until May.

Alpinschule Ausseer Land. Alpine instruction for beginners and advanced mountaineers in rock and ice. June to mid-October. **Tours:** One-, three- and six-day rambles. High-alpine ski tours and ski rambles until May.

Bergsteigerschule -Dachstein-Tauern. Basic alpine instruction in rock and ice. June to September. **Tours:** Touring weeks, one-week climbing tours, mountain rambles. Ski tours and long-distance skiing in the high-alpine region until May.

Bergsteigerschule Hochschwab. Basic alpine instruction. June to September. **Tours:** Touring weeks.

Bergsteigerausbildung der Akademischen Sektion Graz des Österreichischen Alpenvereins. Three-, seven- and 12-day courses in rock and ice for beginners and advanced mountaineers.

Bergsteigerzentrum Steiermark. Basic instruction in rock and ice. July to mid-September. **Tours:** One-week climbing tours, private guides. High alpine ski tours until May.

Tirol (Tyrol)

Alpinschule Ausserfern. Basic alpine instruction in rock and ice. Climbing school with one-week courses and two- to four-day short courses. Senior courses. Junior mountain camps (10 to 14 years of age). May to October. High-alpine ski courses until June. **Tours:** Touring weeks, climbing weeks, rambling weeks, weekend tours, one- to four-day glacier tours. Ski touring weeks until June.

Alpinschule Innsbruck. Seven-day courses May to October. Basic alpine instruction. Senior courses for participants over 50 years. Courses for youths up to 17 years of age. High-alpine ski courses until the beginning of June. **Tours:** Touring and mountain rambling weeks. Ski touring weeks until the beginning of June.

Alpin- und Wanderschule St. Anton am Arlberg. Instruction in ice and rock. End of June to mid-September. **Tours:** High-alpine rambles, climbing and mountain touring weeks, ski tours and winter climbing.

Alpin- und Wanderschule Zillertal. Basic and advanced alpine instruction. July to September. **Tours:** High-alpine touring weeks, one-day excursions, mountain rambles, private guides.

Alpin- und Bergsteigerschule Stubai. Alpine instruction in rock and ice for beginners and advanced climbers. March to September. **Tours:** Touring weeks, climbing tours, one-day excursions, glacier tours, rambling weeks in the Stubai Valley and family weeks. Also offers ski touring weeks.

Berg- und Wanderschule Kirchdorf am Wilden Kaiser. Basic alpine instruction in rock and ice. Courses for children and youths. March to September. **Tours:** Rambling weeks, touring weeks, climbing weeks. Ski touring weeks until the beginning of June.

Bergsteigerschule Osttirol. Basic alpine instruction in rock and ice. June to September. **Tours:** High-alpine touring weeks, climbing weeks, three-day tours.

Bergsteigerschule Piz Buin. Basic alpine instruction in rock and ice. April to October. **Tours:** Touring weeks, one-week climbing tours, rambling weeks, private guides. Ski touring weeks until May.

Berg- und Wanderschule Sepp Kröll-Kitzbühel. Basic alpine instruction in rock and ice. Instruction in mountain rescue and tour guiding. Senior and junior courses. March to October. **Tours:** Touring weeks on rock and ice, climbing and high-alpine weeks, alpine rambles, ski touring weeks. Private guided tours all year.

Bergschule Tannheimertal. Information supplied on request. **Tours:** Mountain rambles and climbing tours.

Bergsteiger- und Wanderschule Wetterstein. Basic instruction in climbing and ski mountaineering. December to May and July to October. **Tours:** High-alpine rambles, ascents of peaks, climbing tours, family rambles, ski touring weeks.

Hochalpine Bergsteigerschule Sölden. Basic and advanced courses in rock and ice. Courses for youths (8 to 14 years). End of June to end of September. **Tours:** Touring weeks, mountain rambles. Ski touring weeks from mid-April to the beginning of May.

Hochgebirgsschule Innerpitztal. Basic instruction in rock and ice. Climbing courses for beginners and advanced mountaineers. Beginning of June to the end of September. **Tours:** One-day rambles, circular tours, touring weeks.

Hochgebirgs- und Wanderschule Obergurgl. Basic alpine instruction in rock and ice. April to September. **Tours:** Touring weeks for advanced climbers. Ski touring weeks.

Hochgebirgsschule Tyrol. Six- and seven-day courses mid-June to September. Alpine training for beginners and advanced mountaineers. Senior courses for participants over 45 years. Junior courses. High-alpine ski courses until the end of May. **Tours:** Touring weeks, mountain rambling weeks. Ski touring weeks until the end of May.

Berg- und Wanderschule St. Johann in Tirol. Basic alpine instruction in rock and ice. June to October. Ski touring courses until the end of May. **Tours:** Rambling weeks, one-day rambles, climbing weeks, touring weeks.

Vorarlberg

Alpinschule Montafon. Basic alpine instruction in rock and ice. March to September. **Tours:** Touring weeks, climbing weeks, mountain-rambling weeks, ski touring weeks.

Bergsteigerschule Kleinwalsertal. Basic alpine instruction. Mid-May to mid-October. **Tours:** Climbing weeks, climbing on snow and ice, touring weeks, two- and three-day guided tours, mountain rambles, special interest guided tours (geology), ski tours.

Bergsteigerschule Hochtannberg. Alpine instruction and tours. May to October.

Cross-Country Skiing

The downhill ski run still dominates skiing in Austria. But cross-country skiing—known as *Skilanglauf* or simply *Langlauf*—has become more and more popular. Currently, there are more than 600 ski tracks in the country—each prepared and marked. Some of the tracks are only one kilometer in length. Others are as long as 80 kilometers.

Ski touring equipment can be rented—or for that matter, purchased—in most sport shops. And for beginners, the majority of ski schools in Austria offer instruction in cross-country skiing.

No organization in Austria is concerned solely with cross-country skiing. Information, however, can be obtained from Österreichischer Ski-Verband, which has a section for cross-country skiing.

> **Österreichischer Ski-Verband** (see *Address Directory*). You may write in English or German.

Each year, the Austrian National Tourist Office publishes a list of towns in the country where cross-country ski tracks are located. The list, entitled *Skilanglauf in Österreich,* is broken down by province and includes the length of the tracks, the altitude and postal code of the town, and tells if ski instruction, guided ski tours and equipment rental are available. The list is published in German and is available only from the head office of the Austrian National Tourist Office in Vienna. Many of Austria's provincial tourist boards also publish lists of the ski tracks in their provinces.

In addition, two guidebooks are published on the subject:

- *DSV Langlauf Kompass,* edited by Franz Wölzenmüller. Published by Südwestdeutscher Verlag in cooperation with the Deutscher Skiverband in Munich. Updated each year. Includes locations and lengths of cross-country ski tracks in Austria, Germany, Italy and Switzerland. Lists addresses and telephone numbers where additional information can be obtained, as well as the names of ski schools that offer cross-country instruction and places where equipment can be hired. Well illustrated with maps of the trails. Emphasis is on ski tracks in Germany. Ski tracks in Austria are listed in alphabetical order, according to the name of the place. They are not divided by province. Published only in German. Available by mail from *Südwestdeutscher Verlag* (see *Address Directory*). You may write to the publisher in English or German.

  (A synopsis of this information for Austria is also included in a small booklet available from the Deutscher Skiverband. The booklet is entitled: *DSV Langläufer Leben Länger INFORMATION: Nachtrag Österreich.)*

- *Skilanglauf Atlas,* edited by Claus-Peter Berner, Berner-Verlag.

Updated each year. Includes locations and lengths of more than 1,000 ski tracks in Austria, Finland, France, Germany, Italy, Norway and Switzerland. Sections are divided by province, with the names of the towns in each province listed in alphabetical order. Lists addresses and telephone numbers where additional information can be obtained. Notes where equipment can be rented and which towns have ski schools for cross-country instruction. Includes a short description of each route, plus a liberal scattering of maps and photos. Published only in German. Available by mail from the *Österreichischer Ski-Verband* or *Freytag-Berndt und Artaria* (see *Address Directory*).

Ski Touring & Ski Mountaineering

Ski touring (or, in German, *Skiwandern)* and ski mountaineering *(Skibergsteigen)* were well established in Austria long before the advent of cable cars, chair lifts and lift lines. Ski touring is simply the winter extension of summer rambles in the woodlands and mountains. Ski mountaineering, however, is not without its risks—not the least of which are avalanches. For this reason, you should join one of the tours offered by Austria's climbing schools, hire a guide or—at the very least—go in a party of *at least* four experienced ski mountaineers who are familiar with the area in which you intend to ski.

Information on routes for *Skiwandern* and *Skibergsteigen* and on the availability of guides can be obtained from local tourist offices throughout Austria. To write the offices, address your letter to: Verkehrsverein, then on the next line write a capital A-, followed by the postal code and name of the town about which you wish to obtain information. Example:

Verkehrsverein
A-6370 Kitzbühel
A U S T R I A

Ski Touring Guides

Five guidebooks with 1:50,000 maps are published by Bergverlag Rudolf Rother. They include:

- *Bayerisches Hochland und angr. Nordtirol Skiführer,* Seibert, 1977, 200 pages, 24 color maps. Covers the Lechtal and Ammergau Alps; Wetterstein and Mieminger regions; Karwendel, Rofan and Kaiser massifs; Chiemgau and Berchtesgaden Alps; Silvretta and Samnau massifs; Ötztal and Stubai Alps; Tuxer-Voralpen and the Zillertal and Kitzbühel Alps.

- *Arlberg-Gebiet Skiführer,* Langenmaier, 1975, 40 pages, four panoramas, one color map. Covers the Lechquell Massif and Lechtal Alps in Vorarlberg and Tyrol.
- *Ötztaler Alpen Skiführer,* Prochaska, 1966, 112 pages, one color map. Covers the Ötztal Alps in Tyrol.
- *Rätikon Skiführer,* Flaig, 1974, 480 pages, one color map. Covers the Rätikon Massif in Vorarlberg.
- *Silvretta Skiführer,* Flaig and Pracht, 1977. Covers the Silvretta Range in Vorarlberg.

Rudolf Rother also publishes five maps on which ski routes are marked. They include:

- *Berchtesgadener Alpen.* Full-color map and panorama, 1968. Covers the region southwest of the city of Salzburg.
- *Ötztaler Alpen.* Full-color map and panorama, 1968.
- *Saalbach-Zell am See.* Includes two color maps, 1966. Covers the region around Kitzbühel.
- *Stubaier Alpen.* Includes two color maps, 1965.
- *Zillertaler Alpen.* Includes two color maps, 1966. Covers the Zillertal Alps in southeastern Tirol.

Another book that is useful to the ski tourer is:

- *Abseits der Piste—100 stille Skitouren in den Alpen* by Walter Pause, BLV Verlag, Munich. Describes 100 off-the-beaten-track ski tours throughout the Alps.

The maps and guidebooks can be purchased in local bookstores or by mail from Freytag-Berndt und Artaria (see the *Address Directory*).

Special Train & Bus Fares

If you don't have a car, getting around in Austria is best done by train. Regular second-class fares are not expensive. And there are a variety of fare reductions. Buses are nearly as efficient as the rail network, although they stop at more places and take longer, but if you're not in a hurry, they provide a scenic and cheaper alternative.

The special fares you can take advantage of include:

Austria Ticket. Good for unlimited travel on trains, buses and ships throughout Austria. Discounts are also given with the ticket on many cable cars, chair lifts and mountain railways. First- and second-class tickets available for a duration of 9 or 16 days.

Austria Ticket Junior. For young people up to the age of 23. Provides the same advantages as the Austria Ticket at half price.

Bundes-Netzkarte. Good for unlimited travel on trains throughout Austria. Also provides a 50 percent discount for travel on the buses of the Federal Railways and ships. First- and second-class tickets available for 9 days, 16 days or one month.

Länder-Netzkarten. A great value if you are going to spend a lot of time in one province. Gives you unlimited travel on trains and a 50 percent discount on the buses of the Federal Railways in a single province. First- and second-class tickets available for 9 days, 16 days or one month.

Sechser-Karte. A good ticket to buy if you are going to base yourself in one village and ride back and forth on the train to get to nearby trails. You pay for five trips and get one free—giving you a savings of nearly 17 percent over regular fares. Twelve different tickets are available at twelve different prices. Good for six trips of up to 6, 10, 15, 20, 25, 30, 40, 45, 50, 60 or 70 kilometers one way. To take advantage of the tickets you must ride second class; no first-class tickets are available.

Kilometerbank. This ticket provides a discount of up to 35 percent on rail travel. Also, up to six people can use the same ticket. You can buy 2,000, 5,000 or 10,000 kilometers of rail travel. Each time you travel more than 71 kilometers, the conductor deducts the length of the trip from your kilometer checkbook. The tickets can be purchased for first- or second-class rail travel and are good for six months. The tickets are not valid for trips less than 70 kilometers in length.

Bergsteigerkarten. Provides a 25 percent discount. There is no charge for the ticket. To obtain one you must present a current membership card in the Österreichischer Alpenverein, Österreichischer Tour-istenklub or Österreichischer Ski-Verband. Members of several other clubs in Austria are also eligible for the ticket. It can be used on trains and buses for trips in excess of 71 kilometers *round trip*. It's also good for discounts on cable cars, chair lifts and mountain railways that display the sign: *VAVÖ*. Valid for one year.

These tickets can be purchased at the ticket offices of any train station in Austria. Further information can be obtained from any branch of the Austrian National Tourist Office, as well as from the train information offices in the stations.

Useful Addresses & Telephone Numbers

General Tourist Information

In Austria:

ÖSTERREICH-INFORMATION (Austrian National Tourist Office/ Österreichische Fremdenverkehrswerbung). See *Address Directory.*

Abroad

Branch offices of the Austrian National Tourist Office are located in EUROPE: London, Dublin, Paris, Brussels, Berlin, Cologne, Frankfurt, Hamburg, Copenhagen, Stockholm, Amsterdam, Zurich, Lisbon, Prague and Zagreb; AUSTRALIA and NEW ZEALAND: Sydney, Christchurch and Wellington; SOUTH AFRICA: Johannesburg; JAPAN: Tokyo; CANADA: Montreal, Toronto and Vancouver, B.C.; and in the U.S.A.: New York, Chicago, Los Angeles and Portland, Oregon.

London: Austrian National Tourist Office, 30 St. George Street, London WIR 9FA. Tel. (01) 629 0461.

New York: Austrian National Tourist Office, 545 Fifth Avenue, New York, New York 10017. Tel. (212) 697-0651.

Sport Shops

Throughout Austria you will be able to find sport shops in which you can buy boots, skis, stoves, sleeping bags, ice axes and other mountaineering hardware. Many rent equipment—ice axes and crampons in summer; skis, boots, poles and sealskins in winter. And if you need a pair of boots resoled, or need to have a piece of equipment repaired, they will be able to help.

If you cannot find a sport shop—or you can only find one filled with tennis raquets—ask at the local tourist office. They will be able to tell you where the sport shops that specialize in mountaineering equipment are located.

If you are in Vienna, one mountain shop worth a visit is:

Sporthaus SCHWANDA (see *Address Directory*). A catalog is free on request. People in the shop, for the most part, speak only German.

Search & Rescue

There is no charge for the helicopters and rescue squads that participate in mountain rescues in Austria. The injured person, however, must pay for ambulance transportation and any other incidental expenses, such as telephone tolls, that might be incurred during the rescue.

In Tyrol alone, more than 85 rescue posts are maintained by volunteers of the *Österreichischer Bergrettungsdienst* (Austrian Mountain Rescue Service).

If one of your party becomes lost or injured, you should go to the nearest *staffed* mountain hut or trailside inn for help. The hut wardens have direct contact with the rescue posts. Or, if you can get to a telephone, call the police.

Police Emergency: In most towns, tel. 133.

A few towns may have a different police emergency number. If so, check the first page of the telephone book. The police emergency number in small localities will be listed under *Gendarmerie*. In towns, the number will be listed under *Polizei*.

Many police speak only German. If this poses a difficulty, try to get someone who speaks German to make the phone call. Otherwise, be sure to ask for *Bergrettung*. Then give the name of your precise location and the location of the injured person.

Further information on search and rescue is available from:

Österreichischer Bergrettungsdienst (see *Address Directory*). The staff speaks only German.

Avalanche Warnings

Kärnten: For a recorded message, Tel. (04222) 16. For specific advice, Tel. (04222) 33 6 03.

Oberösterreich: Oberösterreich Lawinenwardienst-Zentrale (Central Avalanche Warning Center), Tel. (0732) 584 24 67 or 584 24 12.

Salzburg: Daily radio broadcasts on local stations from 7:30 to 11:30 a.m. for a recorded message, Tel. (06222) 196. For specific advice, call the Lawinenwarndienst-Zentrale, Tel. (06222) 43 4 35.

Steiermark: For a recorded message, Tel. (0316) 831 61 77. Lawinen-warndienst-Zentrale, Tel. (0316) 25 1 16.

Tirol: Daily radio broadcasts on local stations from 7:45 a.m. For a recorded message, Tel. (05222) 196. Lawinenwarndienst-Zentrale, Tel. (05222) 21 8 39 or 28 7 01.

Vorarlberg: For a recorded message, Tel. (05522) 16.

Austria's Long-Distance Footpaths

The long-distance walker has the choice of numerous footpaths in Austria leading from one border to another within the country. One of the routes passes through the Ötztal Alps and requires *mountaineering experience.* The rest generally are not difficult, although sections of a few paths involve some scrambling and should be avoided by those without mountain experience. In these cases, alternate trails can be followed.

Eventually, 10 long-distance routes—or *Weitwanderwege*—will cross Austria from north to south and from east to west. Since 1972, eight routes have been waymarked—Weitwanderwege 01, 02, 04, 05, 06, 07, 08 and 10, as well as the Austrian section of European Long-Distance Footpath E-5. Two others—Weitwanderwege 03 and 09—are partially marked.

Walking times on the long-distance routes range from two to seven weeks, depending upon the path. Those who walk the full length of the paths—and check in at control points along the way—are awarded a hiking badge at the end of the route.

Accommodation along the routes can be found at most of the control stations as well as in mountain huts and privately owned trail lodgings. Towns are also scattered along the routes and are useful places to begin or end a section if you do not want to walk the entire route.

In addition to basic equipment, a sleeping bag—and on the high-alpine sections of the routes, an ice axe and crampons—will be required. A 50-meter length of 9-mm (⅜-inch) climbing rope also should be carried on the high-alpine sections.

Information on walking the routes can be obtained from the following sections of the ÖAV (see *Address Directory):*

Österreichischer Alpenverein—Sektion "Edelweiss." Sells German-language guidebooks to the routes. Enquiries should be in German.

Austrian Alpine Club, U.K. Branch. Route descriptions in English are available from the club for Weitwanderwege 01 and 05, as well as for the Kamptalseenweg and Nordwaldkammweg, which make up portions of the long-distance routes. Maps for walking the routes also can be obtained from the club. In addition, the club organizes many hiking and climbing tours.

Vlaamse Bergsportvereniging (Belgian Section of the ÖAV).

Nederlandse Bergsportvereniging (Dutch Section of the ÖAV).

Österreichischer Alpenverein—Sektion Dänemark (Danish Section of the ÖAV).

AUSTRIA'S LONG DISTANCE FOOT PATHS

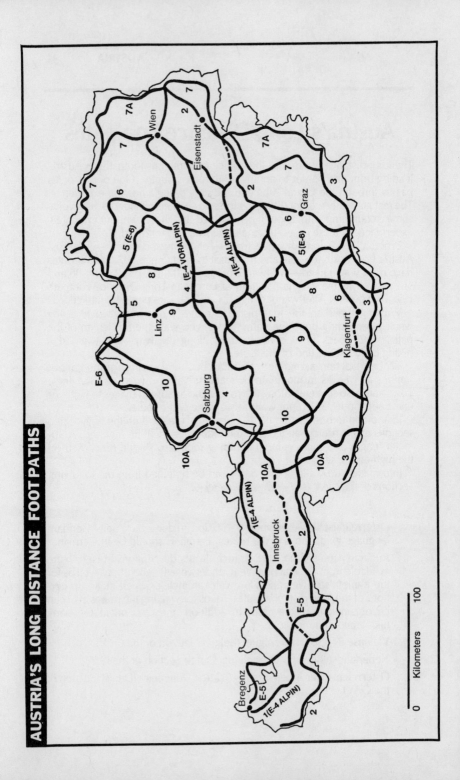

0   Kilometers   100

Weitwanderweg 01—Nordalpenweg

Through the Northern Limestone Alps from Bregenz on the Bodensee (Lake Constance) to Rust on the Neusiedler See. Forms the alpine section of European Long-Distance Footpath E-4. **Status:** Completed. **Length:** 1,404 kilometers. **Walking Time:** 55 days. **Difficulty:** Some sections of the trail are moderately difficult; others require mountaineering experience. The most difficult sections of path are in the Lechquellengebirge between Damüls and Biberacher-Hütte (18 kilometers) and between Göppinger-Hütte and Ravensburger-Hütte (31 kilometers); in the Lechtal Alps between Stuttgarter-Hütte and Steinsee-Hütte (79 kilometers); in the Steinernes Meer between Riemann-Haus and Matras-Haus (25 kilometers); and in the Dachstein between Lungötz and Simony-Hütte (41 kilometers). These sections are for experienced mountaineers only. **Path Markings:** Red-white-red bars with black route numbers. Follows path numbers 201, 401, 601, 801, 801A and 901A.

Maps:
- Freytag-Berndt Wanderkarten 1:100,000, sheets 1, 2, 4, 6, 8, 9, 10, 27, 28, 30, 31, 32, 33, 34, 35 and 36. Or:
- Österreichische Karte 1:50,000, sheets 77, 78, 88, 89, 90, 91, 92, 93, 95, 96, 97, 98, 99, 100, 101, 102, 103, 104, 105, 106, 107, 111, 112, 115, 116, 117, 118, 119, 124, 125, 126, 127, 142, 143, 144 and 145.

Guidebook:
- *Vom Neusiedler See zum Bodensee/Nordalpiner Weitwanderweg 01* by Dr. Robert Wurst, Dipl. Ing. Werner Rachoy and Franz Groissböck, Verlag Styria, 1978. Available from Freytag-Berndt u. Artaria.
- Short route description in English available from the U.K. Branch of the ÖAV.

Further Information: ÖAV—Sektionenverband Niederösterreich (see *Address Directory*). You may write in English or German.

Weitwanderweg 02—Zentralalpenweg

Through the Central Alps from Feldkirch to Hainburg on the Danube, Austria's easternmost town on the Czech-Austrian border, 60 kilometers from Vienna. One of the most spectacular—and difficult—trails in the Alps. **Status:** Both the main route and its easier alternates, 02A and 02B, are completed. **Length:** ca. 1,200 kilometers. **Walking Time:** 50 to 60 days. **Difficulty:** Most of the path is a high-alpine route for experienced mountaineers *only*. Only between Mixnitz and Hainburg is the footpath easy. Less difficult alternate routes, however, have been established to allow walkers to follow the path, yet avoid its most difficult sections. **Path Markings:** Red-white-red bars with black route numbers.

Main Route:
- In VORARLBERG, path numbers 102 through the Rätikon, 302 through Silvretta and 502 through the Ferwall Massif.
- In Tyrol, path numbers 702 through the Samnaun Massif, 902 through the Ötzal Alps, 102 through the Stubai Alps and 502 along the Zillertaler Höhenweg to the Krimmler Ache Valley. The path then continues along the *Tauernhöhenweg* zigzagging between Salzburg, Osttirol and Kärnten.
- In SALZBURG, OSTTIROL and KÄRNTEN, path numbers 902 through the Venediger Massif, 502 through the Granatspitz Massif, 702 through the Glockner Massif, 102 through the Goldberg Massif (intersection at Hagener Hütte with Weitwanderweg 10—Rupertiweg), and 502 through the Ankogel Massif to Murtörl on the Tappenkarsee (junction with the less difficult variant, Weitwanderweg 02A). The route then enters a lower mountain region, following path number 702 through the Radstädter Tauern, Obertauern and Schladminger Tauern in Steiermark.
- In STEIERMARK, path numbers 702 through the Schladminger Tauern; 902 through the Wölzer Tauern, Rottenmanner Tauern and Seckau Alps; and 502 from Knittelfeld to Mixnitz. The route then becomes easy, following path numbers 702 through the Fischbach Alps to Pfaffensattel and 902 through the Bucklige Welt to Burgenland.
- In BURGENLAND, it follows path number 902 to the route's terminus at Hainburg on the Danube.

A less difficult alternate route:
- In VORARLBERG, path number 502A through the Ferwall Massif (not indicated on maps).
- In TIROL, path numbers 702A through the Samnaun Massif (not indicated on maps), 902A from Prutz via Jerzens to Ötz, 102A from Fulpmes in the Stubai Valley to Matrei am Brenner, 302A through the Tuxer Alps to Zell on the Ziller River and 702A through the Kitzbühel Alps to Zell on the Zeller See in Salzburg.
- In SALZBURG, path numbers 402A to Taxenbach in the Salzach Valley, 102A to Hofgastein, 502A to Hüttschlag and 702A to the junction with the main route at Murtörl on the Tappenkarsee.

Maps:
For the Main Route:
- Freytag-Berndt Wanderkarten 1:100,000, sheets 2, 13, 19, 20, 21, 27, and 37. Also:
- Freytag-Berndt Wanderkarten 1:50,000, sheets 021, 362, 371 and 372. Also: Alpenvereinskarten 1:25,000 and 1:50,000, sheets 26, 30/1, 30/2, 30/3, 30/4, 31/1, 31/3, 35/1, 35/2, 35/3, 36, 39, 40 and 42.

For the 02A variant:
- Freytag-Berndt Wanderkarten 1:100,000, sheets 2, 13, 19, 20, 21, 25, 27, 33 and 38. Also:
- Freytag-Berndt Wanderkarten 1:50,000, sheets 021, 362, 371 and 372. Also: Alpenvereinskarten 1:25,000 and 1:50,000, sheets 30/3, 31/2, 31/5 and 61.

Guidebooks:
* A provisional guide, *Zentralalpiner Weitwanderweg 02* by Fritz Peterka, is available from Verlag Styria, Graz. Sections of the route also are described in:
* *Tauernhöhenweg* by Prof. Dr. Ernst Herrmann, available from ÖAV— Sektion "Edelweiss."
* *Die Höhe Route der Ostalpen* by Schnürer, Bergverlag Rudolf Rother.
* *Berg Heil, 100 schöne Bergtouren in den Alpen* by Walter Pause, BLV Verlag, Munich.

Further Information: Fritz Peterka (see *Address Directory*). Best to write in German.

Weitwanderweg 03—Südalpinweg

Also known as the *Südösterreichischer Grenzlandweg*. Stretches through the southern Limestone Alps along the Austrian-Italian border from Sillian im Pustertal (30 kilometers west of Lienz) to Bad Radkersburg (on the Austrian-Yugoslav border at the headwaters of the Mur River). Follows portions of the *Karawankenweg*. It also links up with several spectacular trails in Italy and Yugoslavia. **Status:** Much of the path can be walked. A few sections remain to be marked. **Length:** ca. 500 kilometers. **Walking Time:** 20 days. **Difficulty:** Ranges from moderately difficult to difficult. **Path Markings:** Red-white-red bars with black path numbers.
Maps:
* Freytag-Berndt Wanderkarten 1:100,000, sheets 18, 23, 41 and 44, and 1:500,000, sheets 223, 224, 232, 233 and 234.
* Österreichische Karte 1:50,000, sheets 195-209 and 211-213.

Guidebook:
* A provisional guide, *Karnischer Höhenweg* by Walter Schaumann, is available from ÖAV—Sektion "Edelweiss."

Further Information: Dr. Hermann Doujak (see *Address Directory*). Best to write in German.

Weitwanderweg 04—Voralpinweg

Through the alpine foothills from Salzburg to Vienna. Passes through the Salzkammergut Lake region and the Vienna Woods. This is the principal route of European Long-Distance Footpath E-4 in Austria. **Status:** Completed. **Length:** 734 kilometers. **Walking Time:** 30 days. **Difficulty:** Moderately difficult. **Path Markings:** Red-white-red bars with black route numbers. Follows path numbers 204, 404, 444, 604 and 804.
Maps:
* Freytag-Berndt Wanderkarten 1:100,000, sheets 1, 2, 3, 5, 8 and 9.

Guidebooks:
* *Wienerwald – Salzkammergut – Berchtesgadenerland / Voralpiner Weit-wanderweg 04* by Dr. Robert Wurst, Dipl. Ing. Werner Rachoy and Dr. Josef Steffan, Verlag Styria, 1979. Available from Freytag-Berndt u. Artaria. Or:
* *Europäischer Fernwanderweg 4*, available by mail from Deutscher Wanderverlag, Stuttgart, Germany.

Weitwanderweg 05—Nord–Südweg

From Dreisesselberg on the German-Austrian border to Eibiswald (50 kilometers south of Graz). Across the Mühlviertel in Oberösterreich and the Waldviertel in Niederösterreich, over the Hochschwab and through the mountains of Steiermark. Forms Austrian section of European Long-Distance Footpath E-6. **Status:** Completed. **Length:** Nordwaldkammweg, 144 kilometers; Nord-Süd Weitwanderweg, 460 kilometers. **Walking Time:** Nordwaldkammweg, 5 days; Nord-Süd Weitwanderweg, 17-21 days. **Difficulty:** Nordwaldkammweg, easy; on the Nord-Süd Weitwan-derweg there is a difficult section of trail on the crossing of the Reichenstein (2,166 meters) in Steiermark; it should be attempted only by experienced mountain walkers. **Path Markings:** Nordwaldkammweg, white-blue-white bars, path number 105; Nord-Süd Weitwanderweg, red-white-red bars, path numbers 605, 405, 805 and 505.
Maps:
* Freytag-Berndt Wanderkarten 1:100,000, sheets 26 and 11 (Nord-waldkammweg) and sheets 3, 4, 7, 11, 13, 21 and 41 (Nord-Süd Weitwanderweg). Or:
* Österreichische Karte 1:50,000, sheets 2, 3, 14, 15, 16 and 17 (Nordwaldkammweg) and 17, 18, 34, 35, 36, 37, 54, 72, 73, 101, 102, 103, 132, 162, 163, 188, 189 and 206 (Nord-Süd Weitwanderweg).
Guidebooks:
* *Nordwaldkammweg Führer* and *Nord-Süd Weitwanderweg Führer*, both available by mail from Freytag-Berndt u. Artaria.
* Short route descriptions in English available from the U.K. Branch of the ÖAV.
Further Information (see *Address Directory*):
On the Nordwaldkammweg: ÖAV—Sektion Freistadt, Freistadt.
On the Nord-Süd Weitwanderweg, from Nebelstein to Mariazell: Sektion Waldviertel des Österreichischen Alpenvereins, Gmünd.
From Mariazell to Eibiswald: ÖAV—Sektionenverband Steiermark, Graz.
Best to write in German.

Weitwanderweg 06—Mariazellerweg

From Nebelstein to Klagenfurt through the Vienna Woods and the mountains of Steiermark. Follows portions of the *Kamptal-Seenweg* and *Kremstalweg* in Niederösterreich and *Unterkärntner Hügellandweg* in Kärnten. **Status:** Completed. **Length:** ca. 800 kilometers. **Walking Time:** 32 days. **Difficulty:** Ranges from easy to moderately difficult. **Path Markings:** Red-white-red bars with black route numbers. Follows path numbers 406, 706A, 706, 506, 306 and 106. An alternate route between Mittendorf and Walster can also be followed on path numbers 406A, 606, 406 and 206.

Maps:
- Freytag-Berndt Wanderkarten 1:100,000, sheets 1, 3, 4, 7, 11, 13, 23 and 41.

Guidebooks:
- A temporary guidebook to the route in Kärnten and Steiermark can be obtained from the ÖAV-Sektionenverband Steiermark, Graz.
- A guidebook to the entire route has also been published by Styria Verlag, Graz.

Further Information (see *Address Directory*):
For the section in Niederösterreich: ÖAV—Sektion Waldviertel, Gmünd.
For the section in Steiermark: ÖAV—Sektionenverband Steiermark, Graz.
And for the section in Kärnten: Hofrat Dr. Hermann Doujak, Klagenfurt.

Weitwanderweg 07—Ostösterreichischer Grenzlandweg

From Nebelstein to Eibiswald through Niederösterreich, Burgenland and the foothills of Steiermark. A variant from Mailberg to Bad Radkersburg follows the Austro-Hungarian border and links up with trails in Yugoslavia. **Status:** Both the main route and the variant along the Austro-Hungarian border—known as the *Südburgenlandisch Route*—are completed. **Length:** 750 kilometers. **Walking Time:** 30 days. **Difficulty:** Easy. **Path Markings:** Red-white-red bars with black route numbers. Completed sections follow path numbers 607 and 907.

Maps:
- Freytag-Berndt Wanderkarten 1:100,000, sheets 1, 7, 11, 27, 41, 42 and 44.

Guidebook:
- *Vom Thayatal über den Seewinkel zu den Muraen/Ost- Österreichischer Grenzlandweg 07* by Kreutzer and Wallner, Styria Verlag, Graz, 1979. Available by mail from Freytag-Berndt u. Artaria.

Further Information: Ernst Kreutzer (see *Address Directory*). Best to write in German.

Weitwanderweg 08—Eisenwurzenweg

From Litschau at Austria's northernmost point to the Kärntner Seebergsattel at its southernmost point. Across the Waldviertel through Naturpark Blockheide, Naturpark Grosspertholz and Naturpark Weinserger Forst; into the mountains of Steiermark, thence to the Drau Valley in Kärnten. Follows a section of the *Lavanttaler Höhenweg* through the Saualpe above Klagenfurt. **Status:** Completed. **Length:** 750 kilometers. **Walking time:** 30 days. **Difficulty:** Ranges from easy to moderately difficult. **Path Markings:** Red-white-red bars with black route numbers. Follows path numbers 608, 208, 908, 608, 308 and 608.
Maps:
• Freytag-Berndt Wanderkarten 1:100,000, sheets 3, 5, 6, 11, 21 and 23.
Guidebook:
• *Vom Nördlichsten Waldviertel ins Südlichste Kärnten/Der Eisenwurzenweg 08* by Wurst, Rachoy and Steffan, Verlag Styria, 1980. Available by mail from Freytag-Berndt u. Artaria.

Weitwanderweg 09—Salzsteigweg

From Bad Leonfelden (30 kilometers north of Linz) to the Wurzenpass region above Villach. Through the Sensengebirge, the Niedere Tauern and the Gurktaler Alpen. **Status:** Completed from Bad Leonfelden to Tauplitzalm. The portions of the route in Steiermark and Kärnten are currently marked. **Length:** 600 kilometers. **Walking Time:** 24 days. **Difficulty:** Moderately difficult. **Path Markings:** Red-white-red bars with black route numbers. Follows path numbers 109, 409, 209, 609, 909, 109 and 609.
Maps:
• Freytag-Berndt Wanderkarten 1:100,000, sheets 5, 6, 8, 20, 26 and 40, and 1:50,000, sheets 222, 224 and 233.
Guidebook:
• In preparation.
Further Information: Franz Kosina (see *Address Directory*).

Weitwanderweg 10—Rupertiweg

From the Bohemian Forest to the Nassfeld Hütte above Hermagor in Kärnten. Passes through the Berchtesgadener region and a portion of the Hohe Tauern. **Status:** Completed. **Length:** 800 kilometers. **Walking Time:** 32 days. **Difficulty:** Moderately difficult. **Path Markings:** Red-white-red bars with black route numbers. Follows path numbers 110, 810, 410, 110, 210 and 410.
Maps:
• Freytag-Berndt Wanderkarten 1:100,000, sheets 19, 22, 26, 39 and 43.

Guidebook:
• In preparation.

Austria's Hauptwanderwege

In addition to the Weitwanderwege, there are several shorter long-distance
paths known as the *Hauptwanderwege*—or principal paths—in the various
provinces of Austria. These include:

In Vorarlberg & Tyrol:

European Long-Distance Footpath E-5: The Austrian section stretches
from Bregenz to Timmelsjoch above the Ötz Valley in Tyrol. **Walking
Time:** 11 days. **Difficulty:** Moderately difficult. **Path Markings:** White
crosses.
Maps:
• Freytag-Berndt Wanderkarten 1:100,000, sheets 25, 35, 36 and 46.
Guidebook:
• *Europäischer Fernwanderweg 5, Bodensee—Adria* by Hans Schmidt,
Fink-Kümmerly + Frey, Stuttgart, 1977. Available by mail from Freytag-
Berndt u. Artaria.

In Kärnten:

Karnische Alpen-Weg: From Arnbach/Sillian (near the Italian border,
about 35 kilometers east of Lienz) to Egger Alm, above the village of Egg in
the Gail Valley (40 kilometers east of Villach). Follows the ridge of the
Karnische Alpen along the Italian-Austrian border for ca. 100 kilometers.
Walking Time: 6 days. **Difficulty:** Moderately difficult, with some difficult
sections. **Path Markings:** Red-white-red bars. Follows path number 402.
Maps:
• Freytag-Berndt Wanderkarten 1:100,000, sheets 18 and 22. Or:
• Österreichische Karte 1:50,000, sheets 195, 196, 197, 198 and 199.
Guidebook:
• *Karnischer Hauptkamm* by Peter Holl, Bergverlag Rudolf Rother,
Munich. Available by mail from Freytag-Berndt u. Artaria.

Karawankenweg: From Feistritz i. Rosental (10 kilometers south of
Klagenfurt) to Bleiburg. **Walking time:** 7 days. **Difficulty:** Moderately
difficult. **Path Markings:** Red-white-red bars, path number 603.
Maps:
• Österreichische Karte 1:50,000, sheets 203, 204, 211, 212 and 213.

Guidebooks:
• *Karawankenführer* by Jahne, and *Karawankenführer* (Hochstuhl Section) by Zopp and Frick, Heyn-Verlag, Klagenfurt. Available by mail from Freytag-Berndt u. Artaria.

Lavanttaler Höhenweg: A circular walk in the mountains above the Lavant Valley. Begins and ends in Wolfsburg. 135 kilometers. **Walking Time:** 6 days. **Difficulty:** Moderately difficult. **Path Markings:** Red-white-red bars.
Maps:
• Österreichische Karte 1:50,000, sheets 187, 188, 204 and 205.
Guidebook:
• *Lavanttaler Höhenweg Führer*, available from the ÖAV—Sektion Wolfsberg and Freytag-Berndt u. Artaria.

In Niederösterreich:

Grosser Pielachtaler Rundwanderweg: A circular path through the Pielach Valley starting in Baumgarten, 107 kilometers. **Walking Time:** 5 days. **Difficulty:** Moderately difficult. **Path Markings:** Red-white-red bars, path number 652.
Maps:
• Freytag-Berndt Wanderkarten 1:100,000, sheet 3. Or:
• Österreichische Karte 1:50,000, sheets 54, 55, 72 and 73.
Guidebook:
• *Grosser Pielachtaler Rundwanderweg Führer*, published by Fremdenverkehrsverband Pielachtal. Available by mail from the tourist office or Freytag-Berndt u. Artaria.

Kamptalseenweg: From Rosenburg to Nebelstein, 85 kilometers. **Walking Time:** 4 days. **Difficulty:** Easy. **Path Markings:** Red-white-red bars, path number 620. Follows a portion of Weitwanderweg 06.
Maps:
• Österreichische Karte 1:50,000, sheets 17, 18, 19, 20 and 21.
Guidebook:
• *Kamptal-Seenweg-Führer* by Rieder and Mück, ÖAV—Sektion Horn, 1972. Available from Freytag-Berndt u. Artaria. Translations available from foreign sections of the ÖAV.

Kuenringerweg: From Arbesbach to Raabs on the Thaya River, 70 kilometers. **Walking Time:** 4 days. **Difficulty:** Easy. **Path Markings:** Red-white-red bars, path number 611. Follows a portion of Weitwanderweg 08.
Maps:
• Österreichische Karte 1:50,000, sheets 7, 18, 19 and 20.
Guidebook:
• *Kuenringerweg Führer*, ÖAV—Sektion Waldviertel, Gmünd. A description of the Waldviertler-Vier-Märkte-Weg also is included in the guide.

Römerweg: A circular walk through the Texing Valley. Begins in Rammersdorf, 100 kilometers. **Walking Time:** 4 days. **Difficulty:** Easy. **Path Markings:** Red-white-red bars, path number 651.
Maps:
• Österreichische Karte 1:50,000, sheets 54 and 55.
Guidebook:
• *Römerweg Führer,* available from Freytag-Berndt u. Artaria.

Thaya-Kamp-Weg: From Raabs on the Thaya River to the Rosenburg on the Kamp River, 45 kilometers. **Walking Time:** 2 days. **Difficulty:** Easy. **Path Markings:** Red-white-red bars, path number 631. Follows a portion of Weitwanderweg 07.
Maps:
• Österreichische Karte 1:50,000, sheets 7, 20 and 21.
Guidebook:
• *Thaya-Kamp-Weg Führer,* from the ÖAV—Sektion Horn.

Thayatalweg: From Nebelstein to Retz, 170 kilometers. **Walking Time:** 7 days. **Difficulty:** Easy. **Path Markings:** Red-white-red bars, path number 630. Follows a portion of Weitwanderweg 07.
Maps:
• Österreichische Karte 1:50,000, sheets 5, 6, 7, 8, 9, 17 and 18.
Guidebook:
• *Thayatalweg Führer* by Carl Hermann, ÖAV—Sektion Waldviertel, Gmünd. Also available from Freytag-Berndt u. Artaria.

Waldviertler-Vier-Märkte-Weg: Circular walk from Grossgerungs through Rappottenstein, Schönbach, Arbesbach and Griesbach, 54 kilometers. A shorter alternate route of 17 kilometers can also be walked. **Walking Time:** 2 days. **Difficulty:** Easy. **Path Markings:** Red-white-red bars, path numbers 612 and 613. Follows a portion of Weitwanderweg 08.
Maps:
• Freytag-Berndt Wanderkarten 1:100,000, sheet 11. Or:
• Österreichische Karte 1:50,000, sheets 17, 18, 19 and 35.
Guidebook:
• *Waldviertler-Vier-Märkte-Weg/Kuenringerweg Führer,* ÖAV—Sektion Waldviertel. Also available from Freytag-Berndt u. Artaria.

Waldviertler Weitwanderweg: From Grein to Krems, 130 kilometers. **Walking Time:** 6 days. **Difficulty:** Easy. **Path Markings:** Red-white-red bars, path number 606.
Maps:
• Freytag-Berndt Wanderkarten 1:100,000, sheets 11 and 7. Or:
• Österreichische Karte 1:50,000, sheets 52, 53, 35, 36, 37 and 38.
Guidebook:
• *Waldviertler Weitwanderweg Führer,* available by mail from Freytag-Berndt u. Artaria.

Weinviertelweg: From Langenzersdorf to Drasenhofen, 120 kilometers. **Walking Time:** 5 days. **Difficulty:** Easy. **Path Markings:** Red-white-red bars, path number 632. Follows a portion of Weitwanderweg 07
Maps:
• Österreichische Karte 1:50,000, sheets 11, 22, 23, 24, 25, 39 and 40.
Guidebook:
• *Weinviertelweg Führer,* available by mail from Freytag-Berndt u. Artaria.

Wienerwald Weitwanderweg 04: Circuitous route through the Wienerwald from Grinzing to Mödling, 220 kilometers. **Walking Time:** 9 days. **Difficulty:** Easy. **Path Markings:** Red-white-red bars, path number 404.
Maps:
• Freytag-Berndt Wanderkarte 1:100,000, sheet 1. Or:
• Österreichische Karte 1:50,000, sheets 40, 56, 57, 58, 74 and 75.
Guidebook:
• *Wienerwald Weitwanderweg 404* by Glaser, Europäischer Verlag, Vienna, 1977. Available from Freytag-Berndt u. Artaria.

In Oberösterreich

Nordwaldkammwanderweg: From Aigen to Sandl, 100 kilometers. **Walking Time:** 5 days. **Difficulty:** Easy. **Path Markings:** White-blue-white bars.
Maps and Guidebook:
• See the description of Weitwanderweg 05, above.

Mittellandweg: From Oberkappel to Waldhausen, 109 kilometers. **Walking Time:** 5 days. **Difficulty:** Easy. **Path Markings:** Red-white-red bars, path number 150.
Maps:
• Freytag-Berndt Wanderkarte 1:100,000, sheets 11 and 26.
Guidebook:
• *Mühlviertler Mittellandweg Führer,* ÖAV—Sektionsverband Oberösterreich, Linz.

Mühlviertler Nord-Süd-Wanderweg: From Aigen to Neufelden, 60 kilometers. **Walking Time:** 3 days. **Difficulty:** Easy. **Path Markings:** Not entirely marked.
Map:
• Freytag-Berndt Wanderkarte 1:100,000, sheet 26.
Guidebook:
• A short route description in German is available on request from: Fremdenverkehrsverband Oberösterreich, Linz. Ask for the *Routenvorschläge* for the *Weitwanderwege im Mühlviertel.* Also available from: Fremdenverkehrsverband Mühlviertel, Linz.

Naturfreunde-Wanderweg: From Mauthausen to Karlstift, 90 kilometers.
Walking Time: 4 days. **Difficulty:** Easy. **Path Markings:** Red-white-red
bars, path number 170.
Maps:
• Freytag-Berndt Wanderkarte 1:100,000, sheets 11 and 40.
Guidebook:
• *Mühlviertel-Naturfreunde-Wanderweg-Führer*, available from Freytag-
Berndt u. Artaria.

In Salzburg & Osttirol:

Tauernhöhenweg: From the Ennstal to the Grossvenediger, 100 kilome-
ters. **Walking Time:** 5 days. **Difficulty:** Difficult. For experienced moun-
tain walkers only. **Path Markings:** Red-white-red bars, path numbers 502,
702 and 902.
Maps:
• Alpenvereinskarten 1:25,000, sheets 36, 39, 40, 41, 42 and 1:50,000,
sheets Ankogelgruppe, Niedere Tauern II and Schladminger Tauern.
• Österreichische Karte 1:50,000, sheets 122-129, 151-158 and 178-181.
Guidebook:
• *Tauernhöhenweg* by Prof. Dr. Ernst Herrmann, available from ÖAV—
Sektion Edelweiss and Freytag-Berndt u. Artaria.

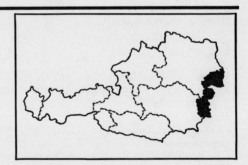

Burgenland

Burgenland, Austria's easternmost province, is a narrow plain along the
Czech and Hungarian frontiers. It is the only flat region in Austria. Here,
acacias and poppies grow wild, flocks of geese waddle through peaceful
pastoral villages and oxen pull wagons past cottages thatched with straw.
This is Austria's least developed walking area, although European Long-
Distance Footpath E-4 (Weitwanderweg 01) ends on the shores of the
Neusiedler See, Austria's largest lake and its lowest point (115 meters).
Also, portions of two other long-distance paths—Weitwanderwege 02 and
07—will eventually cross the province.

Useful Addresses

See *Address Directory:*

> **Landesfremdenverkehrsverband für das Burgenland.** Provides general tourist information on the province.
>
> **ÖAV—Sektion Burgenland,** Eisenstadt.

Maps

Burgenland is covered by Freytag-Berndt Wanderkarten 1:100,000, sheets 2, 27, 42 and 44, as well as by Österreichische Karte 1:50,000, sheets 61, 77, 78, 79, 107, 108, 137, 167 and 168.

Guidebooks

Descriptions of the portions of Weitwanderwege 01, 02, 07 and 07A that pass through Burgenland are included in the guidebooks for these paths (see the section on *Austria's Long-Distance Footpaths).* Several hikes in Burgenland are also described in the *Burgenländisches Wanderbuch,* available from Freytag-Berndt und Artaria.

Hiking Routes

Several hikes can be planned in Burgenland by referring to the maps that cover the province.

Suggested Walks

Burgenländischer Nord-Süd-Weg: From the Neusiedlersee to Güssing, 155 kilometers. Forms a portion of Weitwanderweg 07. **Walking Time:** 6 days. **Difficulty:** Easy.
Maps:
• Freytag-Berndt Wanderkarte 1:100,000, sheets 27 and 42.
Guidebook:
• *Burgenländisches Wanderbuch,* Burgenlandverlag, Eisenstadt. Available by mail from Freytag-Berndt u. Artaria.

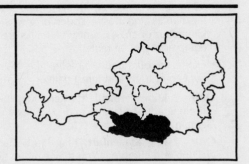

Kärnten (Carinthia)

Carinthia is Austria's southernmost province, bordering Italy and Yugoslavia. It has more lakes than any other province in Austria and the warmest, driest weather. Surrounding the lakes are broad river valleys, forested mountainsides and meadows, as well as the craggy peaks of the Central Alps and the Southern Limestone Alps. Tucked away in the province's mountains are two nature reserves with rare plants. At Lendorf, there are large bushes of yellow rhododendrons, a relic of the Cenozoic Age. And the Gartnerkofel, a mountain south of Hermagor, is one of the few places outside of the Himalayas on which the brilliant blue flower *Wulfenia* grows.

Trails in Kärnten range from gentle woodland paths through isolated valleys to high-alpine routes in the Hohe Tauern, the Karnische Alps and the Karawanken Mountains. There also are paths in the nature reserves and protected land areas abutting many of the province's lakes.

Useful Addresses

See *Address Directory:*

> **Landesfremdenverkehrsamt Kärnten.** Provides general tourist information on the province. Also issues several useful German-language publications for walkers and skiers:
>
> * *Kärnten—Wanderfreuden, "Bergwandern."* Outlines nine suggested hikes and one spring ski tour in the province. Lists the trails for which hiking badges are awarded. Also lists the addresses and telephone numbers of 13 organizations that offer walking tours.
> * *Kärnten—Wanderfreuden, "Einfache Unterkünfte-Schutzhütten-Jugendherbergen."* Lists the opening and closing dates, number of sleeping spaces, addresses and telephone numbers of the mountain huts, guesthouses and youth hostels along the province's trails.
> * *Kärnten—Winterhobbies, "Spazier- und Wanderwege."* Lists the locations of Carinthia's 510 kilometers of cleared winter footpaths.

- *Kärnten—Wintersport, "Langlauf und Skiwandern in Kärnten."* Lists the names and postal codes of towns in which Carinthia's 650 kilometers of cross-country ski tracks are located. Also notes where equipment can be rented.
- *Fitnessparcours und Waldlehrpfade.* Lists the lengths and locations of keep-fit trails and forest paths.

ÖAV—Sektionsverband Kärnten, Klagenfurt. Can answer specific questions about walking and climbing in Kärnten. Best to write in German.

ÖAV—Zweig Klagenfurt, Klagenfurt. Can provide information on walking and climbing. You may write in German or English.

Maps

Kärnten is covered by Freytag-Berndt Wanderkarten 1:50,000, sheets 221, 222, 223, 224, 231, 232, 233 and 234; 1:100,000, sheets 18, 19, 20, 22 and 23; and Österreichische Karte 1:50,000, sheets 153-157, 159, 161, 179-188, 196-205 and 211-213.

Guidebooks

Numerous trail guides are available. Bergverlag Rudolf Rother alone publishes 12 guides to the various mountain massifs. One general book on walking in Kärnten is:

- *Kärntner Wanderbuch,* Tyrolia Verlag, 362 pages. Describes 70 mountain hikes in the province. Provides all necessary information about maps, trail lodgings and approach routes.

A complete list of guidebooks, entitled *Bücher für den Bergfreund,* is available on request from Freytag-Berndt u. Artaria.

Suggested Walks

The six-day-long hikes and spring ski tour described in the Austrian National Tourist Office booklet, *Mountain Rambles in Austria* (see the section on *Where to Get Walking Information* earlier in this chapter), are all highly recommended. They range in difficulty from easy to three tours with sections that require a guide or mountaineering experience. The booklet lists the names of trail lodgings along the way and provides a brief day-to-day description of each route. The recommended guidebooks and maps for the routes can be purchased in local bookstores or by mail from Freytag-Berndt und Artaria.

In the Gurktaler Alpen north of Villach, a spectacular circular hike is:

Hochrindl Rundkurs: From Villach, take the train to Feldkirchen, then change to the postbus for Sirnitz-Turracher Höhe. Get off at Hochrindl. **Walking Time:** 6 days. **Difficulty:** Moderately difficult to difficult. Superb views.
Maps:
• *Ausflugskarte der Turracher Höhe,* 1:50,000, sheet 6, available from Bergverlag Rudolf Rother. Or:
• Freytag-Berndt Wanderkarten 1:50,000, sheet 222.
Both can be purchased at Kaufhaus Ski Sepp Turracher Höhe, a climbing shop and office of the local ÖAV, in the community of Albeck near Sirnitz.
Guidebook:
• *Kurzführer Sommerkurort und Wintersportzentrum—Turracher Höhe* by Sepp Huber, Verlag Rudolf Rother. Available from Kaufhaus Ski Sepp.
Day 1: Six hours. From Hochrindl, 1580 m, to Turracher Höhe by way of Messanegger Alm, Neuwirt Hütte, Grosser Speikkofel, 2270 m, Brett Höhe, 2320 m, Gruft and Schoberriegel. Overnight at Turracher Höhe in Gasthof Gangl.
Day 2: Six hours. From Turracher Höhe to Falkert See by way of Rinsennock, 2334 m, Pregat Scharte and Windeben. Overnight at Falkert See in Falkert Haus.
Day 3: Eight hours. From Falkert See to Dr. J. Mehrl Hütte by way of Falkertspitze, 2308 m, Falkert Schutzhaus, 1552 m, Mallnock, Grund, 1688 m, Karlbad, Seenock, 2260 m, and Stubennock. Overnight at Dr. Mehrl Hütte (ÖAV).
Day 4: Six hours. From Dr. Mehrl Hütte to Wildbach Hütte by way of Rosanin Alm, Friesenhals Höhe, 2246 m, Gr. Königstuhl, Stangboden, Stangscharte, Kothütte and Talentschger Alm. Overnight at Wildbach Hütte.
Day 5: Six hours. From Wildbach Hütte to Flattnitz by way of Hannebauer, Perner Alm, 1683 m, Diesling See, Michleben, 1852 m, and Fürsten Alm. Overnight at Flattnitz in Hotel Ladinig.
Day 6: Five hours. From Flattnitz to Hochrindl by way of Spitzer Alm, Haidner Höhe, 1799 m, Weisses Kreuz and Pölling. Overnight at Hochrindl in Hotel Kärntner Hof.

Information on three *Hauptwanderwege* in Kärnten is included in the section on *Austria's Long-Distance Footpaths.*

Cross-Country Skiing

Sketch maps of many routes can be obtained from local tourist offices. For the postal codes and names of towns in which the routes are located, refer to the provincial tourist office list, *Kärnten—Wintersport.*

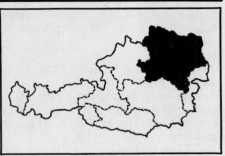

Niederösterreich (Lower Austria)

Niederösterreich is Austria's largest province—19,170 square kilometers. It is also the most varied. At its southern border with Steiermark the peaks of the Rax and Schneeberg rise to altitudes in excess of 2,000 meters, marking the eastern terminus of the Central Alps. Its southeast corner is covered by the forested slopes of the Alpine foothills and is cut by the narrow river valleys of the Ybbs, Erlauf, Pielach and Traisen. Further north are the Vienna Woods and the Wachau with its wooded hills, Baroque towers and steeply terraced vineyards above the banks of the Danube. Here, Austria's first dynasty, the Babenbergs, erected their first residence in the year 976, and during the Crusades King Richard the Lionhearted was imprisoned in the riverside town of Dürnstein. Along Austria's northern border with Czechoslovakia is the high granite plateau of the Waldviertel, an area of dark forests, and the rolling pastureland and fields of the Weinviertel—the wine district. Scattered throughout the province are prehistoric potsherds, Roman remains, medieval castles, fortified churches and the ornate facades of Baroque abbeys and monasteries. There also are streams, lakes and quiet, tule-rimmed ponds. And there is the city of Vienna. In all, the province is divided into 21 districts—each with its own special rewards for the walker.

Trails in Niederösterreich are as varied as the terrain. Portions of six of Austria's Weitwanderwege cross the province. And it has 10 Hauptwanderwege—principal paths. There also are innumerable shorter paths criss-crossing its various regions. A few of the paths in the southern region of the province have steep sections, but none are difficult. In fact, Niederösterreich offers some of the gentlest walking in Austria.

Useful Addresses

See *Address Directory:*
   Niederösterreichische Fremdenverkehrswerbung. Provides general tourist information on Niederösterreich. German is primarily spoken

in the office. Only one person on the staff speaks English. Useful German-language publications available through the office include:

- *Wanderbares Niederösterreich Rundwanderwege.* Describes 120 circular walks in the province. Also provides details on nearly 30 long-distance footpaths.

- *Wir wandern—Ausflugtips und Wandervorschläge.* Describes 20 day hikes in various regions of the province. All can be reached on bus, train and car. Includes sketch maps. Also lists the maps needed for each hike and the names, addresses and telephone numbers of inns along the routes. Published by Universitätsbuchhandlung Wilhelm Braumüller & Sohn, Vienna.

- *Wanderkarte der Gemeinde Wienerwald.* A hiking map in a scale of 1:40,000 with trails marked in red, blue, green and yellow. Five circular hikes in the Vienna Woods are described on the back. The hikes range in length from 37 to 54 kilometers.

- *Wanderkarte Semmering-Rax-Schneealpe.* A hiking and ski-trail map in a scale of 1:50,000. Trails are numbered and marked in red; ski routes are marked in blue. On the back, 13 towns in the mountain region are described. The descriptions list principal tourist attractions, number of lodgings, hiking possibilities and the addresses and telephone numbers of tourist offices. Published by the Fremdenverkehrsverband Semmering-Rax-Schneealpe.

- *Rundwanderwege im Westlichen Weinviertel.* Describes 22 circular hikes in the Weinviertel—the wine district. Walking times range from one to four hours. Published by the Fremdenverkehrsverband Westliches Weinviertel.

- *Seilbahnen, Bergbahnen, Sessellift, Schlepplift und Schiwanderwege in Niederösterreich.* Lists the towns where the province's 470 kilometers of marked cross-country and ski touring tracks are located. Notes which towns have facilities for instruction and equipment rental.

- *Naturparks, Tierparks, Fitnessparcours, Waldlehrpfade und Weinlehrpfade in Niederösterreich.* Describes the province's 13 nature parks and lists the locations of its keep-fit trails, nature paths and wine-identification paths (where hikers sample wines along the way).

- *Fremdenverkehrsgebietsverbände.* Gives the addresses and telephone numbers of the regional tourist offices in the 21 regions of Niederösterreich.

ÖAV—Sektionenverband Niederösterreich. Can provide specific information on Weitwanderweg 01 and trails in the Vienna Woods. You may write in English or German.

ÖAV—Sektionsverband Niederösterreich. Can refer you to the appropriate ÖAV sections for answers to specific questions on hiking in the various regions of Niederösterreich. Best to write in German.

ÖAV—Sektionenverband Wien, Vienna. Can provide information on walking around Vienna. Best to write in German.

Hiking information can also be obtained from many local tourist offices. Among the most helpful are:

Fremdenverkehrsverband Kamptal. Issues a list entitled *Wanderwege in Gars am Kamp* that describes 15 short walks. Also sells the guidebook to the *Kamptal-Seenweg* (see the description of *Austria's Hauptwanderwege* under the section on *Austria's Long-Distance Footpaths*).

Fremdenverkehrsverband Oberes Waldviertel. The staff is extremely helpful. Among the publications available through the office are: *Nordwald-Loipen,* a sketch map, elevation profile and route description of three cross-country ski tracks in the Nordwald; and *Schutzgebiete und Naturparks in Niederösterreich,* a map in a scale of 1:25,000 that shows the locations of nature parks, long-distance paths and many of the principal footpaths in the province. The office also sells the guidebooks to the *Thayatalweg, Waldviertler-Vier-Märkte-Weg, Küenringerweg* and *Nord-Süd Weitwanderweg.*

Fremdenverkehrsverband Pielachtal. Publishes the guidebook to the *Grosser Pielachtaler Rundwanderweg* (see the section on *Austria's Long-Distance Footpaths*).

Fremdenverkehrsverband Semmering-Rax-Schneealpe. Issues a list of mountain walks. Also publishes the 1:50,000 *Semmering-Rax-Schneealpe Wanderkarte.*

Fremdenverkehrsverband Thayatal. Issues a list entitled *Informationsblatt* that describes 14 short circular walks. Also stocks guidebooks to the *Thaya-Kamp-Weg* and *Thayatalweg* (see the section on *Austria's Long-Distance Footpaths*).

Fremdenverkehrsbüro Krems. Oversees the *Kremser Wanderweg,* a 12-kilometer path in the hills above the Danube River.

Fremdenverkehrsverein Mödling. Can provide information about the Wienerwald-Wandertag, the Internationale Mödlinger Föhrenberge-Wanderung and the Internationale Wienerwald Wanderung. Issues a list entitled *Rundwanderwege im Anningerraum* that outlines 25 short walks in the Vienna Woods. Also sells the guidebook to the *Wienerwald Weitwander Weg 404* (see the section on *Austria's Long-Distance Footpaths*).

Fremdenverkehrsverband Ybbstaler-Alpenvorland-Mostviertel. Issues a list entitled *Wandern und Wanderferien im schönen Ybbstal* that describes 56 short walks in the Alpine foothills. Includes sketch maps.

Fremdenverkehrsverband Ysper-Weitental. Sells the 1:25,000 *Wanderkarte Strudengau* on which seven hikes of up to 20 kilometers are marked, and the 1:10,000 *Yspertal-Wanderkarte* that shows paths in the Ysper Valley. Also provides sketch maps of ski touring routes in the area.

Similar information can be obtained from many other local tourist offices.

Maps

Niederösterreich is covered by the Freytag-Berndt Wanderkarten 1:50,000, sheets 021 and 022; 1:100,000, sheets 1, 2, 3, 5, 7 and 11; and Österreichische Karte 1:50,000, sheets 5-11, 17-26, 35-43, 51-61, 70-78, 104-106 and 137.

Guidebooks

* *Die Voralpen an Traisen und Gölsen,* Baumgartner, Verlag Niederösterreichisches Presshaus, St. Pölten, 1976. Describes 235 day hikes and mountain tours, 20 ski tours and 5 long-distance hikes of from 2 to 10 days in the Alpine foothills.
* *Ötscherland und Pielachtal,* Baumgartner and Tippelt, Verlag Nö. Presshaus, St. Pölten, 1977. Describes 164 day hikes and ski tours in the region surrounding the river valleys of the Erlauf, Ybbs and Pielach. Also describes six long-distance hikes.
* *Mariazeller Bergland mit Schneealpe, Veitsch und Hochschwab,* Baumgartner and Tippelt, Verlag Nö. Presshaus, St. Pölten, 1977. Describes 138 day hikes, 68 ski tours and 3 long-distance hikes in the mountain region between Steiermark and Niederösterreich.
* *Wanderungen rings um Wien,* Tyrolia Verlag. Describes 50 hikes around Vienna.
* *Weitwanderwege in Niederösterreich* by Fritz Peterka, Verlag Niederösterreichisches Presshaus, St. Pölten. Describes the long-distance footpaths in Niederösterreich.

In addition, Bergverlag Rudolf Rother publishes several trail guides that cover portions of Niederösterreich. These include: *Nördliche Kalkalpen, Wienerwald und Salzkammergut, Türnitzer und Gutensteiner Alpen* and *Ybbstaler Alpen.* A complete list of guide books, entitled *Bücher für den Bergfreund,* is available on request from Freytag-Berndt u. Artaria.

Suggested Walks

The hikes suggested in the Austrian National Tourist Office's booklet, *Mountain Rambles in Austria*, are hard to beat—at least as an introduction to walking in Niederösterreich. Of the eight hikes suggested in the booklet, the four most spectacular are:

1. From Schneeberg via Raxalpe to Göller.
2. From the Vienna Woods to the Foothills of the Alps.
3. Through the Waldviertel Region to the Danube.
4. Spring Ramble from the Kamp Valley to the Wachau.

Another highly recommended walk is the section of the Nord-Süd Weitwanderweg 05 from Nebelstein to Mariazell. To hike this section of the trail takes eight days. You will need the Freytag-Berndt Wanderkarten 1:100,000, sheets 3, 7 and 11, and the *Nord-Süd Weitwanderweg Führer*, available by mail from Freytag-Berndt und Artaria. This is perhaps the best single hike for an overview of Niederösterreich.

Cross-Country Skiing

Sketch maps for many cross-country and ski touring routes are available from local tourist offices. For the postal codes and names of towns in the areas in which the routes are located, refer to the *Schiwanderwege* list published by the provincial tourist board.

One of the most spectacular ski tours is along the ridge of the Raxalpe, beginning at the upper terminal of the Raxseilbahn (cable car), 1545 m, and continuing for more than 10 kilometers past Otto Haus (ÖAV hut), 1644 m, Karl Ludwig Haus, 1804 m and below Heukuppe, 2007 m, to Zahmes Gamseck, 1894 m. The route should be attempted only by experienced skiers. For further information, write the Fremdenverkehrsverband Semmering-Rax-Schneealpe.

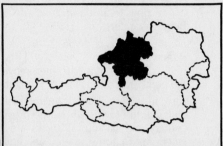

Oberösterreich
(Upper Austria)

Oberösterreich is divided into five distinct regions: to the north is the Mühlviertel, a wooded hill region between the Bohemian Forest and the Danube River. To the east is the Inn-Hausruckviertel, an expansive plain of fields and meadows surrounded by gentle hills and forests. In the center is Linz-Donauraum, a region of low hills below the city of Linz. To the southeast is the Krems-Steyr-Enns-Tal, a mountain region dominated by the peaks of the Totes Gebirge and Sengsengebirge. And to the southwest is the spectacular Salzkammergut.

In the Salzkammergut, two chains of lakes are set among the limestone peaks of the Höllengebirge and the Dachstein. Within the steep, glaciated slopes of the Dachstein is a network of huge rock caverns, tunnels and ice caves (2½ hours by footpath from Obertraun). Below its slopes lie the Hallstätter See and the town of Hallstatt, where hunters came more than 4,500 years ago to hunt game around its salt-bearing springs. When the spring waters evaporated, it became the site of a famous salt mine that, at one point, was worked by the Romans.

Oberösterreich has four *Hauptwanderwege*, which take from five to seven days to walk. In addition, two of Austria's *Weitwanderwege* will eventually cross the province from north to south. Other paths crisscross the various regions of the province.

Useful Addresses

See *Address Directory:*

> **Oberösterreichisches Landesfremdenverkehrsamt.** Provides general tourist information on the province. German-language publications that are useful to walkers include:
>
> - *Weitwanderwege im Mühlviertel.* Has brief day-by-day descriptions of four major trails in the province: the Nordwaldkammwanderweg, Mittellandwanderweg, Naturfreunde-Wanderweg and Mühlviertel

Nord-Süd-Wanderweg. Lists overnight lodgings and bus and train connections to and from the trails. The area is covered by Freytag-Berndt Wanderkarten 1:100,000, sheets 11 and 26.

• *Fitness-Parcours, Gymnastik-Wanderwege, Markierte Wanderwege, Rundwanderwege, Lehrpfade.* Lists the towns in which keep-fit trails, circular paths and interpretive paths are located. Also notes the number of kilometers of footpaths near the towns.

• *Langlaufloipen, Hallenschwimmbäder.* Lists the names and postal codes of the towns where the province's 550 kilometers of cross-country and ski touring tracks are located. Also notes the towns where instruction is offered and equipment can be rented. Second half of the brochure lists indoor swimming pools.

The office also provides information on various *Wanderwochen*—rambling weeks—that are organized in the province each year.

ÖAV—Sektion Oberösterreich. Can answer specific questions on walking and climbing in the province. Sells the *Mühlviertler Mittellandweg Führer.*

Maps

For climbs and rambles in the Dachstein and Totes Gebirge, the 1:25,000 Alpenvereinskarten, sheets 14, 15/1, 15/2 and 15/3, are recommended. The remainder of Oberösterreich is covered by the Freytag-Berndt Wanderkarten 1:50,000, sheet 281; 1:100,000, sheets 5, 6, 8, 26, 40 and 43; and Österreichische Karte 1:50,000, sheets 12-17, 28-35, 44-51, 64-70, 95-99 and 127.

Guidebooks

• *Wandern in Oberösterreich 1,* Tyrolia Verlag, 336 pages. Describes 50 hikes in the Salzkammergut and Enns Valley.

• *Wandern in Oberösterreich 2,* Tyrolia Verlag, 240 pages. Describes 35 hikes in the Hausruck and Mühlviertel. Includes a description of the Mühlviertler Mittellandweg.

In addition, Bergverlag Rudolf Rother publishes 11 trail guides that cover the Dachstein, Sengsengebirge, Totes Gebirge and the Alpine foothill region. A complete list of guidebooks may be obtained from Freytag-Berndt u. Artaria.

Suggested Walks

The Austrian National Tourist Office booklet, *Mountain Rambles in Austria,* gives seven day-by-day descriptions of spectacular walks in

Oberösterreich, in addition to one high-alpine spring ski tour for experienced high-altitude skiers. All are highly recommended. Two of the routes, the "Ramble through the Northern Alps" and "Rambling through the Totes Gebirge," can be linked up by walking the Totes Gebirge ramble in reverse, then continuing on the "Ramble through the Northern Alps" from Hinterstoder. The total walking time for this route is nine days.

The most spectacular mountain walk of the bunch is the "High Altitude Rambles in the Dachstein Area." It is, however, not an easy walk. For gentle walks, both the Mühlviertler Mittellandweg and Nordwaldkammweg are recommended (see the section on *Austria's Long-Distance Footpaths*).

Cross-Country Skiing

Many local tourist offices publish sketch maps of the cross-country ski tracks and ski touring routes in their areas. The postal codes and names of the towns are listed in the provincial tourist office's publication, *Langlaufloipen Hallenschwimmbäder*.

For expert ski tourers, the route described in *Mountain Rambles in Austria* is recommended.

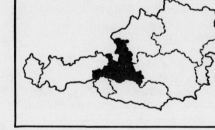

Salzburg Province

Salzburg is one of Austria's smallest provinces. What it lacks in size, however, it makes up for in natural beauty. Mountains ring its borders and tower above deep green valleys in the southern part of the province. On its southern border with Osttirol is the Grossglockner, Austria's highest peak. To the north are the Alpine foothills and the Salzkammergut Lakes. The province also includes the Eisriesenwelt, the world's largest accessible ice cave, and the Krimml Waterfalls, the highest in Europe. In addition, there are eight other notable waterfalls and gorges in the province, a wildlife refuge and four nature parks. And, of course, there is the city of Salzburg, birthplace of Mozart, seat of archbishops for nearly 1,000 years and home of the Salzburg Summer Festival, Europe's first—and most important— music festival.

For walkers, 51 localities in the province distribute hiking badges as a distinction for accomplishing a pre-established hiking performance. Twenty resorts have mountain guides available. Six guides run private mountaineering schools. There are keep-fit trails in 14 localities. And for cross-country skiers, there are marked tracks near 37 towns.

Useful Addresses

See *Address Directory:*

> **Landesverkehrsamt in Salzburg.** Provides general tourist information on the province. Useful German-language publications for walkers include:
>
> * *Fitness-Parcours.* Describes the locations, lengths and facilities of the province's keep-fit trails.
> * *Schneegeräumte Wanderwege im Salzburger Land.* Lists the locations and lengths of the paths that are cleared during the winter.
> * *Langlauf im Salzburger Land.* Lists the names and postal codes of the towns where the province's 1,490 kilometers of cross-country and ski touring routes are located. Also notes which towns offer instruction and equipment rental. Includes prices.
>
> **ÖAV—Sektionenverband Salzburg.** Can answer specific questions about walking and climbing in Salzburg. Best to write in German.

Maps

The Alpensvereinskarten 1:25,000, sheets 9/1, 9/2, 10/1 and 10/2 are recommended for hikes and climbs in the Loferer Steinberge, Leoganger Steinberge, Steinernes Meer and Hochkönig-Hagengebirge in the western part of Salzburg Province; for the Niedere Tauern and Glockner-Gruppe in the south, sheets 36, 39, 40 and 61 are recommended. Maps in a scale of 1:50,000 are also published by Bergverlag Rudolf Rother to the Berchtesgadener Alps *(BV–Tourenblätter, Mappe 2)* and the Glockner-Gruppe *(BV/Tourenblätter, Mappe 7)*. The remainder of Salzburg Province is covered by the Freytag-Berndt Wanderkarten 1:50,000, sheets 101, 102, 103, 281 and 382; 1:100,000, sheets 9, 10, 19, 20, 28, 30, 38 and 39; and Österreichische Karte 1:50,000, sheets 63-65, 92-95, 122-126 and 151-158.

Guidebooks

Numerous guidebooks are available. Bergverlag Rudolf Rother alone publishes more than 15 guides to the mountain regions in Salzburg. Several other publishers also have walking guides. Tyrolia Verlag, for instance, has two books that describe several hikes in the mountains and foothills, *Salzburger Wanderungen 1* and *Salzburger Wanderungen 2*. A complete list of guides is available from Freytag-Berndt u. Artaria. Or you can browse the shelves in one of the local bookstores.

Suggested Walks

Again, the hikes suggested in the Austrian National Tourist Office's booklet, *Mountain Rambles in Austria,* are recommended—especially "From Hut to Hut in the Hohe Tauern, including ascent of Grossvenediger" (for experts only—includes glacier crossings and climbing) and "Via Steinernes Meer to Loferer Steinberge" in the Pinzgauer Saalachtal region in the eastern part of the province.

A variation on this route is:

Three-day ramble through the Leoganger Steinberge and Steinernes Meer: Begins at the train station in Leogang (on the train line between Kitzbühel and Salzburg). Trail well marked. Moderately difficult.

Maps:
• *Zinner Wanderkarte* 1:30,000. Available from the tourist office in Leogang. Also:
• Alpenvereinskarten 1:20,000, sheets 9/2 and 10/1.

Day 1: Up the trail from Leogang to Passauer Hütte, 2033 m (3-4 hours). A steep climb. Beautiful view from the refuge to the Grossglockner and Grossvenediger mountains. Excursions from the refuge to Hochzinn (1 hour) and the Birnhorn (2 hours). Overnight at Passauer Hütte. **Note:** The refuge is attended on weekends only from June until September.

Day 2: Descend via the Hochgrub to Diesbach-Stausee (2 hours). A private road leads from Diesbach to the Diesbach Reservoir. The Loferer taxi company in Weissbach is authorized to take guests along the road to the reservoir. You can call the taxi from a nearby farmhouse, Tel. 25 81 15. From the reservoir, follow the path along the eastern shore up to Ingolstädter-Haus, 2132 m (2½ hours). Excursion from the refuge to Grossen-Hundstod (1½ hours). Overnight at Ingolstädter-Haus.

Day 3: From the Ingolstädter-Haus along the Eichstätter-Weg to Riemannhaus, 2177 m (3 hours). Excursions from the refuge to Breithorn (1 hour) and the Schönfeldspitze (2 hours). From Riemannhaus you can then:
a. Descend to Maria Alm (2½ hours), lodgings, bus connections.
b. Descend to Saalfelden (2½ hours), lodgings, train connections to all points.
c. Continue to Kärlinger Haus, 1630 m (2½ hours). This hut is in Germany; you will need your passport. Overnight at Kärlinger Haus, then descend to St. Bartholomä, Germany, on the Königsee (3 hours) and continue to the town of Königsee for lodgings and train connections.

In the same region, there is a spectacular day hike:

Saalachtaler Höhenweg: From Bibergalm, 1453 m, to Spielberghorn, 2044 m, along a high ridge of the Kitzbühler Alpen. The path leads through vast fields of alpine roses. Magnificent panoramas. **Walking Time:** 1 to 2 days. **Difficulty:** Moderately difficult. **Path Markings:** Stylized arrow in a circle.

Map:
• *Zinner-Wanderkarte*, 1:30,000, available from the tourist offices in Saalfelden, Viehhofen and Saalbach.

Guidebook:
• A leaflet entitled *Saalachtaler Höhenweg* is available from the tourist offices. It includes a sketch map of the route and shows the locations of lodgings, cable cars and chair lifts along the route.

Approach: By chair lift from Saalfelden to Bibergalm.

Return: By cable car to Saalbach.

Further Information: Fremdenverkehrs-Gebietsverband Pinzgauer Saalachtal (see *Address Directory*).

Cross-Country Skiing

Many local tourist offices publish sketch maps of the routes in their area. For the postal codes and names of towns in the areas in which the routes are located, refer to *Langlauf im Salzburger Land*, available from the provincial tourist board.

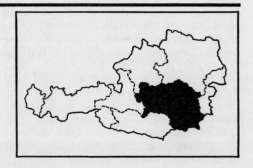

Steiermark (Styria)

Steiermark is Austria's second-largest province. It encompasses 12 major mountain massifs, is cut by two major rivers—the Mur and Enns—and is more than half covered by forests. Patchworks of woods, pastures and fields stretch up valleys in the foothills of the mountains, surrounding small villages clustered around church spires. In the north, there are noted climbing regions—the Gesäuse and Dachstein—and Styria's highest peak, the 2,995-meter (9,826-foot) Dachstein. And in the south, some of Austria's best-known wines are grown in vast vineyards. The province also is dotted with stalactite caves, lakes, numerous waterfalls and gorges.

Although the mountains of Steiermark are not as high as those in western Austria, they are no less spectacular. They are, however, less well known and tend to be less crowded in midsummer. In addition, there are gentle woodland paths in the Alpine foothills and paths that wander through the vineyards in the south. Mountain guides are available in 47 communities. There also are five climbing schools in the province. And there are 57 communities in which cross-country-ski and ski touring tracks are located.

Useful Addresses

See *Address Directory:*

Amt der Steiermärkischen Landesregierung, Landesfremdenverkehrsabteilung. Provides general tourist information on the province. Useful German-language publications for walkers include:

* *Steiermark Panorama Karte.* Gives you a birds-eye view of the mountains, valleys and lakes in the province. Useful for orientation. On the back of the map, towns in the province are listed in alphabetical order. Various columns give the towns' postal codes, altitudes, number of hotel room beds and tell which have mountain guides, campgrounds, and various tourist facilities.

* *Skiwandern und Skilanglauf in Österreich—Steiermark.* Lists the locations and lengths of the province's 550 kilometers of cross-country ski tracks and ski touring routes. Notes where instruction is offered and equipment can be rented.

* *Steiermark Hotelpreisliste.* Gives general travel information on Steiermark. Lists each town alphabetically, with the telephone prefixes, postal codes, addresses and telephone numbers of tourist offices. Short descriptions of each town include the number of kilometers of nearby walking paths. In the back is a list of hotels, inns and pensions.

ÖAV—Sektion Graz. A most helpful section of the ÖAV. Can answer queries in English, French and German.

Maps

Steiermark is covered by the Freytag-Berndt Wanderkarten 1:100,000, sheets 2, 4, 6, 8, 13, 20, 21, 41, 42 and 44; and Österreichische Karte 1:50,000, sheets 72, 73, 96-105, 127-136, 158-166, 188-192 and 205-209.

Guidebooks

Numerous guidebooks are available including:

- *Wandern um Graz* by Günther Auferbauer, Verlag Styria. Describes hikes in the mountain and foothill area around Graz. Recommended.
- *Hochschwab Wanderführer* by Günther Auferbauer, Verlag Styria. A well-done guide to the trails in the Hochschwab Massif in northern Steiermark. Recommended.
- *Wanderführer Hartberg und Wechselgebiet* by Josef Wallner, Verlag Styria. A good guide to the trails in the rolling countryside and foothills in eastern Steiermark.
- *Eisenerzer Alpen* by Scharfetter and Buchenauer, Verlag Styria. A guide to mountain hiking, climbing and ski touring in the mountains of northern Steiermark.
- *Bergwandern in der Steiermark* by Buchenauer, Tyrolia Verlag. Describes numerous mountain hikes throughout Steiermark.
- *Wandern in der Steiermark* by Buchenauer, Tyrolia Verlag. Describes numerous rambles throughout Steiermark.
- *Mariazeller Bergland* by Baumgartner and Tippet, Verlag Nö. Pressehaus. Describes day hikes, ski tours and long-distance hikes in the mountain region surrounding Mariazell.

Eight guidebooks are also available from Bergverlag Rudolf Rother: *Fischbacher Alpen, Bucklige Welt; Admont-Gesäuse; Gleinalpe, Koralpe, Packalpe; Hochschwab; Mürztal: Niedere Tauern; Wienerwald und Salzkammergut,* and *Nördliche Kalkalpen.* A complete list of guidebooks is available from Freytag-Berndt u. Artaria.

Suggested Walks

Of the hikes suggested in the Austrian National Tourist Office booklet, *Mountain Rambles in Austria,* parts of three can be linked up for a spectacular 11-day walk along high ridges and past lakes and waterfalls. The route also can be extended for another six days. The route follows sections of one of Austria's west-east long-distance footpaths, *Weitwanderweg 02.* While much of the route is only moderately difficult, mountain walking experience is necessary to traverse several of the ridges along the route.
Maps:
- Freytag-Berndt Wanderkarten 1:100,000, sheets 6 and 20.
Guidebook:
- *Wandern in der Steiermark* by Buchenauer, Tyrolia Verlag.
Day 1: Six hours. From Schladming railway station by bus via the mountain road to Hochwurzen-Hütte, 1852 m. Take high-altitude path number 773 via Schiedeck, 2339 m, to Ignaz-Mattis Hütte, 1986 m, on the Giglachsee. Overnight at Ignaz-Mattis Hütte (open June 15 to September 25).

Day 2: Six hours. Via Rotmannlscharte, 2433 m, on path 702 to Krugeckscharte, 2303 m. Descend to Keinprechthütte, 1872 m. Continue on path numbers 702 and 775 via Trockenbrotscharte, 2227 m, to Landwierseehütte, 1985 m. Overnight at Landwierseehütte (open June 15 to September 8).

Day 3: Six hours. Return along route number 702, then continue on the Höhenweg to Gollingscharte, 2326 m, and to Hochgolling (western ridge), 2863 m. Descend via the Historic Path to Gollingscharte and to Gollinghütte, 1651 m. Overnight at Gollinghütte.

Day 4: Six hours. On path number 702 via Greifenberg, 2618 m, to Klafferkessel and to Preintalerhütte, 1656 m. Overnight at Preintalerhütte.

Day 5: Six hours. On path number 782 to Neualmscharte, 2347 m, up Hochwildstelle, 2747 m, and descend (steep! requires a rope) to Trattenscharte, 2408 m, then via path number 702 to Breitlahnhütte, 1104 m. As an alternative, follow path 702 from Preintalerhütte via Trattenscharte to Breitlahnhütte (4 hours). Overnight at Breitlahnhütte.

Day 6: Nine hours. Follow path number 786 up the Schwarzenseebach Valley to Grafenalm, 1150 m, then via path numbers 702 and 793 to Predigtstuhl, 2545 m. Descend on path 702 to Rudolf-Schober-Hütte, 1650 m. Overnight at Rudolf-Schober-Hütte.

Day 7: Eight to nine hours. Descend on path 702 to St. Nikolai (lodgings), 1126 m, and walk along the road on path 902 to Mössna, 1023 m. Continue up path number 902 via Gstemmerscharte, 1908 m, and descend to Mörsbachhütte, 1300 m. Many nearby streams and waterfalls. Overnight at Mörsbachhütte.

Day 8: Seven to eight hours. On path 902 via Donnersbachwald to Karlspitze, 2080 m, and descend to Alte Plannerhütte, 1575 m. Overnight at Plannerhütte.

Day 9: Ten hours. A long day on a poorly marked path along a high ridge without lodgings. An early start is essential. Continue on path number 902 via Breiteckkoppe, 2142 m; Seitner Zinken, 2165 m; Hochschwung, 2199 m; Polster, 1815 m and Grosser Hengst, 2154 m, to Edelrautehütte. Overnight at Edelrautehütte.

Day 10: Eight to nine hours. On path number 946 to Grosser Bösenstein, 2449 m. Descend along a high ridge on path 944 (climbing tour; rope advisable) via Drei Stecken, 2387 m, and Hochhaide, 2363 m. Descend via Singsdorferalm to Rottenmanner Hütte, 1561 m. Overnight at Rottenmanner Hütte.

Day 11: On route 943 via Steinernes Mandl, 2042 m. Descend via Kamplalm to Rottenmann-Stadt railway station, 674 m (3 hours). The tour can be ended here. Or you can continue on the green-marked path to Dürrenschöberl, 1783 m, and descend on path number 651 to the town of Admont, 639 m (several possibilities for lodgings), then continue for another six days on the Gesäuse Mountains tour described in *Mountain Rambles*.

For a less strenuous mountain tour, try the "Mountain Ramble in Totes

Gebirge," along a section of *Weitwanderweg 01,* or the six-day ramble along *Nord-Süd-Weitwanderweg 05,* "Rambling through Gleinalpe, Stubalpe, Packalpe and Koralpe." Both are described in *Mountain Rambles.* Better yet, hike the entire 12-day section of *Nord-Süd-Weitwanderweg 05* in Steiermark (see the section on *Austria's Long-Distance Footpaths).*

Still another possibility is:

Five-day ramble in the Hochlantsch and Fischbacher Alpen: A circular hike from Mixnitz (on the train line between Graz and Bruck an der Mur). Moderately difficult.

Maps:
• Österreichische Karte 1:50,000, sheet 133, 134 and 135. A sketch map of trails and lodgings in the area, entitled *Wanderkarte Teichalm, Hochlantsch Rennfeld,* is available from ÖAV—Sektion Mixnitz.

Guidebook:
• *Wandern um Graz* by Günter Auferbauer, Verlag Styria.

Day 1: 2½ hours. From the railway station at Mixnitz on path number 745 up a narrow gorge with rapids and waterfalls to the Vorauer Gasthof on Teichalm. Overnight at Vorauer Gasthof.

Day 2: Six hours. Continue on path 745 to Weizerhütte (intersection with the Mariazellerweg). Return to Teichalm via Siebenkögel and Osser. Overnight at Teichalmhütte or Vorauer Gasthof.

Day 3: Four hours. On path number 7 via Heulantsch and Mooskögel to path number 730 (Mariazellerweg). Follow path 730 via Zechnerschlag to Strassegg Gasthof. Overnight at Strassegg.

day 4: Six hours. On path numbers 730, 740 and 715 via Maisshöhe, Tirolerschlag, Ebenschlag, Eiwegsattel and Bucheck to Ottokar-Kernstock-Haus. Along a high ridge. Overnight at Ottokar-Kernstock-Haus.

Day 5: Six hours. Return on path number 715 to its intersection with path number 714. Follow path numbers 714 and 4 south via Feisterer, Feisterergraben, and Schafferwerke to Schüsserlbrun (Gasthof). Descend to Mixnitz on path numbers 746, 702 and 745.

Cross-Country Skiing

Many local tourist offices publish sketch maps to the routes in their areas. For the addresses of the offices, refer to the *Steiermark Hotelpreisliste* or *Skiwandern und Skilanglauf in Österreich—Steiermark,* available from the provincial tourist board.

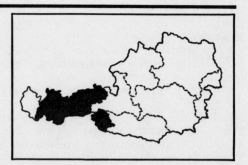

Tirol (Tyrol)

Mountains—and the juxtaposition between green rolling pastures and sheer rock cliffs—dominate Tyrol. Between the Arlberg in the west and Tyrol's eastern boundary with Salzburg, the Northern Limestone Alps and Central Alps stretch across the province, separated by the deep furrows of the Stanzer and Inn valleys. In the Central Alps are the granitic massifs of the Ötztal, Stubai and Zillertal Alps. The Ötztal Alps contain the largest glacier region in the East Alps which, together with the Stubai Alps, extends over an area of nearly 480 square kilometers. Parallel with the Ötztal is Tyrol's narrowest valley, the Pitztal, which ends at the base of the 3,744-meter high Wildspitze, Tyrol's highest peak. In the east, between the two mountain chains, is a third chain of mountains, the Kitzbühel Alps, a gently undulating range of slate rocks covered with Alpine pastures. Northeast of Innsbruck is Tyrol's largest lake, the Achensee, a nine-kilometer-long "fjord" between the rock walls of the Karwendel and Rofan mountains. And between the provinces of Salzburg and Kärnten is Osttirol—cut off from the rest of the province when Südtirol was ceded to Italy in 1919—a region dominated by the so-called Lienz Dolomites.

Nowhere else in the East Alps are there as many peaks over 3,000 meters in altitude. And nowhere else in Austria are there as many facilities for walkers, climbers and skiers. There are more than 350 alpine inns and mountain huts in Tyrol's mountains. The province also has 75 keep-fit trails, 16 climbing schools and more than 400 mountain guides and ski guides. There are nearly 3,000 kilometers of marked cross-country ski tracks and ski touring routes, as well as 3,200 kilometers of paths that are kept clear in winter. And for winter campers, there are 30 campgrounds that remain open.

Footpaths lace the entire province. Level or only gently rising paths lead from every village into the surrounding countryside. There also are hiking routes in the valley basins, on the terraces of the Central Alps and high up on the Alpine pastures. Even in the most remote valleys you will find inns and small restaurants where you can eat. Fresh milk also can be purchased from many herders on the Alpine pastures.

The weather, however, can be very unpredictable—and wet—especially in the early summer. And this can make even moderately difficult paths in the mountains treacherous.

Useful Addresses

See *Address Directory:*

Tiroler Fremdenverkehrswerbung. Provides general tourist information on the province. Also issues several useful publications for
walkers in English, French, German and Dutch. Among them:

• *Schutzhütten Alpengasthöfe/Chalets-Refuges Auberges Alpines/Re-
fuge Chalets and Mountain Inns.* Lists the trail lodgings in the
province by mountain group. Gives approach routes, altitudes,
opening and closing dates and tells which have winter rooms.

• *Guidebook for Travellers, Tyrol, Austria.* A 74-page booklet that lists
all the towns in the province. Gives altitudes, postal codes, number
of hotel room beds and lists tourist attractions and facilities. Also
tells which have mountain guides, where trails are located and how
nearby mountain huts can be reached.

• *Tyrol informs, Summer/Autumn.* Includes a list of the mountaineering schools, campgrounds, the towns with keep-fit trails, cable cars
and chair lifts, and other tourist facilities as well as the addresses
and telephone numbers of local tourist offices.

• *Tyrol informs, Winter.* Includes a list of towns with cross-country
tracks and ski touring routes, cleared winter paths, ski and mountain
guides and winter campgrounds. Full information is given on each.

• *Der Zirbenweg in Tirol.* A small leaflet describing the approach and
return routes to a popular, 2½-hour-long ramble through the Tulfein
Alm above Innsbruck. Begins at the upper station of the Pat-
scherkofel cableway, 1960 m, and ends at the upper end of the
Glungezer chair lift, 2100 m. The *Alpenvereinskarte* 1:50,000,
sheet number 31/5 should be carried on the walk.

Alpine Auskunft (Alpine Information). An office set up specifically to
provide information on walking and climbing in Tyrol. Located in the
Innsbruck tourist office. If the staff cannot answer your question, they
will refer you to the appropriate section of the ÖAV for an answer.
The staff speaks English, French and German. A handy publication
available from the office is:

• *Ausflüge und Wanderungen in Tirol,* published by the Österreichische Bundesbahnen, Innsbruck. Available only in German. A
36-page booklet that describes numerous day hikes that can be
reached by bus. Includes bus schedules.

Maps

Most of the principal walking and climbing areas in Tyrol and East Tyrol are covered by the 1:25,000 Alpenvereinskarten: sheets 2/1 and 2/2 cover the Allgäu-Lechtaler Alpen; sheets 4/1, 4/2 and 4/3 cover the Wetterstein-Mieminger-Gebirge; sheets 5/1, 5/2 and 5/3 cover the Karwendelgebirge; sheet 6 covers the Rofangebirge; sheet 8 covers the Kaisergebirge; sheets 30/1, 30/2, 30/3 and 30/4 cover the Ötztaler Alpen; sheets 31/1, 31/2 and 31/3 cover the Stubaier Alpen and Brenner; sheet 31/5 (in a scale of 1:50,000) covers the region surrounding Innsbruck; sheets 35/1, 35/2 and 35/3 cover the Zillertaler Alpen; sheet 36 covers the Venedigergruppe; sheet 39 covers the Granatspitzgruppe; sheet 40 covers the Glockner-Gruppe, sheet 41 covers the Schobergruppe; and sheet 56 covers the Lienzer Dolomiten surrounding the town of Lienz.

Most of these areas are also covered by Bergverlag Rudolf Rother's 1:50,000 Tourenblätter, an excellent series of maps on which footpaths (and sometimes ski touring and climbing routes) are marked. Each Tourenblatt also includes photos and route descriptions and comes in a plastic binder so individual pages and map sections can be taken out to be carried on the trail. The Tourenblätter covering Tyrol are: BV–Tourenblätter, Mappe 1 (Karwendel, Rofan and Wetterstein); Mappe 2 (Kaisergebirge/Berchtesgadener Alpen); Mappe 3 (Allgäuer Alpen, Lechtaler Alpen and Bregenzerwald); Mappe 5 (Ötztaler and Stubaier Alpen); and Mappe 7 (Zillertaler Alpen, Glockner-Venediger).

In addition, Tyrol is covered by the Freytag-Berndt Wanderkarten 1:50,000, sheets 121, 122, 123, 301, 381 and 382; 1:100,000, sheets 12, 18, 24, 25, 30, 31, 32, 33, 34, 35 and 38; and Österreichische Karte 1:50,000, sheets 84-92, 113-123, 143-153, 170-175, 177-180, 195 and 196.

Guidebooks

Numerous guidebooks are available to Tyrol's mountain regions. Tyrolia Verlag publishes four books, each of which describes 50 hikes in various regions of Tyrol: *Tiroler Wanderbuch 1* covers the western section of the province, *Tiroler Wanderbuch 2* covers the area surrounding Innsbruck, *Tiroler Wanderbuch 3* covers the eastern part of the province and *Osttiroler Wanderbuch* covers East Tyrol. Many guides also are published by Bergverlag Rudolf Rother.

A visit to the Freytag-Berndt und Artaria bookstore in Innsbruck to browse the shelves is worthwhile.

Suggested Walks

The hikes described in the Austrian National Tourist Office booklet *Mountain Rambles in Austria* are all recommended. They range in difficulty from easy to tours that require a guide or mountain experience.

Cross-Country Skiing

Your best source of information is the *Tyrol informs, Winter* brochure, published by the provincial tourist board. It also includes the addresses of local tourist offices throughout Tyrol where you can write for sketch maps of the routes.

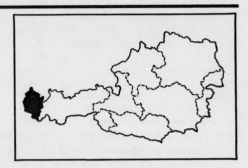

Vorarlberg

Vorarlberg is Austria's westernmost province. It also is the smallest—2,602 square kilometers—stretching from the Bodensee (Lake Constance) on Austria's border with Germany and Switzerland to the Silvretta. Despite its small size, it has a varied terrain. There are the wide green valleys of the Walgau and Rheintal, the wooded, moderately mountainous regions of the Bregenzerwald and Oberland, and the high mountains of the Arlberg, Brandnertal, Grosses Walsertal, Kleinwalsertal, Klostertal and Montafon. Surrounding the Montafon Valley are the peaks of the Silvretta, Verwall and Rätikon mountains, topped by the 3312-meter-high Piz Buin.

Trails range in difficulty from easy valley-floor paths to high-mountain routes across glaciers and along sheer rock precipices. The latter paths should be attempted only by experienced mountaineers. Path markings vary more than elsewhere in Austria. Each trail has its own color and may be marked with squares, triangles and parallelograms in addition to the typical paint stripes. Trails in the valleys are marked and maintained by local tourist authorities; those at high altitudes are kept up by the ÖAV.

There are four mountaineering schools in the province, and mountain guides can be hired in numerous localities. In addition, Vorarlberg has 400 kilometers of cross-country ski tracks and 670 kilometers of winter hiking trails that are snow-cleared.

Useful Addresses

See *Address Directory:*

Landesfremdenverkehrsamt Vorarlberg. Provides general tourist information on the province. Also issues numerous publications. Among the most useful are:

➤ *Vorarlberg—Sports, Hobby and Entertainment.* Lists the addresses and telephone numbers of mountaineering schools, gives the locations of keep-fit trails, cable railways and chair lifts, provides useful information on mountain huts in the province and lists the towns where guided walking tours are available. Written in French, English, German and Dutch.

• *Vorarlberg—Wintersport.* Lists the lengths and locations of cleared winter paths and cross-country ski trails. Also gives the addresses, courses and prices for instruction in ski schools and full information—including prices—on equipment full information—including prices—on equipment rental.

ÖAV—Sektion Vorarlberg. Can answer specific questions about hiking and climbing in the province.

ÖAV—Sektionenverband Vorarlberg. Also very helpful.

Maps

Vorarlberg is covered by the 1:25,000 Alpenvereinskarten, sheets 3/2 (Lechtaler Alpen) and 26 (Silvrettagruppe); Bergverlag Rudolf Rother's 1:50,000 BV-Tourenblätter, Mappe 3 (Allgäuer Alpen, Lechtaler Alpen and Bregenzerwald) and Mappe 4 (Rätikon, Silvretta, Ferwall and Samnaun); Freytag-Berndt Wanderkarten 1:50,000, sheets 361, 362, 363, 371, 372 and 373; Freytag-Berndt Wanderkarten 1:100,000, sheets 35, 36 and 37; and Österreichishe Karte 1:50,000, sheets 82, 83, 110, 111, 112, 113, 141, 142, 143, 169 and 170.

Guidebooks

Bergverlag Rudolf Rother publishes 14 mountain guides and 4 ski guides to Vorarlberg. Other guidebooks include the *Führer Alpenpark Montafon* by W. and H. Flaig, published by the Verkehrsverband Montafon, A-6780 Schruns; *Sommerführer durch das Kleinwalsertal*, published by A. Köberle, A-6991 Riezlern; and the *Vorarlberger Wanderbuch*, published by Tyrolia Verlag, Innsbruck.

A good general guide to the province is:

• *Kleiner Führer, Vorarlberg* by Jörg Heine, Bergverlag Rudolf Rother.

Most of the guidebooks are stocked by local bookstores. They also can be purchased at Buchhandlung J.N. Teutsch, Bregenz (see *Address Directory)* or by mail from Freytag-Berndt und Artaria.

Suggested Walks

The section of West-Ost Weitwanderweg 01, "From the Arlberg to the Bregenz Woods," described in *Mountain Rambles in Austria* is highly recommended. The route is normally moderately difficult. The degree of difficulty, however, depends strongly upon the weather. In bad weather several of the ridges it follows can become treacherous. Hence, you should check the route conditions before you start out. Also, owing to the route's high altitude, some mountaineering experience and good equipment are indispensable.

Cross-Country Skiing

The best source of information is *Vorarlberg—Wintersport,* published by the provincial tourist board. The brochure also includes the addresses of local tourist offices, many of which can provide sketch maps to the ski routes in their areas.

For experienced skiers, the six-day route described in *Mountain Rambles,* "Spring Skiing in the Hoch-Silvretta," is recommended.

Address Directory

A

- *Alpin- und Bergsteigerschule Stubai,* A-6167 Neustift im Stubaital. Tel. (05226) 2218. Director: Horst Fankhauser.
- *Alpin- und Wanderschule St. Anton Am Arlberg,* Haus Scherer, Oberndorf 79, A-6580 St. Anton am Arlberg. Tel. (05446) 2336. Director: Walter Strolz.
- *Alpin- und Wanderschule Zillertal,* A-6290 Mayrhofen 119. Tel. (05285) 2563 or 2528. Director: Peter Habeler.
- *Alpine Auskunft* (Alpine Information), Tiroler Landesreisebüro, Boznerplatz 7, A-6010 Innsbruck. Tel. (05222) 34 9 85.
- *Alpine Ski- und Bergsteigerschule Reisseck,* Halleggerstrasse 10, A-9201 Krumpendorf. Tel. (04229) 701. Director: Hias Kumning. Bookings also through: Fremdenverkehrsamt, A-9815 Kolbnitz, Tel. (04783) 252 and Sporthotel Reisseck, A-9815 Kolbnitz, Tel. (04783) 420.
- *Alpinschule Ausseer Land,* Fischerndorf 161, A-8992 Altausee. Tel. (06152) 7310. Director: Karl Jansenberger.
- *Alpinschule Ausserfern,* Allgäuer Strasse 15, A-6600 Reutte. Tel. (05672) 2232. Director: Sepp Paulweber.

• *Alpinschule Dachstein,* Alpengasthof Peter Rosegger, A-8972 Ramsau am Dachstein 233. Tel. (03687) 8223. Director: Fritz Walcher.

• *Alpinschule Glockner-Heiligenblut,* A-9844 Heiligenblut. Tel. (04824) 2263. Director: Helmuth Damith.

• *Alpinschule Innsbruck,* Müllerstrasse 27/III, A-6010 Innsbruck. Tel. (05222) 35 3 40. Director: Hannes Gasser.

• *Alpinschule Montafon,* Im Feld 1041, A-6780 Schruns/Montafon. Tel. (05556) 29 9 75. Director: Wendelin Tschugmell.

• *Alpinschule Oberösterreich,* Gruberstrasse 47, A-4020 Linz. Tel. (0732) 20 62 33. Director: Dipl. Ing. Eduard Koblmüller.

• *Amt der Steiermärkischen Landesregierung, Landesfremdenverkehrsabteilung,* Herrengasse 16, Landhaus, A-8010 Graz. Tel. (03122) 831 2287.

• *Austrian Alpine Club, Innsbruck,* see *Österreichischer Alpenverein.*

• *Austrian Alpine Club, U.K. Branch,* 13 Longcroft House, Fretherne Road, Welwyn Garden City, Hertfordshire AL8 6PQ, England.

• *Austrian National Tourist Office, London:* 30 St. George Street, London W1R 9FA, England. Tel. (01) 629 0461.

• *Austrian National Tourist Office, New York:* 545 Fifth Avenue, New York, New York 10017, U.S.A. Tel. (212) 697-0651.

• *Austrian National Tourist Office, Vienna:* see *ÖSTERREICH-INFORMATION.*

• *Avalanche Warnings, Kärnten:* For a recorded message, Tel. (04222) 16. For specific advice, Tel. (04222) 33 6 03.

• *Avalanche Warnings, Oberösterreich:* Oberösterreich Lawinenwarndienst-Zentrale (Central Avalanche Warning Center), Tel. (0732) 584 24 67 or 584 24 12.

• *Avalanche Warnings, Salzburg:* For a recorded message, Tel. (06222) 196. For specific advice, call the Lawinenwarndienst-Zentrale, Tel. (06222) 43 4 35.

• *Avalanche Warnings, Steiermark:* For a recorded message, Tel. (0316) 831 61 77. Lawinenwarndienst-Zentrale, Tel. (0316) 25 1 16.

• *Avalanche Warnings, Tirol:* For a recorded message, Tel. (05222) 196. Lawinenwarndienst-Zentrale, Tel. (05222) 21 8 39 or 28 7 01.

• *Avalanche Warnings, Vorarlberg:* For a recorded message, Tel. (05522) 16.

B

• *BLV Verlagsgesellschaft,* Lothstrasse 29, Postfach 40 03 20, D-8000 Munich 40, Germany.

- *Berg- und Wanderschule Kirchdorf am Wilden Kaiser,* A-6382 Kirchdorf im Tirol 556. Tel. (05352) 3180. Director: Adi Bichler.
- *Berg- und Wanderschule Sepp Kröll-Kitzbühel,* Zwickerleiten 3a, A-6370 Kitzbühel-Sonnberg. Tel. (05356) 51 0 02. Director: Sepp Kröll.
- *Berg-und Wanderschule St. Johann in Tirol,* Velbenstrasse 30, A-6380 St. Johann in Tirol. Tel. (05352) 2052. Director: Lois Jöchl.
- *Bergschule Tannheimertal,* Lechtaler Strasse 27, A-6600 Lechaschau. Tel. (05672) 3625. Director: Franz Feuerstein.
- *Bergsteiger- und Wanderschule Wetterstein,* A-6105 Leutasch. Tel. (05214) 6207. Director: Helmut Wagner.
- *Bergsteigerausbildung der Akademischen Sektion Graz des Österreichischen Alpenvereins,* Jahngasse 2, A-8020 Graz. Tel. (0316) 63 4 18. Director: Hermann Bratschko.
- *Bergsteigerschule Dachstein-Tauern,* Café-Pension Herold, A-8972 Ramsau am Dachstein 2733. Tel. (03687) 8282. Director: Albert Prugger.
- *Bergsteigerschule des Österreichischen Alpenvereins,* Postfach 282, Wilhelm-Greil-Strasse 15/V, A-6010 Innsbruck. Tel. (05222) 23 1 71.
- *Bergsteigerschule des Österreichischen Touristenklubs,* Bäckerstrasse 16, A-1010 Vienna. Tel. (0222) 52 38 44.
- *Bergsteigerschule Filzmoos,* Verkehrsverein, A-5532 Filzmoos. Tel. (06469) 8135. Director: Lois Huber.
- *Bergsteigerschule Hochschwab,* A-8624 Grassnitz. Tel. (03863) 263. Director: Franz Ogrinz.
- *Bergsteigerschule Hochtannberg,* A-6886 Schoppernau 281. Tel. (05515) 2196. Director: Wilfried Stelzhammer.
- *Bergsteigerschule Hohe Tauern,* Reitlehen 18, A-5731 Hollersbach im Pinzgau. Tel. (06562) 8223. Director: Ferdinand Rieder.
- *Bergsteigerschule Karawanken,* Touristenverein "Die Naturfreunde," Bahnhofstrasse 44, A-9020 Klagenfurt. Tel. (04222) 86 7 55. Director: Rainer Ottowitz.
- *Bergsteigerschule Kleinwalsertal,* Sonnhalde 6, A-6993 Mittelberg. Tel. (05517) 5969. Director: Walter Heim.
- *Bergsteigerschule Leogang,* Sonnberg 23, A-5771 Leogang. Tel. (06583) 221. Director: Sepp Freudenthaler.
- *Bergsteigerschule Oberpinzgau,* A-5742 Wald Königsleiten. Tel. (06564) 34 2 01. Director: Toni Hölzl. Bookings: Verkehrsverein, A-5741 Neunkirchen/Grossvenendiger. Tel. (06565) 256.
- *Bergsteigerschule Osttirol,* Postfach 117, A-9900 Lienz. Tel. (04852) 4100. Director: Sepp Mayer. Information also available

from: Pension Lhotse-shar, Göriach 38, A-9991 Dölsach. Tel. (04852) 4100.

• *Bergsteigerschule Piz Buin,* Haus Vereina, A-6563 Galtür. Tel. (05443) 260. Director: Hugo Walter.

• *Bergsteigerschule Schladminger Tauern,* Touristenverein "Die Naturfreunde," Südtiroler Platz 13, A-8020 Graz. Tel. (0316) 91 36 65. Director: Othmar Kucera.

• *Bergsteigerschule Schneeberg,* Wasserfallweg 6, A-2734 Puchberg am Schneeberg. Tel. (02636) 22 05 59. Director: Hans Gross.

• *Bergsteigerschule Wilder Kaiser,* Touristenverein "Die Naturfreunde," Salurner Strasse 1, A-6020 Innsbruck. Tel. (05222) 24 1 44. Director: Adi Huber.

• *Bergsteigerzentrum Steiermark,* Pension Sonnberg, A-8960 Öblarn. Tel. (03684) 221. Director: Klaus Hoi.

• *Berner-Verlag,* D-8311 Velden, Germany.

• *Bibliographisches Institut,* Hardturmstrasse 76, Postfach 130, CH-8021 Zürich, Switzerland.

• *Buchhandlung J.N. Teutsch,* Kirchstrasse 2, A-6900 Bregenz. Tel. (05574) 22 6 66.

D

• *Deutscher Alpenverein,* Praterinsel 5, D-8000 Munich 22, Germany. Tel. (089) 29 30 86.

• *Deutscher Skiverband,* Postfach 20 18 27, D-8000 Munich 2, Germany.

• *Deutscher Wanderverlag,* Haussmanstrasse 66, D-7000 Stuttgart 1, Germany.

• *Doujak, Dr. Hermann,* Festungsweg, A-9020 Klagenfurt.

E

• *Emergency:* In most towns, Tel. 133.

• *Ernst Kreutzer,* see *Kreutzer, Ernst.*

F

• *Fink-Kümmerly + Frey,* Gebelsbergstrasse 41, D-7000 Stuttgart 1, Germany.

• *Fritz Peterka,* see *Peterka, Fritz.*

• *Franz Kosina,* see *Kosina, Franz.*

• *Fremdenverkehrsbüro Krems,* Wichnerstrasse (Künstlerhaus), A-3500 Krems an der Donau. Tel. (02732) 2676.

- *Fremdenverkehrs-Gebietsverband Pinzgauer Saalachtal*, A-5760 Saalfelden.
- *Fremdenverkehrsverband Kamptal*, A-3571 Gars am Kamp. Tel. (02985) 2225.
- *Fremdenverkehrsverband Mühlviertel*, Dinghoferstrasse 4, A-4020 Linz. Tel. (0732) 76 6 16.
- *Fremdenverkehrsverband Oberes Waldviertel*, Stadtplatz 19, A-3950 Gmünd. Tel. (02852) 3212.
- *Fremdenverkehrsverband Oberösterreich*, Postfach 8000, A-4010 Linz.
- *Fremdenverkehrsverband Pielachtal*, Schlosstrasse 1, A-3204 Kirchberg an der Pielach. Tel. (02722) 7533.
- *Fremdenverkehrsverband Semmering-Rax-Schneealpe*, Hochstrasse 91, A-2680 Semmering. Tel. (02664) 326.
- *Fremdenverkehrsverband Thayatal*, A-3820 Raabs an der Thaya. Tel. (02846) 238.
- *Fremdenverkehrsverband Westliches Wienviertel*, A-2072 Ober-Markersdorf 75.
- *Fremdenverkehrsverband Ybbstaler-Alpenvorland-Mostviertel*, Freisingerberg 2-4, A-3340 Waidhofen an der Ybbs. Tel. (07442) 25 11 17.
- *Fremdenverkehrsverband Ysper-Weitental*, A-3682 Altenmarkt im Yspertal. Tel. (07415) 224.
- *Fremdenverkehrsverein Mödling*, Postfach (P.B.) 34, A-2340 Mödling bei Wien. Tel. (02236) 6727.
- *Freytag-Berndt & Artaria KG*, Wilhelm-Greil-Strasse 15, A-6020 Innsbruck. Tel. (05222) 25 1 30.
- *Freytag-Berndt & Artaria KG*, Kohlmarkt 9, A-1010 Vienna. Tel. (0222) 52 24 21 or 52 24 22.
- *Freytag-Berndt und Artaria*, see *Freytag-Berndt & Artaria KG*.

G

- *George G. Harrap & Company Ltd.*, 182-184 High Holborn, London WC1V 7AX, England.

H

- *Dr. Hermann Doujak*, see *Doujak, Dr. Hermann*.
- *Hochalpine Bergsteigerschule Sölden*, A-6450 Sölden-Windau Nr. 153. Tel. (05254) 2364 or 2546. Director: Martin Gstrein.
- *Hochalpinschule Dachstein*, A-8972 Ramsau am Dachstein 81. Tel. (03687) 8253. Director: Heinrich Perner.

- *Hochgebirgs- und Wanderschule Obergurgl,* Haus Schönblick, A-6456 Obergurgl 53. Tel. (05256) 251. Director: Karl Giacomelli.
- *Hochgebirgsschule Glockner-Kaprun,* A-5710 Kaprun. Tel. (06547) 271. In winter: Touristenverein "Die Naturfreunde," Viktoriagasse 6, A-1150 Vienna. Tel. (0222) 83 86 08. Director: Fritz Moravec.
- *Hochgebirgsschule Innerpitztal,* Neurur 97, A-6481 St. Leonhard im Pitztal. Tel. (05413 270. Director: Franz Auer.
- *Hochgebirgsschule Sonnblick,* Touristenverein "Die Naturfreunde," Diefenbachgasse 36, A-1150 Vienna. Tel. (0222) 83 14 40.
- *Hochgebirgsschule Tyrol,* Innrain 67, A-6020 Innsbruck. Tel. (05222) 25 9 86. Director: Ernst Senn.
- *Hofrat Dr. Hermann Doujak,* see *Doujak, Dr. Hermann.*

K

- *Kaufhaus Ski Sepp Turracher Höhe,* A-9571 Gemeinde Albeck/ Sirnitz.
- *Klettergarten Kanzianiberg,* Information: Verkehrsamt, A-9583 Faak am See. Tel. (04254) 2110.
- *Kosina, Franz,* Flötzerweg 110, A-4020 Linz.
- *Kreutzer, Ernst,* Englischfeldgasse 9, A-1228 Wien-Essling.

L

- *Landesfremdenverkehrsamt Kärnten,* Kaufmanngasse 13, A-9010 Klagenfurt. Tel. (04222) 80 5 11.
- *Landesfremdenverkehrsamt Vorarlberg,* Römerstrasse 7/I, Postfach 104, A-6901 Bregenz. Tel. (05574) 22 5 25.
- *Landesfremdenverkehrsverband für das Burgenland,* Schloss Esterhazy, Postfach 90, A-7000 Eisenstadt. Tel. (02682) 3384.
- *Landesverkehrsamt in Salzburg,* Mozartplatz 1, Postfach 562, A-5010 Salzburg. Tel. (06222) 43 2 64.

M

- *Mountaineers Books,* 719 Pike Street, Seattle, Washington 98101, U.S.A.

N

- *Nederlandse Bergsport Vereniging,* Laan van Meerdervoot 503, Den Haag, The Netherlands.
- *Niederösterreichische Fremdenverkehrswerbung,* Paulanergasse 11, A-1041 Vienna IV. Tel. (0222) 57 67 18.

74 AUSTRIA

O

- *ÖAV*, see *Österreichischer Alpenverein.*
- *ÖAV—Sektion Burgenland,* Herrn Franz Kubiska, Ing. Sylvester Strasse 18, A-7000 Eisenstadt.
- *ÖAV—Sektion Edelweiss,* see *Österreichischer Alpenverein—Sektion "Edelweiss."*
- *ÖAV—Sektion Freistadt,* Rathaus (3. Stock), A-4240 Friestadt.
- *ÖAV—Sektion Graz,* Sackstrasse 16, A-8010 Graz. Tel. (0316) 72 2 66.
- *ÖAV—Sektion Horn,* Bei der Kapelle 18, A-3580 Horn.
- *ÖAV—Sektion Innsbruck,* see *Österreichischer Alpenverein—Sektion Innsbruck.*
- *ÖAV—Sektion Mixnitz,* Gasthof Sarklet, A-8131 Mixnitz. Tel (03867) 279.
- *ÖAV—Sektion Oberösterreich,* Hauptplatz 23, A-4020 Linz. Tel. (0732) 73 2 95 or 24 2 95.
- *ÖAV—Sektion Vorarlberg,* Hermann-Sander-Strasse 12, A-6700 Bludenz. Tel. (05552) 2639.
- *ÖAV—Sektion Waldviertel,* Grillenstein 58, A-3950 Gmünd.
- *ÖAV—Sektion Wolfsberg,* St. Jacob 15, A-9400 Wolfsberg.
- *ÖAV—Sektionsverband Kärnten,* Dr. Kurt Dellisch, Vorsitzender, Villacher Ring 59, A-9020 Klagenfurt. Tel. (04222) 70 5 74.
- *ÖAV—Sektionsverband Niederosterreich, Tulln,* Dipl. Ing. Werner Rachoy, Vorsitzender, Brachmannstrasse 1, A-3430 Tulln. Tel (0222) 82 36 38.
- *ÖAV—Sektionsverband Oberösterreich,* Hauptplatz 23, A-4020 Linz.
- *ÖAV—Sektionenverband Niederosterreich,* Franz Groissbock, Wegereferent, Petzoldstrasse 57, A-3100 St. Polten.
- *ÖAV—Sektionenverband Salzburg,* Nonntaler Hauptstrasse 86, A-5020 Salzburg. Tel. (06222) 46 6 44.
- *ÖAV—Sektionenverband Steiermark,* Färbergasse 6-1, A-8010 Graz.
- *ÖAV—Sektionenverband Vorarlberg,* Montfortstrasse 4, Postfach 104, A-6900 Bregenz. Tel. (05574) 22 3 25.
- *ÖAV—Sektionenverband Wien,* Dir. Walter Miedler, Vorsitzender, Mitisgasse 5, A-1140, Vienna.
- *ÖAV—Zweig Klagenfurt,* Lidmanskygasse 2-1, A-9020 Klagenfurt.
- *ÖTK,* see *Österreichischer Touristenklub.*

- *Oberösterreichisches Landesfremdenverkehrsamt,* Johann-Konrad-Vogel-Strasse 2, Postfach 142, A-4010 Linz. Tel. (07222) 72 8 88.
- *Organisation der Internationalen Wienerwald-Wanderung,* Postfach 595, A-1011 Vienna.
- *ÖSTERREICH-INFORMATION* (Austrian National Tourist Office/ Österreichische Fremdenverkehrswerbung), Margaretenstrasse 1, A-1040 Vienna. Tel. (0222) 57 57 14 or 57 57 15.
- *Österreichische Bundesbahnen,* Karwendelstrasse 15, A-6020 Innsbruck.
- *Österreichische Fremdenverkehrswerbung,* see *ÖSTERREICH-INFORMATION.*
- *Österreichischer Alpenklub,* Getreidemarkt 3, A-1060 Vienna. Tel. (0222) 563 86 73.
- *Österreichischer Alpenverein* (Austrian Alpine Club), Wilhelm-Greil-Strasse 15, A-6010 Innsbruck. Tel. (05222) 23 1 71.
- *Österreichischer Alpenverein—Sektion Dänemark,* Lone Christensen, Fuglesangsvej 42, DK-3460 Birkerøl, Denmark.
- *Österreichischer Alpenverein—Sektion "Edelweiss,"* Walfischgasse 12, A-1010 Vienna.
- *Österreichischer Alpenverein—Sektion Innsbruck,* Wilhelm-Greil-Strasse 15, A-6020 Innsbruck.
- *Österreichischer Bergrettungsdienst,* Wilhelm-Greil-Strasse 15, A-6010 Innsbruck. Tel. (05222) 21 9 19.
- *Österreichischer Gebirgsverein,* Lerchenfelder Strasse 28, A-1080 Vienna. Tel. (0222) 42 26 57.
- *Österreichischer Naturschutzbund* (Gesellschaft für Naturkunde und Naturschutz), Messeplatz 1, Stiege 14, A-1070 Vienna. Tel. (0222) 93 64 78.
- *Österreichischer Ski-Verband,* Maria-Theresien-Strasse 53, A-6020 Innsbruck. Tel. (05222) 25 9 46 or 33 7 66.
- *Österreichischer Touristenklub (ÖTK),* Bäckerstrasse 16, A-1010 Vienna. Tel. (0222) 52 38 44.
- *Österreichisches Jugendherbergswerk,* Freyung 6-11, A-1010 Vienna. Tel. (0222) 63 18 33.

P

- *Peterka, Fritz,* Adolf Loos Gasse 8, Steige 38, A-1121 Vienna.
- *Pongauer Wander- und Alpinschule,* Maximilian-Siedlung 3, A-5500 Birschofshofen. Tel. (06462) 21 4 52. Director: Siegfried Bernegger.

R

- *Ringier-Verlag,* Spitalgasse 5, Postfach 206, CH-8025 Zurich, Switzerland.

S

- *Salzburger Bergsteiger- und Wanderschule,* Neutorstrasse 55, A-5020 Salzburg. Tel. (06222) 44 1 29. Director: Walter Niederreiter.
- *Sektion Waldviertel des Österreichischen Alpenvereins,* Grillenstein 58, A-3950 Gmünd.
- *Sierra Club Books,* 530 Bush Street, San Francisco, California 94108, U.S.A.
- *Sporthaus SCHWANDA,* Bäckerstrasse 7, A-1010 Vienna. Tel. (0222) 52 53 20.
- *Südwestdeutscher Verlag,* Postfach 5760, D-6800 Mannheim 1, Germany.

T

- *TVN,* see *Touristenverein "Die Naturfreunde."*
- *Tiroler Fremdenverkehrswerbung,* Bozner Platz 6, A-6010 Innsbruck. Tel. (05222) 20 7 77.
- *Touristenverein "Die Naturfreunde" (TVN),* Viktoriagasse 6, A-1150 Vienna. Tel. (0222) 83 86 08.
- *Touristenverein "Die Naturfreunde," Sektion Graz,* Südtiroler Platz 13, A-8020 Graz. Tel. (0316) 91 36 65.
- *Touristenverein "Die Naturfreunde," Sektion Innsbruck,* Salurner Strasse 1, A-6020 Innsbruck. Tel. (05222) 24 1 44.
- *Touristenverein "Die Naturfreunde," Sektion Klagenfurt,* Bahnhofstrasse 44, A-9020 Klagenfurt. Tel. (04222) 86 7 55.
- *Tyrolia Verlag,* Exlgasse 20, Postfach 220, A-6010 Innsbruck.

U

- *Universitätsbuchhandlung Wilhelm Braumüller & Sohn,* Schottenfeldgasse 24, A-1070 Vienna.

V

- *Verband der Österreichischen Berg- und Skiführer,* Postfach, A-6010 Innsbruck. Tel. (05222) 20 9 15.
- *Verkehrsamt,* A-9583 Faak am See. Tel. (04254) 2110.
- *Verlag F. Bruckmann KG,* Nymphenburger Strasse 86, Postfach 27, D-8000 Munich 20, Germany.

- *Verlag Kremayr & Scheriau,* Niederhofstrasse 37, A-1120 Vienna.
- *Verlag Karl Thiemig,* Pilgersheimer Strasse 38, Postfach D-8, Munich 90, Germany.
- *Verlag Niederösterreich Pressehaus* (Verlag Nö. Pressehaus), Gutenbergstrasse 12, A-3100 St. Pölten.
- *Verlag Nö. Pressehaus,* see *Verlag Niederösterreich Pressehaus.*
- *Verlag Styria,* Schönaugasse 64, Postfach 435, A-8011 Graz.
- *Vlaamse Bergsportvereniging,* c/o Werner Aghten, Meeuwenhoflei 94, B-2100 Deurne-Antwerp, Belgium.

W

- *Wander- und Bergsteigerschule Schwarzatal,* Information: Sport Gruber, Bundesstrasse 14, A-2632 Wimpassing. Tel. (02630) 8395.
- *Weather Forecasts* (Wetterauskunft): Tel. (0222) 15 66 in Vienna and the rest of Niederösterreich; Tel. 16 in the larger places of all the other federal provinces.
- *West Col Productions,* 1 Meadow Close, Goring-on-Thames, Reading, Berkshire RG8 9AA, England.

A Quick Reference

In a hurry? Turn to the pages listed below. They will give you the most important information on walking in Austria.

Search & Rescue, page 30.
Weather Forecasts, page 9.
Associations to Contact for Information:
    On Walking, page 9.
    On Climbing, page 19.
    On Skiing, page 25.
    General Tourist Information, page 29.
Maps:
    For Walking, page 12.
    For Ski Touring page 27.
Guidebooks:
    For Walking, page 13.
    For Cross-Country Skiing, page 25.
    For Ski Mountaineering, page 26.
Equipment, page 18.
Address Directory, page 68.

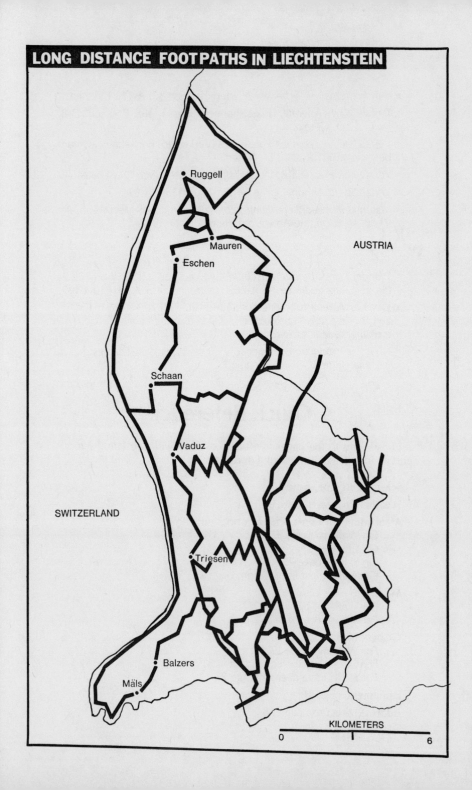

LONG DISTANCE FOOTPATHS IN LIECHTENSTEIN

Ruggell

Mauren

Eschen

AUSTRIA

Schaan

Vaduz

SWITZERLAND

Triesen

Balzers

Mäls

KILOMETERS

0   6

Liechtenstein

T HE TINY PRINCIPALITY of Liechtenstein is a beautiful alpine country situated on the banks of the upper Rhine River between Austria and Switzerland. It is the fourth smallest country in Europe, covering only 160 square kilometers (62 square miles). Its greatest north-south distance is only 25 kilometers (15.5 miles); east-west, 10 kilometers (6.2 miles). Within this space, however, are crammed some 300 kilometers (186 miles) of marked footpaths and a grand array of mountain scenery.

Most of Liechtenstein's 26,000 residents live in a series of villages strung along the Rhine Valley and backed by the sheer western wall of the Rätikon Massif, which is part of the Central Alps. Vaduz, the capital and largest town, has less than 5,000 residents. On a wooded bluff overlooking the town sits the massive Schloss Vaduz, the 700-year-old castle that serves as the official residence of Prince Franz Josef II and his family.

The Rhine flows from south to north through Liechtenstein, and the average elevation of its valley floor is roughly 460 meters (1,500 feet). The lowest point in the country—at 432 meters elevation—is near the village of Ruggell at the lower end of the Rhine Valley. The five parishes of northern Liechtenstein are together known as the Unterland (Lower Country); the six parishes of the south, the Oberland (Upper Country).

The front range of the Rätikon Massif rises steeply from the valley floor, its slopes densely swathed in forest. Drei Schwestern (the Three Sisters), the highest peak on this ridge, rises some 1,800 meters above the valley floor to an elevation of 2,052 meters (6,732 feet). Altogether, Liechtenstein has about 30 peaks in excess of 1,829 meters (6,000 feet). The highest in the country is Grauspitz (2,599 meters; 8,525 feet), followed by Naafkopf (2,570 meters; 8,431 feet) and Falknis (2,560 meters; 8,398 feet).

Beyond the front range lies the valley of the Samina River and two tributary valleys, the Valórschtal and the Malbuntal. Here you find a mosaic of deep-green forests and emerald meadows crowned by rocky, ice-carved peaks, and numerous paths leading into the backcountry. Ski resorts are located at Steg and Malbun, the only two villages in the region, which are linked to the Rhine Valley by a highway that passes through a long tunnel beneath the front range of mountains to Triesenberg.

Liechtenstein's excellent system of marked footpaths offers numerous possibilities for both day walks and longer excursions. Lowland paths and more difficult mountain tracks each have their own distinctive markings, and nearly all grades of walking difficulty exist in the country. You can wander through the open farmlands of the Rhine Valley or follow ridgecrests from peak to peak. Quiet, shady forest paths suddenly leave the trees to cross vast alpine lawns garlanded with flowers and flanked by lofty peaks. Here and there you may stumble on a medieval chapel or the ruins of a castle or Roman villa. And everywhere, whether in the Rhine Valley or the mountains, the views are fabulous.

Forests cover 27 percent of Liechtenstein's total land area. Ninety-one percent of the forest land is public property, belonging to Liechtenstein's 11 communes and 8 alp cooperatives, and is fully protected by law. On the higher mountain slopes dense stands of fir and spruce alternate with expanses of open meadow, which extend above timberline to the steep, rocky flanks of the peaks. Meadows also cover the gentle mountain valleys of the Samina River watershed. Together, lowland and alpine meadows cover 46 percent of the country. On the lower mountain slopes spruce and fir are elements in a mixed forest that also contains pine, copper beech, common and Norway maple and other deciduous trees.

Liechtenstein's mountains support a good variety of wildlife, including red and roe deer, chamois, hare, marmot, fox, badger, marten, polecat, stoat and weasel. Game birds include blackcock, pheasant, hazel grouse and partridge. The poisonous adder also occurs in Liechtenstein, though this snake seldom presents a problem. In case of a bite, however, you should immediately seek medical attention. Mosquitoes and other biting insects do not occur in the country.

Climate

Liechtenstein's climate is fairly mild considering the country's mountain location. Winter temperatures, which rarely drop below *minus* 15°C. (5°F.), are moderated by the *Föhn,* a warm, dry wind which commonly blows down the Rhine Valley from the south. Summers are warm, even at higher elevations, with temperatures averaging between 20° and 28°C. (68° to 82°F.).

Precipitation normally ranges between 914 and 1,143 mm (36 to 45 inches) per year, although as much as 1,981 mm (78 inches) may fall in the uplands. The heaviest rainfall occurs from June through August. Snow falls an average of 35 days during the winter.

As in any mountainous region the weather can change drastically within a few hours. A warm morning of clear blue skies can turn quickly into a cold, stormy afternoon. At higher elevations snow is possible even during the summer, and nighttime frosts can be expected any time of year. Hikers venturing into the mountains should carry warm clothes and raingear at all times.

Weather Forecasts

You can obtain a recorded weather forecast in German by telephoning the following number:

Wettervorhersage (weather forecast): Tel. 162.

For information on road conditions during the winter, as well as ski reports, telephone 163.

Where to Get Walking Information

Information on walking in Liechtenstein is available from the National Tourist Office:

Liechtensteinische Fremdenverkehrszentrale (for its address and telephone number, see the *Address Directory* at the back of this chapter). Staff speaks German, English, French, Italian and Spanish. Handles written requests only.

For personal visits you should go to:

Verkehrsbüro Vaduz (see the *Address Directory*). Operated by the Liechtenstein National Tourist Office. Staff speaks German, English, French, Italian and Spanish.

In addition to supplying general tourist information, the National Tourist Office can recommend places to walk, tell you how to get there and sell you the necessary maps and guidebooks. During the winter, the office can also provide information on cross-country skiing.

Walking & Mountaineering Clubs

Liechtenstein's only walking and mountaineering club is the:

Liechtensteiner Alpenverein (LAV). See *Address Directory*. Correspondence should be in German.

The club maintains several mountain paths, operates two mountain huts and conducts walking and ski touring trips in Liechtenstein and abroad. Membership is open to non-residents of Liechtenstein. Benefits include reduced rates for overnight stays in club huts and receipt of the club's yearbook *Bergheimat* (Mountain Home), which it has published since 1951. The LAV has reciprocal membership agreements with the Swiss Alpine Club, German Alpine Club, Austrian Alpine Club and Austrian Friends of Nature Society, which allows LAV members to stay at reduced rates in huts operated by these clubs.

Maps

Owing to its small size, all of Liechtenstein can be shown on a single map sheet. The best map for walkers is the:

Wanderkarte Fürstentum Liechtenstein (1:50,000). This special-edition walking map covers all of Liechtenstein as well as adjacent parts of Switzerland and Austria. Solid red lines show the routes of easy, lowland paths; red dashes mark steeper, more difficult mountain tracks. Secondary routes are shown in black. Relief is indicated by 100-meter contour lines supplemented by shading. The key to map symbols is in German, French and English and includes pictures of path markings. The map is published by and may be purchased from the Liechtensteinische Fremdenverkehrszentrale, the Verkehrsbüro Vaduz or from any bookstore.

If you plan to follow mountain paths or cross-country routes, you may also want to carry the 1:25,000 **Landeskarte Fürstentum Liechtenstein** published by the Regierung des Fürstentums Liechtenstein—the Liechtenstein government. This map shows topographical relief in greater detail than the *Wanderkarte* and will therefore prove more useful for choosing routes across rugged terrain. It may also be purchased from the Liechtensteinische Fremdenverkehrszentrale (see *Address Directory*).

The following maps are not intended for use on the trail, but are helpful for planning walks in the areas they cover:

Agfa Tourenkarte Fürstentum Liechtenstein (1:50,000). A four-color, shaded-relief map published by the manufacturers of Agfa film. Shows footpaths, mountain tracks and cross-country skiing routes as well as towns and roads. On the back of the map is information in German, French and English on various towns and points of interest, along with suggested walks in each area. The key to map symbols is also in German, French and English. A pictorial inset on the front of the map shows the Swiss mountains across the Rhine Valley as seen from high on the slopes of the Rätikon Massif. A similar inset on the back of the map shows the mountains to the east. Available for a nominal charge from the Liechtensteinische Fremdenverkehrszentrale, the Verkehrsbüro Vaduz or from any souvenir shop in Vaduz.

Wanderkarte Vaduz und Umgebung. A sketch map showing five circular walks in the vicinity of Vaduz. Each route is indicated on the map in a different color. A list of symbols at the bottom of the map shows the path markings used along each route, and the locations of viewtowers, parking places and fire pits with grills. Landmarks, sport facilities and places of interest are also listed and keyed to numbers on the map. On the back of the map are route descriptions in German, French and English. Each description mentions points of interest along the way and gives the approximate walking time and difficulty for each route. The locations of restaurants, hotels and cafes are also shown on a sketch map on the back of the sheet. Available for a nominal charge from the Liechtensteinische Fremdenverkehrszentrale.

Historischer Höhenweg Eschnerberg. Shows five circular walks in the forested hills separating the villages of Eschen and Ruggell in northern Liechtenstein. Each route and its corresponding path marking are shown in a different color. Brief descriptions of each walk and of nearby points of interest are given on the back of the map. All information is in German. Available free of charge from the Liechtensteinische Fremdenverkehrszentrale.

Guidebooks

The most comprehensive guide to walks in Liechtenstein is:

- *Wanderbuch Fürstentum Liechtenstein* (in German), published by Kümmerly + Frey, Bern, Switzerland, 1979. Describes 85 easy walks on marked footpaths and 15 longer, more difficult walks on marked mountain tracks. A list, set off from the rest of the text at the beginning of the descriptions, gives the departure point, approximate walking time and a brief route outline for each walk. Sketch maps show many of the routes. Includes numerous photographs, plus introductory essays on geology, flora and fauna and the development of footpaths in Liechtenstein.

If you are more fluent in English than German, the following booklet—though not nearly so complete as the above—may prove more helpful:

- *Excursions in the Principality of Liechtenstein* (in English), published by Buchhandlung und Souvenirs Haas, Vaduz. Gives a brief description of 86 walks throughout Liechtenstein. Approximate walking times are given. Includes several photographs, but no maps. Should be used in conjunction with the *Wanderkarte Fürstentum Liechtenstein*.

Both guides may be purchased from the Verkehrsbüro Vaduz or the Liechtensteinische Fremdenverkehrszentrale (see the *Address Directory*). For descriptions of walking routes in the vicinity of Vaduz, the map folder,

Wanderkarte Vaduz und Umgebund (see the section on *Maps*, above), is a good substitute for the above guides.

Trailside Lodgings

No matter where you walk in Liechtenstein, even in the remotest corner of the mountains, you are never more than a few hours from lodgings. As a result, it is never necessary to camp, and you can walk everywhere unencumbered by a heavy pack. Hotels and pensions are located in virtually all towns and villages, including the mountain hamlets of Gaflei, Masescha, Silum, Sücka, Steg and Malbun, all of which offer easy access to the alpine high country. A complete list of hotels and pensions giving their prices, opening dates and available facilities can be obtained from the Liechtensteinische Fremdenverkehrszentrale. The National Tourist Office can also provide details on Liechtenstein's first youth hostel, an attractive wood and stucco building opened in 1978:

> **Jugendherberge Schaan-Vaduz** (for its address and telephone number, see the *Address Directory*). A well-equipped hostel with a game room, clothes-drying room, meeting room and members' kitchen for those who wish to cook their own meals. Warm meals are also served by the hostel. Sleeping facilities include 4 rooms with 2 beds each and 12 rooms with 8 beds each. Located about a 10-minute walk from the train station in Schaan. Footpaths leading into the mountains begin near the hostel.

Accommodation is also available in the two mountain huts operated by the Liechtensteiner Alpenverein (see the *Address Directory*):

> **Pfälzer-Hütte.** Located near the Austrian border in extreme southeastern Liechtenstein, high on the slopes of 2,108-meter Bettlerjoch. To the south rises 2,570-meter Naafkopf, which stands on the shared border of Switzerland, Austria and Liechtenstein and is known as the *Dreiländergipfel*—the three-country peak. North of the hut rises 2,360-meter Augstenberg.

> **Gafadura-Hütte.** Located in northern Liechtenstein in the mountains above Planken. Sits at 1,428 meters elevation amid the forest and meadows on the northern slope of 2,052-meter Drei Schwestern—the Three Sisters Mountain.

The huts are normally open from mid-June to late September. If conditions are favorable they sometimes open at the beginning of June and may remain open until the middle of October. The Pfälzer-Hütte has a winter room in a nearby building which is kept unlocked during the off-season. The Gafadura-Hütte may be used only during the months it is open. It has no winter room and no key is available to the hut. Anyone is welcome to stay in the huts, although members of the LAV and clubs with which it has reciprocal agreements enjoy reduced rates. You have the choice of renting either a bed or—for about half the price—a mattress on the floor. Warm meals are served in the huts. No facilities for self-cooking exist. During the off-season, however, you may cook your own meals in the winter room of the Pfälzer-Hütte.

Camping

Liechtenstein has three official campgrounds, one at Bendern and two near Triesen. You may obtain information on these sites from the Verkehrsbüro Vaduz or the Liechtensteinische Fremdenverkehrszentrale.

Although camping is discouraged outside the official campgrounds, you may presently do so if you obtain the permission of landowners. Nonetheless, it's wise to first check with the tourist office on the legality of this. The *Diet*—Liechtenstein's parliament—may soon pass a law forbidding camping outside of designated sites.

Water

When walking in the Rhine Valley or anywhere near populated areas, you should rely on tap water rather than streams. Mountain streams, however, are safe sources of drinking water except perhaps in areas of summer grazing.

Equipment Notes

Because food and lodgings are always available within a few hours' walk, relatively little equipment is needed to walk anywhere in Liechtenstein. If you plan to stay in LAV huts you will need to carry a sheet sleeping bag and personal items. For the campgrounds you will also need a sleeping bag, tent, cooking gear and food. But for day walks little is required beyond appropriate clothing and perhaps your lunch. Street clothes and comfortable shoes will suffice on most marked footpaths in the lowlands. In the mountains, however, sturdy hiking boots are recommended, as is additional clothing for protection against wind and rain. On a warm summer day, you may want to dress lightly for your mountain walk—and so you should—but at the same time, you should also carry a warm change of clothing in your pack, along with woolen cap and mittens, a wind jacket and raingear. Mountain weather is notoriously changeable, and you should be prepared for the worst even on short jaunts. A good compass and appropriate map are also recommended.

Walking Tours, Climbing Courses & Guides

Several guided walking excursions and ski tours are conducted each year by the Liechtensteiner Alpenverein. Information on the tours is available from either the LAV or the Liechtensteinische Fremdenverkehrszentrale. No climbing courses or guide services are currently available in Liechtenstein.

Cross-Country Skiing

Liechtenstein has about 37 kilometers of cross-country ski trails. Most of the routes are in the vicinity of the mountain hamlets of Steg (1,300 meters elevation) and Malbun (1,600 meters elevation), both of which also have downhill skiing facilities, including seven lifts and two ski schools between them, as well as the usual complement of resort hotels. Cross-country skiing is also possible at Masescha (1,250 meters elevation) in the mountains directly above Vaduz. From Masescha you can ski to the summit of 1,944-meter Alpspitz overlooking the Rhine Valley. From Steg a ski trail leads up the Samina Valley to the Pfälzer-Hütte, on the slopes of Bettlerjoch. Trails from Malbun lead, among other places, to the summits of Galinakopf, Schönberg, Sareiserjoch and Hahnenspiel.

The best map for cross-country skiers is the Agfa Tourenkarte (see the section on *Maps),* which shows most existing routes. Brochures describing ski facilities at Malbun and Steg include sketch maps of cross-country routes. The brochures are available from the Liechtensteinische Fremdenverkehrszentrale.

Cross-country skiing equipment may be rented from:

Schweizer Skischule, located in Malbun (see *Address Directory).*

Or from:

Pic-Sport, also located in Malbun (see *Address Directory).*

Transportation

Bus service is available to and from all towns and villages in Liechtenstein. A schedule can be obtained on request from the Liechtensteinische

Fremdenverkehrszentrale or from any post office in Liechtenstein. Three discount tickets are available:

Inhaber–Abonnement.

Allgemeines Abonnement.

Postauto-Wochenkarte.

Useful Addresses & Telephone Numbers

General Tourist Information

In Liechtenstein:

Liechtensteinische Fremdenverkehrszentrale, Vaduz

Verkehrsbüro Vaduz

Or:

Verkehrsbüro Malbun. See *Address Directory.*

Abroad:

The Swiss National Tourist Office in your country (for their locations, see the section on *Useful Addresses & Telephone Numbers* in the chapter on Switzerland).

Sport Shops

Sport Stoffel. Located in Schaan.

Pic-Sport. Located in Malbun. See *Address Directory.*

Sporthaus Bruhl AG. Located in Eschen. See *Address Directory.*

Sport + Mode, Ender AG. Located in Vaduz. See *Address Directory.*

Sporthaus Eberle. Located in Vaduz. See *Address Directory.*

Search & Rescue

In case of an emergency: Tel. 117 (police) or 2 44 55 (Rettungsdienst des Liechtensteinisch. en Roten Kreuzes—Rescue office of the Liechtenstein Red Cross).

Search and rescue costs are borne wholly by the party being rescued (or, in the case of a fatality, the next of kin). The cost depends on the difficulty of the task and the amount of time it takes. But it can add up quickly. Rescue personnel are paid on an hourly basis, and several may be required—not to mention possible helicopter support. If you plan to venture off the trail in the remoter mountain areas or if you intend to do some climbing, you would do well to obtain insurance covering the costs of search and rescue beforehand.

Suggested Walks In Liechtenstein

Liechtenstein contains some 300 kilometers of marked footpaths. Many offer short, easy rambles requiring no special equipment or experience. Others are more difficult mountain tracks through steep, rugged terrain. You have the choice of numerous short day walks or of combining the paths to form longer routes. Several long mountain circuits are possible, as are extended walks into the mountains of neighboring Austria. The following suggested walks represent only a small sample and were selected to show the variety of scenery, terrain and walking conditions found in Liechtenstein.

From Balzers–Mäls to Ruggell

Follows the Rhine River from the southernmost to the northernmost village in Liechtenstein. Through the broad, open farmlands along the river, with unobstructed views of the mountains of both Liechtenstein and neighboring Switzerland on the west. The route follows footpaths, roads and the river dike. **Walking Time:** 6-8 hours. **Difficulty:** Easy. **Path Markings:** Yellow bars, arrows and diamonds on trees, rocks and signposts.
Maps:
• Wanderkarte Fürstentum Liechtenstein 1:50,000.

From Planken to Falknis

From the town of Planken on a steeply ascending mountain path to the LAV hut at Gafadura, then up switchbacks to the ridgecrest at Sarojasattel. From there the route heads south, sticking close to the crest of the mountains overlooking the Rhine Valley, ascending such peaks as Drei Schwestern, Gafleispitz, Alpspitz, Goldlochspitz, Mazorahöhe and, finally, Falknis, on the southern border with Switzerland. Alpine meadows, forests of spruce and fir, rocky summits and fabulous views in all directions. **Walking Time:** 12 to 15 hours. **Difficulty:** Moderately difficult

to difficult (some steep ascents). **Path Markings:** White-red-white arrows, bars and triangles on rocks, trees and signposts.
Special Note: Carry water, which is available only at intervals along the route.
Maps:
• Wanderkarte Fürstentum Liechtenstein 1:50,000.

From Malbun to Galinakopf

Through alpine meadows and timberline forest to the summit of 2,198-meter Galinakopf, then back via the Valórsch Valley. Splendid mountain scenery throughout; grand views from the summit of Galinakopf. **Walking Time:** 6 hours. **Difficulty:** Easy to difficult (some steep ascents). **Path Markings:** White-red-white arrows, bars and triangles on rocks, trees and signposts.
Maps:
• Wanderkarte Fürstentum Liechtenstein 1:50,000.

Steg to Malbun via the Pfälzer-Hütte

Up the glacially scoured trench of the Samina River to the LAV hut high on the slopes of Bettlerjoch. Then north along the ridgecrest to Augstenberg and around the rim of the cirque at the headwaters of the Malbuner River, descending at last to Malbun. Easy one-hour walk from there to Steg. Magnificent mountain scenery throughout, including close-up views of 2,570-meter Naafkopf, Liechtenstein's second-highest peak. **Walking Time:** 5 to 6 hours. **Difficulty:** Easy to difficult (some steep ascents and rocky stretches). **Path Markings:** White-red-white arrows, bars and triangles on rocks, trees and signposts.
Maps:
• Wanderkarte Fürstentum Liechtenstein 1:50,000.

Vaduz to Gaflei

Through forest and meadow in the mountains above Vaduz to a lookout tower at Gaflei (elevation 1,483 meters), with its magnificent views across the Rhine Valley to the mountains of Switzerland. Ruined castle ("Wildschloss") of Schalun; chamois often seen near Seliwald. **Walking Time:** 3 to 4½ hours. **Difficulty:** Easy to moderately difficult (some fairly steep ascents). **Path Markings:** A stylized gentian on a heart-shaped wooden plaque.
Maps:
• Wanderkarte Fürstentum Liechtenstein 1:50,000.

- The map folder, *Wanderkarte Vaduz und Umgebung* (see the section on *Maps* earlier in this chapter), is also recommended.

Historischer Höhenweg Eschnerberg

Five circular routes in the hills separating Eschen and Mauren from Ruggell. Forest, fields, small villages and farms. Prehistoric settlements at Malanser and Schneller; foundations of a Roman villa at Nendeln; other historical points of interest. **Walking Time:** ¾ hour to 2½ hours, depending upon the route you choose. **Difficulty:** Easy. **Path Markings:** Each circular route has its own distinctive marking: horse and rider, urn, linden leaf, ammonit (mollusc) or castle ruins.

Maps:
- Wanderkarte Fürstentum Liechtenstein 1:50,000.
- The map folder, *Historischer Höhenweg Eschnerberg* (see the section on *Maps* earlier in this chapter), is also recommended.

Address Directory

E

- *Emergency:* Tel. 117 (police) or 2 44 55 (rescue office of the Liechtenstein Red Cross).

G

- *Gafadura-Hütte,* FL-9494 Planken. Tel. (075) 3 24 42.

J

- *Jugendherberge Schaan-Vaduz,* Untere Rüttigasse 6, FL-9494 Schaan. Tel. (075) 2 50 22

L

- *LAV,* see *Liechtensteiner Alpenverein.*
- *Liechtensteiner Alpenverein (LAV),* Ramschwagweg, FL-9496 Balzers. Tel. (075) 4 12 49.
- *Liechtensteinische Fremdenverkehrszentrale,* P.O.B. 139, FL-9490 Vaduz. Tel. (075) 2 14 43 or 6 62 88.

P

- *Pfälzer-Hütte,* FL-9497 Triesenberg. Tel. (075) 2 36 79.
- *Pic-Sport,* FL-9497 Malbun. Tel. (075) 2 37 55.

S

- *Schweizer Skischule,* FL-9497 Malbun. Tel. (075) 2 29 34 or 2 26 36.
- *Sporthaus Brühl AG, Essanestrasse* 513, FL-9492 Eschen, Tel. (075) 3 37 88
- *Sporthaus Eberle, Herrengasse 11,* FL-9490 Vaduz, Tel. (075) 2 27 05.
- *Sport + Mode,* Ender AG, Städtle 2, FL-9490 Vaduz, Tel. (075) 2 33 11.
- *Sport Stoffel,* Landstrasse 94, FL-9494 Schaan. Tel. (075) 2 18 93.

V

- *Verkehrsbüro Malbun,* FL-9497 Triesenberg/Malbun. Tel. (075) 2 65 77.

W

- *Verkehrsbüro Vaduz,* Engländerbau, Städtle 37, FL-9490 Vaduz. Tel. (075) 2 14 43.
- *Weather forecasts* (Wettervorhersage): Tel. 162.
- *Winter road condition and ski reports:* Tel. 163.

A Quick Reference

In a hurry? Turn to the pages listed below. They will give you the most important information on walking in Liechtenstein.

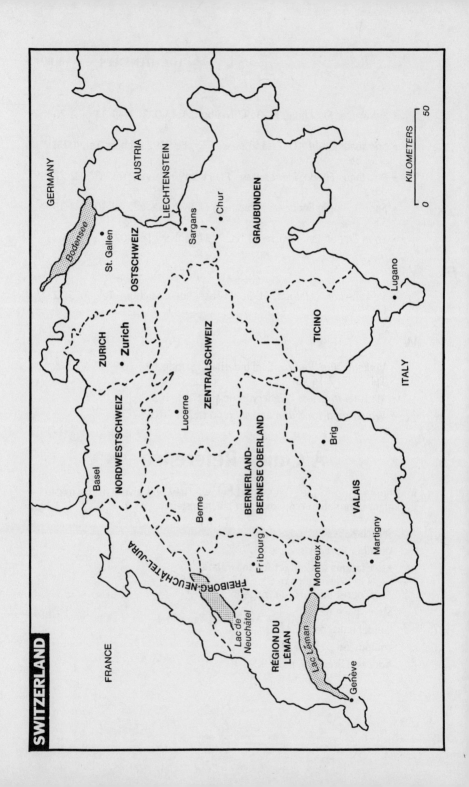

SWITZERLAND

Switzerland

SWITZERLAND COMES AS close to being a walker's paradise as any country in the world. The footpath network is more extensive than the rail and road systems combined. It includes some 50,000 kilometers of marked paths in addition to unmarked rural lanes, mountain tracks and primitive paths—this in a country covering only 41,287 square kilometers (15,937 square miles). Paths radiate from every town and village, linking all parts of the country, no matter how remote. Six long-distance footpaths now cross Switzerland, and more are being planned. Most footpaths are well maintained and clearly marked. Nearly every kilometer is lovingly described in a staggering array of guidebooks, walking maps, pamphlets and leaflets. The main problem confronting the walker is sorting through the overwhelming number of possibilities.

Notoriously punctual rail and postal bus systems serve the entire country, including the most remote Alpine villages. Consequently, you can walk from anywhere to anywhere and always be assured of reliable public transportation when you arrive. Along the way are numerous hotels, pensions, inns, chalets, mountain shelters and campgrounds, rarely more than a day's walk apart and all displaying the cleanliness and efficiency for which the Swiss are justly famous.

The rail and bus systems even publish walking guides to routes served by their lines. And posted on the wall of virtually every train station is a 1:50,000 topographical map of the surrounding district showing footpaths in red. From the station's edge, numerous paths strike off into the countryside, their destinations indicated by thick clumps—sometimes virtual forests—of yellow directional signs.

Switzerland's model footpath system reflects the Swiss' high regard for walking and the fact that they are themselves inveterate walkers. Footpaths are regarded as public rights-of-way, and walking is simply presumed to be one of several legitimate modes of transportation, often the preferable one. A foreigner may sometimes be surprised to discover that a footpath passes unusually close to a private dwelling—through a backyard garden or between a farmhouse and barn—but any misgivings will be quickly allayed by the owner's friendly greeting and natural acceptance of the passing wayfarer. The Swiss ask only that walkers respect private property and conduct themselves in a courteous, considerate fashion. They assume such behavior and—perhaps as a result—are rarely disappointed.

Then there is the scenery, which is spectacular, a happy wedding of natural grandeur and human charm unsurpassed anywhere. The Alps, of course, form the centerpiece. Covering the southern three-fifths of the country, they consist of high, rugged, east-west trending massifs separated by broad, awesomely deep valleys. The central knot of the Alps is the Gotthard Massif, headwaters of the Rhine, Rhône, Aar, Reuss and Ticino rivers, which between them drain all but a small portion of Switzerland. The valleys of the Rhine-Rhône and Reuss-Ticino divide the Alps into four geographic groups. The northeastern ranges include the Urner, Glarner, Schwyzer and Eastern Urner Alps. The northwestern ranges encompass the Western Urner, Unterwaldner, Berner, Fribourg and Vaudois Alps. The southwestern ranges include the Pennine, or Valais, Alps and the Lepontine Alps of Ticino. The southeastern ranges comprise the Rhaetian Alps of Graubünden.

More than 50 summits top 4,000 meters (13,100 feet). The highest is Dufourspitze (Monte Rosa) at 4,634 meters (15,203 feet). It, along with the country's next two highest peaks, Dom and the Matterhorn, are found along the Italian border in the Valais Alps. To the north, across the Rhône Valley, rise the Berner Alps, the second highest range. Its peaks include the monumental Jungfrau and the Eiger, whose awesome north wall is considered one of the most difficult climbs in the world.

Composed of a slate and granite core overlain in places by thick deformed beds of sedimentary rocks, today's Alps are remnants of a once higher range that was worn down by erosion. During the Ice Age, the mountains were overwhelmed by glaciers, which sculpted the ridges and quarried the profound valleys between them. The peaks are boldly chiseled, flanked by steep, sometimes sheer, walls and mantled with perennial snow and ice. There are still 140 glaciers left in the Swiss Alps, but they are of geologically recent origin and have played only minor roles in shaping the range.

The grandeur of the entire Alpine chain, from France east to Austria and Yugoslavia, seems to reach a climax in Switzerland, where the mountains seem bolder and snowier, the valleys deeper and more finely sculpted. You can scale sheer cliffs laced with waterfalls, climb through rock and forest to high, flowery pastures, follow impatient torrents and serene lakeshores, skirt or cross glaciers and snowfields, and ascend to passes and peaks where the ranges seem to run on forever.

Yet the distinctive charm of the Swiss Alps is not merely the handiwork of nature, but also of the Swiss themselves. Whoever walks these mountains will come away with vivid memories of bright, clean villages at the foot of the great peaks, rustic mountain chalets of wood and stone, and everywhere in the high meadows, the wind-chime music of cowbells floating upward in the thin air.

Switzerland, however, is not merely the Alps. North of the range lies the Central Plateau—or *Mittelland*—a region of hills, lakes, river valleys and rolling farmlands stretching from Lac Léman (Lake Geneva) in the west to the Bodensee (Lake Constance) in the east. Known as the Garden of Switzerland, the Mittelland is the center of Swiss agriculture. Here too reside the majority of the 6.3-million Swiss, notably in the cities of Zürich and Bern, but also in dozens of smaller communities scattered throughout the region. Footpaths wind through fields and pastures, orchards and woods, past small, manicured farms and storybook villages, by lakes and streams, along ridge tops and valley bottoms, often within view of the snowy peaks arrayed along the southern horizon.

North of the Central Plateau, the Jura Mountains extend along the Swiss border from Lac Léman to the canton of Schaffhausen. By Alpine standards, the Jura are merely high, rugged hills, the loftiest summits barely topping 1,675 meters (5,500 feet). The southern Jura, where the highest peaks are found, are a series of parallel limestone ridges and deep valleys. Many of the higher peaks have rocky, ice-carved summits. The northern Jura is lower and less rugged, consisting of limestone tablelands bounded by river valleys. Jura footpaths cross valley farmlands; follow white-water streams through narrow, cliff-bound gorges; climb steep, forested slopes; and meander along high, meadowy ridge tops offering spectacular views of the Alps toward the south.

With an apparent native genius for taming the land without destroying it in the process, the Swiss have fashioned a garden from the wilderness. The human touch is everywhere evident, even in the remotest corners of the Alps. Yet the transformation was carried out with such deftness of touch and sensitivity to natural beauty that the human presence seems in most cases less an intrusion than a complement. There may be little true wilderness left in the country, but neither are there large areas of urban blight or great tracts of scarred land. When you walk in Switzerland, you walk in the world's largest and grandest park. Enjoy.

Scenery aside, one of the chief pleasures of walking in Switzerland is its enormous cultural diversity. A confederation of 23 semi-autonomous cantons, Switzerland embraces four official languages, two national religions and a host of local differences in history, customs, architecture and dress. French (spoken by 21 percent of the population) is the official language of the western cantons; German (74 percent), of those in the center and northeast; Italian (4 percent), of the southernmost canton of Ticino; and Romansh—a distinct language of Latin origin—is spoken by 1 percent of the population, residing primarily in the eastern canton of Graubünden, which also includes German and Italian speakers. In addition, English is widely spoken in all but French Switzerland.

To further complicate matters, some Swiss are Catholic and some are Protestant, with religious preferences commonly crossing linguistic frontiers. The result is a uniquely rich cultural stew in which the ingredients are at once distinct yet blended into a unified whole. Despite their many differences, which are cherished and consciously preserved, the Swiss are a single people untroubled by the divisiveness that so often plagues pluralistic societies.

Flora & Fauna

One-quarter of Switzerland consists of glaciers, lakes and barren rock, where vegetation is either scarce or absent. Another quarter—roughly 930,000 hectares (2.3-million acres)—is covered by forest. The remainder of the country is mostly given over to pastures and meadows, with arable lands accounting for a mere 10 percent of the total land area. Switzerland's forests, now confined mainly to the Alps and Jura, with scattered stands in the Mittelland, were once far more extensive. Over the centuries, however, thousands of hectares were cut to supply wood and clear land for farming.

Switzerland has four major vegetation zones, which are arrayed, as in all mountainous regions, according to altitude. The Hill Zone, which includes the Mittelland, part of the Jura, and the lower Alpine valleys, extends upward to between 500 and 1,200 meters, depending on local climatic conditions. Most of the arable farmlands are found in this zone. The chief crops are hardy cereal grains, fodder grasses and cold-tolerant orchard fruits. Vegetables, vineyards, maize and tobacco are locally important.

The Mountain Deciduous Zone occupies a belt between about 700 and 1,500 meters. Beech forests dominate this zone in the northern Alps and Jura. Also present are ash, elm, Alpine maple, box, silver pine and Scots pine. Alder and poplar grow along lakes and streams. The foothills of the southern Alps, in the canton of Ticino, support a quite different forest, one with a more Mediterranean flavor. Here the dominant tree is the Spanish chestnut, with pseudo-acacia, mountain ash, holly and broom as important associates.

The Mountain Coniferous Zone extends from about 1,200 to 2,000 meters, and even higher in the southern Alps. Spruce, a tree introduced for its lumber, dominates the forest. Other common species include silver fir—the dominant tree in native forests—and Scots pine. Larch, a deciduous conifer whose leaves turn gold in autumn, grows in cool subalpine basins, along with Arolla pine, the principal timberline tree in the Swiss Alps. The upper forest limit occurs at elevations ranging from as low as 1,800 meters in the northern Alps to well over 2,000 meters in the south. Scattered, wind-dwarfed Arolla pines commonly range even higher. In places, birch or mountain alder form the last continuous timber stands.

The true Alpine Zone extends from tree limit to about 3,000 meters. Here sprawl the great high Alpine pastures, tundra-like turfs that during late June through early August provide a spectacular floral display. Above the pastures, nearly barren screes, Alpine pavements, boulder fields and *felsenmeer* (frost-riven rubble fields) stretch upward to about 3,000 meters, the lower limit of perennial snow in the Alps.

The distribution and limits of these four vegetation zones vary greatly according to local conditions of soil, climate, human activities and other factors. Meadows and pasturelands, for example, are widely distributed throughout the Mountain Coniferous Zone and are in large measure responsible for the distinctive openness of the Alpine landscape.

These broad grasslands are one of Switzerland's most important resources, for they are ideally suited for raising dairy cattle. The cheeses of Gruyère and Emmental are renowned the world over, and dairy farming remains the country's most important agricultural activity. Throughout the Swiss Alps, you encounter cattle grazing in high pastures. They remain in the meadows throughout the summer, tended all the while by herdsmen, who summer in wooden chalets scattered through the mountains. In autumn, the herds are driven—formerly on foot, now more often by truck—to winter quarters in the valley, where they remain until the following spring. The traditional spring and autumn cattle drives, where the herdsmen accompanied their animals on foot to and from the high pastures—a practice known as *transhumance*—has mostly disappeared from Switzerland. It persists only in a few places, notably some of the remoter valleys in the Valais.

Over the past century the variety and abundance of native wildlife has greatly diminished in the Swiss Alps, thanks to hunting and competition from livestock. The bear, wolf and beaver are extinct in these mountains. The steinbock, or ibex, was once extinct, but has been successfully reintroduced in the Swiss Alps. The lynx has also been successfully reintroduced in the canton of Obwalden. The Alpine stag, which hovered on the edge of extinction, was saved only by last-minute protective measures and is still very scarce. Chamois remain rather common, especially in the Engadin, but are still absent from many areas.

Other alpine mammals include the marmot, Alpine hare, ermine and red deer. Conspicuous birds include the golden eagle, Alpine jackdaw, Alpine titmouse, pine jay and grouse. There are two poisonous snakes, the adder and viper, but the chance of seeing either, much less being bitten, is small. If you are bitten, however, seek medical attention immediately.

Switzerland now has a number of wildlife reserves, the most notable being the Schweizerische Nationalpark, which preserves some 169 square kilometers of forest and mountains above the Engadin Valley in Graubünden. All human works, save footpaths and limited visitor facilities, have been eliminated, and the forest is slowly reclaiming the land. Walking is strictly limited to footpaths and overnight camping is not permitted. The park, however, is the best place in Switzerland to observe native wildlife, such as chamois, steinbock and stag. Knowledgeable local guides familiar with the habits and whereabouts of the animals are available for hire.

Walkers and other visitors to Switzerland should confine themselves to merely looking at, rather than picking, the native Alpine flowers. Many, including Alpine columbine, hairy primrose, edelweiss, fire lily, Alpine aster and Bee orchid, are strictly protected by law.

Further information on Switzerland's flora and fauna can be obtained from the *Schweizerischer Bund für Naturschutz/Ligue Suisse pour la Protection de la Nature*, a membership organization devoted to protecting Switzerland's natural resources. Members receive a club bulletin and discounts on books, posters and other items, as well as the opportunity to participate in club excursions and conferences. They may also gain free admission to the Aletsch Ecological Center in Valais. For information, write:

> **Schweizerischer Bund für Naturschutz** (for its address and telephone number, see the *Address Directory* at the back of this chapter). Staff speaks German and French. Publications, including a catalog of the books and posters sold by the association, are also available in both languages.

Climate

Switzerland has a relatively cool, humid climate that is modified enormously by its vast mountain system. Marked differences in temperature and precipitation occur over short distances, both with changes in altitude and from one side of a mountain mass to another. The country's position in the center of Western Europe also opens it to both maritime and continental influences. As a result, winds are variable, swinging from warm, moist southwesterlies to cold, dry northeasterlies, and weather changes, particularly in the mountains, are often swift and sometimes unpredictable.

Although no part of Switzerland is even semiarid, the driest is the Rhône Valley in the Valais, which is virtually surrounded by moisture-blocking mountain ranges. The town of Sierre in the floor of the valley, for instance, has an average of 84 rainy days per year and receives about 609 mm (24 inches) of precipitation. In contrast, the town of Leukerbad, only 15 kilometers away, but 871 meters (2,857 feet) higher in elevation, receives precipitation on about 110 days out of the year for an average of 1,016 mm (40 inches), half of which comes in the form of snow. On the northern side of the Berner Alps, opposite Sierre and Leukerbad, amounts are even greater, topping more than 2,000 mm (79 inches) of annual precipitation in some locales.

The times of year when precipitation is greatest also vary. On the northern side of the Berner Alps, rainfall is frequent and copious in summer and snowfall is considerable in winter, while the town of Lugano, on the southern side of the Lepontine Alps, receives most of its rainfall in the spring and autumn. Throughout most of the Alps, however, afternoon thunderstorms are common in summer, particularly at higher elevations.

Winters are generally cold and snowy throughout most of Switzerland, with the greatest snowfall and lowest temperatures occurring in the Alps. Fogs are common during this season in the Mittelland and mountain valleys, but between storms the Alps often have relatively long periods of clear skies. The warmest winters occur in southern Ticino, where the moderating influence of the Mediterranean is pronounced. Near Lugano (elevation, 272 meters), winters are typically mild and sunny, more often bringing rain than snow. The average minimum temperature in January is *minus* 4°C. (24°F.); the average maximum, 13°C. (56°F.). By comparison, the average minimum and maximum in January for Bern, situated at 545 meters in the Mittelland, are *minus* 10°C. (14°F.) and 8°C. (47°F.). Increases in elevation, of course, bring lower temperatures. Thus, at St. Moritz (elevation, 1,856 meters), the average minimum for January is *minus* 25°C. *(minus* 13°F.); the average maximum, 3°C. (37°F.).

Summers are pleasantly warm throughout most of Switzerland, although again, the mountains are significantly cooler. Average daytime highs during the summer range from the high 20sC. (low 80sF.) in the Mittelland and lower mountain valleys, such as near Interlaken, down to the low 20sC. (low 70sF.) on the middle mountain slopes. With increasing elevation, temperatures drop further, and near the higher crests may be quite chilly. Moreover, summer storms can arise suddenly and may bring freezing winds, hail and significant amounts of snow at higher elevations. Consequently, walkers venturing into the high Alps should be prepared for any contingency.

During the spring—less often at other times of the year—the northern slopes and valleys of the Alps are visited by the *Föhn,* a hot, dry wind that rushes with great speed down the mountain flanks. Air temperatures rise rapidly, melting great quantities of snow and resulting in numerous avalanches. Trees groan and shutters rattle in the hot wind. People's teeth are set on edge as the scorched air crackles with static electricity. Incidences of crime, sickness and nervous tension are even rumored to increase. Yet for all the human stress created by the Föhn, it also hastens the thaw, stimulates the growth of vegetation and opens the high meadows to herdsmen and their cattle. Skiers, however, should stay off the mountains during the Föhn, when the danger of avalanches is severe.

There is no single best time for walking in Switzerland. All seasons are good. Which one you choose depends upon where you want to go and what you want to see and do. Spring is an excellent season for walking in the Mittelland, Jura and lower Alps, which then enjoy clear, mild weather. Early summer is the best time to roam the high Alpine flower gardens, although some of the higher passes may still be snowed in. Late summer permits you to wander almost at will among the high peaks, the only disadvantage being frequent periods of cloudiness and thunderstorms. Many visitors consider autumn, when the forest becomes a blaze of color, and the air is crisp and bright, to be the finest season for walking in the Alps or Jura. And winter turns Switzerland into a skier's dream.

Further information on the general climatic features of 41 locales throughout the Swiss Alps is contained in a handy booklet entitled:

- *Short Climatic Guide to Switzerland* (in English; also available in French and German), published by the Association Suisse des Stations Climatiques/Schweizerische Vereinigung der Kilmakurorte,

Montreux. Designed for those who wish to visit a climatic health resort, but also of use to walkers. The two-page descriptions of each locale give its location, altitude and general weather features—amount and intensity of sunshine, frequency of cloud cover, susceptibility to fog, seasonal temperatures, wind features, frequency and amount of rainfall and snow, and the times of year when skies are clear, temperatures mild and precipitation low. Suggestions are given on the best season to visit each locale, along with information on access, accommodation facilities and the telephone number and address of its tourist office. Useful for deciding when to visit various parts of Switzerland. Also available from the Schweizerische Verkehrszentrale (see *Address Directory*).

Weather Forecasts

Weather forecasts are printed daily in Swiss newspapers and broadcast several times a day on radio and television stations. Recorded weather forecasts for local areas can also be obtained by telephone:

Wetterbericht-Prévisions: Tel. 162.

In winter, the same number can be telephoned for avalanche bulletins. In addition, you can obtain recorded information on winter road and snow conditions by telephoning: Tel. 163.

Where to Get Walking Information

Walking information for Switzerland is abundant and easily obtained. There are scores of guidebooks and hundreds of brochures, pamphlets, pocket-size cards and maps detailing the country's footpaths, ski tracks, winter walking and skiing routes and climbing routes. A single letter to a local tourist office will swamp you with possibilities, more than you could cover in a year or more. The problem—but a delightful one—is to select from among the vast array of alluring routes. This takes time, so it is best to write for information well in advance of your visit.

Three organizations can supply general walking information for the entire country. All are extremely helpful and will quickly respond to enquiries with whatever information they have available—which is considerable. Because so much information exists, however, you will obtain the best assistance if you specify the particular region or regions you intend to visit when you write. This will help the person answering your letter provide a more complete, targeted response. If you do not yet know where you want to walk or ski in Switzerland, it is best to first write the Schweizerische Verkehrszentrale (Swiss National Tourist Office). More specific information on the activities and areas in which you are interested can then be obtained from the Schweizerische Arbeitsgemeinschaft für Wanderwege (Swiss Ramblers' Association) and Schweizer Alpen-Club (Swiss Alpine Club). In all cases, letters written in German, French, Italian or English can be assured of responses in the same language.

The addresses and telephone numbers of the following associations are listed in the *Address Directory* at the back of this chapter.

Schweizerische Verkehrszentrale/Office National Suisse du Tourisme. Staff speaks German, French, Italian, Spanish and English. Can provide general information on Switzerland's long-distance footpaths and lists of selected walking itineraries throughout the country, including a series of pamphlets published by the Schweizer Reisepost (Swiss Postal Authority) describing walks that can be reached on Switzerland's postal buses—*Wanderungen im Tessin, Wanderungen im Wallis, Wanderungen im Jura, Wanderungen in Graubünden,* etc. The office can also provide lists of organized walking and cross-country skiing tours, mountaineering and ski schools, and places where mountain guides are available for hire and lodgings. Free publications available from the office include:

- *On Foot Through Switzerland* (in English; also available in French and German). An attractively illustrated booklet which provides an overview of walking in Switzerland and briefly describes each of its long-distance footpaths. The descriptions for each footpath are broken down into a series of short sections and include a table listing overnight stops, their elevations and the walking times between them. The booklet also includes a large-scale fold-out map showing the routes of the long-distance footpaths and a card showing how Switzerland's various types of footpaths are signposted and waymarked.

- *Hiking in Switzerland* (in English). A leaflet listing 32 popular walking routes in seven regions. Gives the starting point, destination and walking time for each route. Also outlines a long-distance route from Altdorf, in east-central Switzerland, through the Berner and Vaudois Alps to Montreux, on Lac Léman.

- *Switzerland: 5 Mountaineering Hiking* (in English; also available in French and German). Published annually. A directory to mountaineering and walking tours open to the public. Tour descriptions are arranged alphabetically by town and village. The itinerary and fee for each tour are given along with any optional costs and the names, addresses and telephone numbers of organizations sponsoring the tours. Also includes a directory of mountain guides, guide offices and mountaineering schools.

- *Ferienorte der Schweiz/Lieux de Vacances en Suisse/Swiss Holiday*

Resorts/Luoghi di Vacanza in Svizzera (in German, French, English
and Italian). A brochure listing the activities and facilities available
at Swiss resorts. The resorts are grouped by region, with information
presented in tabular form by means of numbers and symbols.
Information includes the name of each resort, its elevation, the total
kilometrage of cleared winter footpaths, and the availability of
campsites (winter and summer), mountain guide services, cross-
country ski tracks and places to hire sports equipment.

- *Summer in Switzerland* (in English). Lists attractions and activities
  for tourists visiting Switzerland in the summer. Includes a list of
  guided mountain tours, rambles and walking excursions, with the
  dates and locations of each.

**Schweizerische Arbeitsgemeinschaft für Wanderwege (SAW)/Asso-
ciation Suisse de Tourisme Pédestre (ASTP).** Staff speaks German,
French, Italian, Spanish and English. This is Switzerland's principal
walking club, with 25 sections scattered throughout the country. Its
central office can provide information on virtually every aspect of
walking and ski touring in Switzerland—details on Switzerland's
long-distance footpaths; the maps, guidebooks, lodgings, organized
walking and skiing tours, and mountain guides available in each
region; the equipment and clothing you need; and answers to specific
questions you may have. There is no more authoritative source of
information on walking and ski touring in Switzerland. And it is all
centralized in one spot. The SAW also sells walking maps and
guidebooks covering all of Switzerland and will supply a complimentary list on request. In addition, it publishes guidebooks to Switzerland's long-distance footpaths, a directory to club walking activities
and a booklet listing cross-country ski routes. The SAW is good about
answering enquiries, but be sure to specify which region or regions
you are interested in. Useful publications available from the SAW
include:

- *Wanderprogramm der SAW/Programme des courses de l'ASTP* (in
  German and French). Published annually. A booklet listing
  organized walking tours offered by each SAW section. Gives the
  address and telephone number of each section. Also lists the
  walking maps and guidebooks covering each canton that are sold
  by the SAW. Free on request.
- *Ski Wandern/Ski de Randonnée* (in German and French). Published
  annually. A comprehensive directory to marked ski tracks and
  cross-country routes in Switzerland. See full description under the
  section on *Cross-Country Skiing* later in this chapter.
- *Wandern* (in German), edited by Berner Wanderwege, the SAW
  section for Bern. A quarterly magazine with articles of interest to
  walkers. Free to members of the Berner Wanderwege; available for

a nominal charge to non-members. Includes the quarterly bulletin *Mitteilungsblatt*, which contains announcements and news items about walking.

- *Die Schweiz zu Fuss/La Suisse à pied* (available in German or French). A leaflet describing the goals and activities of the SAW. Free on request.
- *SAW Prospekt* (available in German or French). Lists the addresses and telephone numbers of SAW sections. Free on request.

Schweizer Alpen-Club (SAC)/Club Alpin Suisse (CAS). Staff speaks German, French, Italian and English. Switzerland's principal mountaineering club, the Swiss Alpine Club, operates more than 200 mountain refuges, 152 of which are open to the public. It also organizes a variety of mountaineering activities and publishes more than 60 guidebooks to climbing, ski mountaineering and the flora, fauna and minerals of the Swiss mountains. It can provide information on rock and ice climbing, ski mountaineering and mountain walking; give technical advice on specific routes; and supply details on its mountain huts, publications, mountaineering courses and organized walking, climbing and skiing tours.

Once you have decided where you want to walk or ski in Switzerland, you can obtain additional information from the tourist offices in each region. A list of the principal offices, along with descriptions of the useful publications supplied by each, are given in the regional descriptions later in this chapter.

Switzerland's Walking & Climbing Clubs

Although Switzerland's extensive footpath system is a major attraction for thousands of tourists, it exists first of all because the Swiss themselves are enthusiastic walkers. The large and active Swiss Ramblers' Association and Swiss Alpine Club and the regionally active Swiss Jura Association further attest to their love of the sport.

Schweizerischer Juraverein/Association du Jura Suisse (see *Address Directory*). The Swiss Jura Association is the principal driving force behind the footpath network and walking activities in the Swiss Jura. It maintains more than 600 kilometers of marked footpaths, publishes a walkers' lodging list covering the mountains, and edits a series of 1:50,000 walking maps and the French- and German-language guides to the Jura. It also organizes walking excursions, helps promote and protect the Jura's footpaths and acts as a clearinghouse for information on walking in the Jura. In addition, it works closely with the cantonal sections of the SAW in the development of new footpaths. Members receive discounts on the association's publications and notices of its various activities. Foreign members are welcome.

Schweizerische Arbeitsgemeinschaft für Wanderwege (SAW) (see *Address Directory*). Founded in 1934, the Swiss Ramblers' Association is an umbrella organization for walkers that has been instrumental in the development of the Swiss footpath network and the promotion of walking activities. Altogether, its sections are responsible for more than three-fifths of Switzerland's footpaths. A member of the European Ramblers' Association, it has 25 sections, including one in neighboring Liechtenstein, and a membership in excess of 26,000. Each section—in most cases, one per canton—is an autonomous walking club. The secretariat of the SAW's central office promotes walking and nature protection on a national level, assists the sections in their work and coordinates their cooperative activities. It also acts as a clearinghouse for information on walking for the entire country. The sections establish, mark and maintain footpaths in their canton or district. They also work closely with the Schweizerischer Ski-Verband (Swiss Ski Club) to promote cross-country skiing and to establish, mark and maintain ski touring routes. The sections disseminate walking information and assist in compiling and editing—and, in a few cases, publishing—walking guides to their areas. They also organize day walks, weekend rambles, extended treks of a week or more, cross-country ski trips and even foreign tours for their members. In addition, many offer *Radiowanderungen,* walking tours open to the public and announced on the radio.

Schweizer Alpen-Club (SAC) (see *Address Directory*). The Swiss Alpine Club is a mountaineering association founded in 1863 with more than 68,000 members distributed among 140 sections. It encourages the practice of climbing, skiing and walking in the Swiss Alps; the exploration and study of mountains both in Switzerland and abroad; and the protection of Switzerland's scenic resources. It conducts climbing, skiing and walking excursions, both in Switzerland and abroad; operates more than 200 mountain huts in the Swiss Alps; offers courses on rock and ice climbing, ski mountaineering, mountain safety, search and rescue and other mountain-related activities; trains and certifies mountain guides; operates mountain rescue posts and conducts search and rescue operations in the Alps; and publishes a wide selection of guidebooks as well as books on mountain first-aid, climbing techniques and a variety of scientific works on the mountains.

Membership is limited to people 18 years of age and older. Application is made through any of the club's 140 sections. Foreign members are welcome, but membership requirements are, for most sections, rather rigorous and may be difficult or impossible to meet without actually living in Switzerland for a prolonged period. Many sections require sponsorship by two SAC members. In addition, there may be a probationary period of anywhere from three to six months, or even up to a year, during which you are expected to participate regularly in club activities. The Monte Rosa section is probably the easiest to join, requiring only two passport photos, an application form and payment of dues.

Membership benefits include:

1. The right to stay in more than 60 SAC mountain huts open only to members and reduced rates for staying in the 152 club-operated mountain huts open to the public;

2. Priority in bed assignments in the huts;

3. Subscription to the SAC quarterly magazine and monthly bulletin *Les Alpes/Le Alpi/Las Alps/Die Alpen* (described below) and to information bulletins published by each section;

4. Free access to the club's mountaineering library in Bern;

5. Discounts on club publications;

6. Insurance covering death and disability; and

7. The right to participate in courses and excursions offered by SAC sections.

In addition, the SAC has reciprocal membership agreements with 18 mountaineering clubs in 10 countries, more, in fact, than it likes. The problem is that while virtually every national club would, for obvious reasons, like to establish a reciprocal arrangement with the SAC, some simply do not offer SAC members sufficient benefits in return. The Union International des Associations d'Alpinisme (UIAA) is now studying a proposal whereby member clubs, of which the SAC is one, would pay for reciprocal privileges with one another.

Useful SAC publications include:

- *Les Alpes/Le Alpi/Las Alps/Die Alpen* (mostly in German and French). A quarterly magazine and monthly bulletin for club members, featuring articles on mountaineering, club expeditions, climbing routes, official business and other matters of interest to members. Free with membership.

- *Clubhütten/Cabanes/Capanne* (in German and French). A book listing and describing SAC mountain huts. Includes a map showing their locations. (For a full description, see the section on *Trailside Lodgings*.)

Maps

Excellent walking maps—indeed, the finest in the world—cover all of Switzerland. They include topographical maps in scales of 1:25,000 and 1:50,000 published by the Eidgenössische Landestopographie (Topographical Survey of Switzerland) and special walking maps in scales ranging from 1:20,000 to 1:75,000 produced by private publishers. Special walking and ski touring maps are also published by several local tourist offices, local railways and other organizations.

The most important maps for walkers are the following:

Eidgenössische Landestopographie/Service Topographique Fédéral. The Topographical Survey of Switzerland's maps set the standard by which all maps in Switzerland are measured and upon which the vast majority—including the special walking maps—are based. It publishes two map series of particular use to walkers: the *1:25,000 Landeskarten der Schweiz* and the *1:50,000 Landeskarten der Schweiz*. The 1:25,000 series covers the entire country in 248 sheets. It also includes eight special composite sheets covering certain districts. This series shows land features in great detail and is ideal for short walks and climbs, when you need to carry only one or two sheets. For extended excursions, the 1:50,000 series is preferred simply because each sheet covers an area roughly three times the size as that shown on the 1:25,000 maps. There is, of course, some sacrifice of detail, but for the huge majority of walks the 1:50,000 sheets are much more than adequate. Seventy-eight 1:50,000 sheets cover the entire country. There are also 15 special composite sheets covering certain districts—the Berner Oberland and the region surrounding Zermatt, for example.

Both series of maps are models of cartographic excellence, showing the ground with enormous detail and accuracy, yet remaining very easy to read. Relief is indicated by both contour lines and shading. Forests are shown in green, pastures and meadows in yellow and glaciers in white. Cliffs and rock outcrops are indicated by hachure marks. Footpaths and other walking routes are shown in black and are subdivided into footpaths, mule tracks, primitive mountain paths, common routes over glaciers and ice fields, and remains of historic tracks and roads. The maps also show the locations of remote inns, including mountain huts, and campsites, along with a truly incredible number of other natural and man-made features.

These maps can be obtained by mail from:

Eidgenössische Landestopographie/Service Topographique Fédéral (see *Address Directory*). A map index showing the 1:25,000 and 1:50,000 sheets covering Switzerland is free on request. Maps should be ordered by number and name.

The maps are also available from local bookstores throughout Switzerland. In addition, they can be obtained from some Swiss tourist offices abroad.

The Eidgenössische Landestopographie also publishes two useful guides to interpreting map signals:

- *Signaturen in Unseren Karten* (in German; also available in French, Italian and English). A leaflet illustrating selected map symbols— showing roads, bridges, footpaths, forests and the like—with color photographs of the features depicted.

- *Conventional Signs of the Swiss Topographical Maps* (in English; also available in German, French and Italian). A complete index to all shading and symbols used on the Landeskarten der Schweiz. Recommended.

Both map guides are available free of charge from the Eidgenössische Landestopographie, the SAW (see *Address Directory*) and local bookstores.

The Eidgenössische Landestopographie also publishes a series of 1:100,000 *Landeskarten der Schweiz,* as well as maps in scales of 1:200,000, 1:300,000 and 1:500,000. While these maps are unsuitable for use on the trail, they are useful for planning excursions, particularly longer ones.

Kümmerly + Frey. This company publishes more than 60 special walkers' maps—known as *Wanderkarten* or *cartes d'excursion*—covering most principal walking districts in Switzerland. Although these maps are based on the Eidgenössische Landestopographie maps, the Kümmerly + Frey Wanderkarten differ in two important ways: 1) they are not uniform in scale and 2) they contain a good deal more information of special interest to walkers. When available, these maps are the walker's best choice.

Marked footpaths are shown in red. A solid line indicates a gentle, rambler's path; a broken line, a rigorous high-mountain path. Unmarked paths, mule tracks, roads and railroads are shown in black. Marked cross-country ski routes are indicated by a solid blue line. The maps also show the locations of hotels and mountain huts, and the telephone number of each hut is listed on the back of the map.

Large red numerals next to the footpaths shown on the front of the map correspond to numbered route descriptions on the back. Also included are summary lists of walks and ski tours and color photographs of a few of the places covered by the map.

In addition to its Wanderkarten, Kümmerly + Frey publishes:

- *Freizeitland Schweiz.* A 1:300,000 map of Switzerland showing the locations of facilities for a large variety of recreational activities, including walking and cross-country skiing. Symbols indicate the locations of such attractions as the Nationalpark, view points, caves, footpaths, fitness paths, bicycle routes, long-distance ski touring routes, youth hostels, mountain huts, Friends of Nature huts, ski huts, campsites, winter and summer resorts, historical and archeological sites, roads and railways. Symbols are identified in German, French, Italian and English. The back of the map provides additional information, such as lists of principal peaks, mountain passes, lakes, rivers, sites worth visiting and towns—all keyed to the front of the map—as well as a kilometerage table; a traveler's vocabulary in German, French, Italian and English; emergency telephone numbers; and a miscellany of other information. The map also includes a list of the Kümmerly + Frey walking maps and guidebooks. The map is also available along with the recreation guide, *Freizeit in der Schweiz* (see description under "Other Useful Guidebooks" in the section on *Guidebooks*). (Recommended)

The Kümmerly + Frey Wanderkarten and *Freizeitland Schweiz* map are available from bookstores throughout Switzerland. The maps can also be purchased by mail from their publisher:

Kümmerly + Frey (see *Address Directory*). A list of the maps, giving their scales, the areas they cover and their prices, is free on request.

In addition, the Kümmerly + Frey Wanderkarten can be purchased from the SAW.

Other Walkers' Maps. Nearly 60 other Wanderkarten are published by a variety of local associations. Some of these are strip maps showing the route of a single footpath in red; others, such as the 1:50,000 walkers' map published by the SAW section in Neuchâtel, cover an entire canton. A complete list of these maps, and the Kümmerly + Frey Wanderkarten covering each canton, is available on request from the SAW. The maps can also be purchased from the SAW (see *Address Directory*).

Guidebooks

There are scores of guidebooks to the footpaths of Switzerland, so many, in fact, that attempting to list them all is virtually impossible. And more are being published all the time. There are guides to valley paths, mountain paths, long-distance footpaths, city paths, country paths, paths with automobile, bus and rail connections, circular paths, straight paths—in short, there's at least one guide describing virtually every kilometer of marked footpaths in the country. If some stretches perchance have been overlooked, someone will surely write a guidebook for them soon.

The principal publishers of guidebooks covering Switzerland are:

Kümmerly + Frey (see *Address Directory*). This is the most prolific publisher of walking guides for Switzerland. Its series of *Wanderbücher—* which includes more than 90 titles—covers almost the entire country. A few of the books are devoted specifically to easy strolls *(Spazierwege)* and circular walking routes *(Rundwanderungen* or *itinéraires circulaires),* but most describe all the principal walking routes in a particular canton or district.

Each footpath description is detailed and complete, featuring precise route-finding instructions and indicating landmarks and interesting sights along the way. A table preceding each description gives the elevations of points enroute and the cumulative walking times from one to the next. High-quality black and white reproductions of the appropriate Landeskarte show the routes of the footpaths described in the text. Each footpath is also labeled by numbers corresponding to those used in the text, so you can easily refer back and forth between the descriptions and the maps.

Although the maps could be used on the trail in a pinch, they are not really suited for actual route finding. Consequently, the *Wanderbücher* should be used in conjunction with the appropriate *Landeskarten* or *Wanderkarten* (see the preceding section on *Maps).*

In addition to the footpath descriptions, the Kümmerly + Frey guidebooks are loaded with useful supplementary information, including: 1) general information on the region; 2) lists of viewpoints, glaciers, lakes, historic sites and mountain passes; 3) lists of public transportation facilities, restaurants and lodgings; 4) the addresses and telephone numbers of local tourist offices; 5) a table of walking times for principal footpaths in the area; 6) a list of available maps, guidebooks and pictorial panoramas for the district; 7) lists of easy strolls and open winter paths; 8) a bibliography and index of place names; and 9) numerous high-quality black and white photographs. The books are also compact and light so they can be easily carried on the trail. And they are so complete even the novice walker can proceed with confidence.

For a comprehensive overview of walking opportunities throughout Switzerland, the most thorough guidebook is:

- *Grosser Kümmerly + Frey Wander-Atlas der Schweiz* (in German), Kümmerly + Frey, Bern, 1978. A compendium of useful information for walkers, with hundreds of footpath descriptions grouped by region. Each regional section includes brief descriptions of the walking possibilities near each and every town, as well as detailed accounts of up to 30 strolls, longer walks and ski tours. Each route description includes: 1) transportation connections, 2) parking places, 3) the names and altitudes of points enroute, 4) the walking times—in both directions—from point to point, 5) a sketch map showing lodgings and restaurants along the route, and 6) an elevational profile showing the locations of lodgings and forests. The regional sections also list tourist office addresses and provide information on the district's land and life, cuisine, commerce and folk festivals. The walking atlas also features a section with general information on Switzerland, including essays on nature protection, geology, weather, architecture, the Schweizerische Arbeitsgemeinschaft für Wanderwege, cross-country skiing, first aid and map reading, as well as dictionaries of plants, mammals and birds. (Recommended)

The Kümmerly + Frey guidebooks are available in most bookstores in Switzerland and by mail from the SAW. A complete list of the guidebooks and their prices may also be obtained from Kümmerly + Frey or the SAW.

Verlag des SAC/Editions du CAS (see *Address Directory*). This is the official publisher of the Swiss Alpine Club's extensive series of walking, climbing and cross-country skiing guides. Nearly 40 of the SAC guides provide comprehensive coverage of the routes on and below the peaks in a specific district. Twenty other books cover a variety of mountain-related subjects. These include a guide to the SAC's refuges and guides to rock- and ice-climbing technique, mountain rescue, first aid and the Swiss flora, fauna and mineralogy. Each of the climbing and ski touring guides is published in the language corresponding to that spoken in the district covered—German for German-speaking districts, French for French-speaking districts and Italian for Italian-speaking districts. Most of the other guides are available in both French and German. A few are also available in Italian.

The guides can be purchased in most bookstores in Switzerland and by mail from the Verlag des SAC. A complete list of the guidebooks and their prices may be obtained on request from the Verlag des SAC.

Other Major Guidebook Publishers

For the addresses of the following publishers, see the *Address Directory* at the back of this chapter.

Bergverlag Rudolf Rother. Bergverlag Rudolf Rother is probably the largest publisher of guidebooks to walking, climbing and ski touring in the Alps. It is the publisher of the German Alpine Club and Austrian Alpine Club climbing guides. The company also publishes—and sells by mail order—a wide variety of books on subjects such as mountain photography, mountain weather, cave exploring, use of a map and compass, Alpine huts and Alpine plants, animals, mineralogy and geology. In addition, it publishes a high-quality series of maps—the *BV Tourenblätter*—showing footpaths (and in some cases, ski touring and climbing routes). Each *Tourenblatt* includes photos and route descriptions and comes in a plastic binder so individual pages and map sections can be taken out to be carried on the trail. Altogether, Bergverlag Rudolf Rother publishes more than 200 titles which cover 74 regions in the Alps of Germany, Switzerland, Austria, Italy and Yugoslavia. Among the guides and *Tourenblätter* it publishes to Switzerland are:

- *Allgäuer Bergland* (in German) by Kornacher. A guide to circular walks and climbs in Germany's Allgäu and Ostschweiz (eastern Switzerland).
- *Berner Alpen* (in German) by Königer and Munter. A comprehensive guide to walking, climbing and ski touring in the Berner Oberland.
- *Bernina* (in German) by Flaig. A guide to circular walks, easy climbs and high-altitude tours in the Engadin and Bernina-Gruppe south of St. Moritz.
- *Graubünden* (in German) by Condrau. A guide to circular walks, easy climbs and high-altitude tours in the Grissons.
- *Haute Route* (in German) by Hartranft and Königer. A ski mountaineering guide describing the classic Haute Route ski traverse from Chamonix to Zermatt.
- *Walliser Alpen* (in German) by Königer and Weh. A guide to circular walks, easy climbs and high-altitude tours in Valais.
- *BV-Tourenblätter: Mappe 10* (Bernina, Engadin) by Höhne and Siebert.
- *BV-Tourenblätter: Mappe 11* (Schweizer Berge um Rhein und Reuss) by Höhne and Dumler.

All the guides may be purchased by mail from Bergverlag Rudolf Rother. Free catalogs are also available on request.

BLV Verlagsgesellschaft. Publishes the Walter Pause book series of the 100 best: 1) mountain tours in the Alps *(Berg Heil)*, 2) hut-hopping trips in the Alps *(Von Hütte zu Hütte)*, 3) day hikes in the Alps *(Wandern bergab)*, 4) ski tours in the Alps *(Abseits der Piste)*, 5) best ski runs in the Alps *(Ski Heil)*, 6) classic rock and ice climbs in the Alps *(Klassische Alpengipfel)*, 7) easy climbs in the Alps *(Im leichten Fels)*, 8) moderately difficult climbs in the Alps *(Im schweren Fels)*, and 9) difficult climbs in the Alps *(Im extremen Fels)*.

Each of Pause's books gives the length of the tour, its difficulty, lists the necessary maps and guidebooks, mentions nearby climbs and lists places where you can stay along the way. There is also a sketch map and a short description of each route.

BLV Verlagsgesellschaft also publishes several other books on rock and ice climbing in the Alps by authors such as Gaston Rébuffat and Günter Sturm, as well as books on cross-country and downhill skiing, mineralogy and Alpine flora. All the books are in German. They may be purchased from most bookstores in Switzerland and by mail from BLV Verlagsgesellschaft. Free catalogs are available on request from the publisher.

Groupe Haute Montagne. This mountaineering group, which shares its offices with the French Alpine Club in Paris, publishes a series of

French-language guidebooks to selected climbs in the Berner Oberland. The series, entitled *Selection d'Ascensions en Oberland Bernois,* includes:

- *I: Blümlisalp-Balmhorn* (in French) by J. M. Pruvost and G. Tassaux, 1965.
- *II: Bietschhorn-Nesthorn* (in French) by J. M. Pruvost and G. Tassaux, 1966.
- *III: Letschhorn* (in French) by J. M. Pruvost and J. L. Colas, 1973.
- *IV: Petersgrat-Jungfrau* (in French) by J. M. Pruvost and J. L. Colas, 1974.

The guides can be obtained by mail from the Groupe Haute Montagne or Au Vieux Campeur in Paris (see *Address Directory).*

Hallwag Verlag. This is Switzerland's principal publisher of travel guides and touring maps. Hallwag also publishes a guide to ski touring in Switzerland (see "Guidebooks" under the section on *Cross-Country Skiing),* a book by Walter Pause and Hanns Schlüter—*Zürcher Hausberge* —describing mountain walking tours in Switzerland and a series of guidebooks by Walter Schmid, including:

- *Zermatt im Sommer und Winter* (in German), a guide to easy strolls, mountain hikes, climbs and ski tours in the mountains surrounding Zermatt.
- *Komm mit mir ins Wallis* (in German)—Come with Me in Valais—a combination touring guide and walking guide to the valleys and mountains of Valais.
- *Glückliche Tage auf hohen Bergen* (in German)—Happy Days on the High Mountains—a guide to climbing and ski mountaineering in the high, snowy reaches of the Swiss Alps.
- *Menschen am Matterhorn* (in German)—Men on the Matterhorn—a classic history of mountaineering on the Matterhorn which has been translated into several languages.

In addition, Hallwag publishes numerous books on botany, zoology, geography and culture. The books are available in bookstores throughout Switzerland. A free catalog is available on request.

Schweizerische Bundesbahnen (SBB). The Swiss Federal Railway publishes a series of booklets describing one or more walking routes—some suited for an afternoon stroll; others requiring several days—between points with train stations. The route descriptions are divided into walking days—and these, in turn, into shorter segments—and include a list of lodgings and restaurants enroute, with the telephone numbers of each, as well as a notation of where you can leave the route to descend to a train station. You can thus walk the routes either in their entirety or in shorter sections and still use the train to return to your starting point. The paths are shown on a separate map accompanying each booklet. The backs of the maps have a route profile showing the elevations of points enroute, walking times—both coming and going—from point to point, distances in kilometers, forests and the locations of villages, inns, huts and other facilities. The booklets also include a directory of hotels and restaurants, with their telephone numbers and dates of operation, and general information on rail and bus transportation, equipment, lodgings, food and path markings. Many of Switzerland's private railways publish comparable walking guides. There is a nominal charge for some of the booklets; others are free. A list of these booklets, and the addresses of the offices where they can be obtained, appears in the regional descriptions later in this chapter.

Schweizerische Arbeitsgemeinschaft für Wanderwege (SAW). The SAW, along with Kümmerly + Frey, publishes guidebooks to each of Switzerland's long-distance footpaths: Gotthardroute, the Mittellandroute, the Alpenrandroute, Jurahöhenweg, Alpenpassroute and Rhein-Rhone-Route. These guides can be purchased from most bookstores and by mail from the SAW.

In addition, several of the SAW sections publish guidebooks to the paths in their regions. These guidebooks can be purchased directly from the sections, in local bookstores or by mail from the SAW. A complete list of all the guidebooks published by the SAW, its sections and Kümmerly + Frey is available on request.

Schweizer Reisepost. The Swiss Postal Authority publishes a series of guides comparable to those of the Swiss railways, each of which describes two dozen or more walking excursions between bus stops and/or train stations. Each description includes a brief summary of sights enroute, the walking time, information on bus or train connections at each end of the route and a sketch map showing both the suggested walking route and the bus and train lines serving it. Most of the suggested excursions are one-day walks requiring only a few hours to complete. Although the booklets are written in German, French or Italian, the essential information can be deciphered even by people unfamiliar with these languages. The booklets are available free of charge from the post offices and tourist offices in the regions covered. They may also be obtained on request from the Schweizer Reisepost. For a list of titles, see the regional descriptions later in this chapter.

English-Language Guidebooks

For the addresses of the following publishers, see the *Address Directory* at the back of this chapter.

- *Footloose in the Swiss Alps* by William E. Reifsnyder, Sierra Club Books, San Francisco, U.S.A.

- *100 Hikes in the Alps* by Ira Spring and Harvey Edwards, The Mountaineers Books, Seattle, U.S.A.

- *Bernese Alps* (Lötschenpass-Grimselpass), *Bernese Alps West* (Col du Pillon-Lötschenpass), *Bernese Alps Central* (Lötschenpass-Jungfraujoch-Aletschgletscher), *Bernese Alps East* (Jungfraujoch-Grimselpass), *Central Switzerland* (Susten, Furka, Grimsel), *High Level Route* (ski ascents, Chamonix-Zermatt traverse), *Mittel Switzerland* (Lepontine, Ticino, Adula Alps), *Mountains of the Alps, Vol. I: Western Alps* and *Zermatt and District,* all published by West Col Productions, Reading, England. Each guide describes walks, climbs and ski tours. Highly recommended.

- *Salute to the Mountains: The Hundred Best Walks in the Alps* by Walter Pause, translated by Ruth Michaels-Jena and Arthur Ratcliff, George G. Harrap & Company, Ltd., London.

- *Selected Climbs in the Bernese Alps* by R. G. Collomb, The Alpine Club, London, 1968.

Other Useful Guidebooks

In addition to the guidebooks mentioned above, there are countless others available, both from commercial publishers and from local tourist offices. Many of these regional walking guides are listed in the regional descriptions later in this chapter.

There are also numerous specialized guidebooks catering to walkers interested in local history, architecture, flora and fauna, geology and the like. For example, the Schweizerischer Bund für Naturschutz (SBN) publishes:

- *Natur-Lehrpfade in der Schweiz* (in German). A booklet describing more than 80 interpretive nature paths located throughout Switzerland. Each description includes information on access to the path, its length, walking time, interpretive signposts and major attractions; lists the appropriate Landeskarte for the walk; and includes a sketch map showing the route, including possible variants, suggested walking direction, parking place, starting points, roads and railways. Available for a nominal charge from the Schweizerischer Bund für Naturschutz (see *Address Directory*).

Kümmerly + Frey publishes an exhaustive guide to recreational activities and facilities in Switzerland entitled:

- *Freizeit in der Schweiz* (in German), Bern, 1975. A directory to sports activities and facilities, health resorts, opportunities for nature study, historic buildings and monuments, museums, libraries and centers for adult education, music and dramatic arts, and fairs, exhibitions and industrial tours. These activities and facilities are described in detail and shown on 12 special maps. Of particular interest to walkers are the sections on: 1) walking and mountaineering, including information on general walking opportunities, long-distance footpaths, huts, climbing schools and walking clubs; 2) skiing, including a list of places with cross-country ski tracks, ski touring routes and cross-country ski schools; 3) orienteering; 4) physical-fitness courses; and 5) nature reserves. Sports facilities, including climbing schools, ski tracks and orienteering courses, are shown, by means of symbols, on four special maps. The book also includes the addresses and telephone numbers of cantonal tourist offices, information on public transportation—including special train and bus fares—lodgings and food. A separate 1:300,000 map, *Freizeitland Schweiz* (see the section on *Maps),* accompanies the book. Recommended as an excellent planning guide for a holiday in Switzerland. Available from most bookstores.

There are also two comprehensive lexicons for walkers and climbers:

• *Schlag nach!* (in German), Bibliographisches Institut, Zürich. Includes more than 2,500 terms covering virtually all subjects of interest to walkers and climbers. Among the information included is: 1) a brief description and history of each of Europe's alpine clubs and major walking, climbing and cave-exploring associations (addresses are included); 2) a brief description of the major hiking regions of the Alps; 3) address lists of European climbing schools, mountain-rescue organizations and numerous other kinds of organizations, such as those that offer walking tours without packs; 4) explanations of first aid techniques, knot tying, use of a map and compass, understanding contour lines on a map, and predicting mountain weather; and 5) information on mineralogy, geology, flora and fauna, plus much, much more. The book is generously illustrated throughout and includes 30 color plates. And it's compact. At the back is an extensive bibliography that lists, among other publications, the guidebooks covering the major hiking regions in the Alps with—in each case—the name of their publishers and the cities in which they are located. Packed with information. One of the best sourcebooks available anywhere. Available from most bookstores and by mail from the publisher (see *Address Directory).*

• *Grosses Lexikon der Alpen* (in German) by Toni Hiebeler, Hans Huber, Bern. This lexicon is even more massive than *Schlag nach!* and includes information of interest to the general tourist as well as to the walker and climber. It describes nearly 3,500 terms. Available from most bookstores.

Trailside Lodgings

In a sense, all lodgings are "trailside" in Switzerland, because footpaths penetrate virtually every corner of the country. Consequently, your choice of lodgings more often depends upon the type and price range you prefer than on proximity to your route. Except in the remoter sections of the Alps, where the choice may be limited, you are faced with a wide variety of possible accommodation—hotels large and small, guesthouses, inns, chalets, youth hostels, Friends of Nature houses and mountain huts.

Alpine Club Huts

The Schweizer Alpen-Club operates more than 200 mountain huts scattered through the Alps from Valais to Graubünden. Built and financed by local sections, the huts are primarily for member use. But all visitors are welcome on a space-available basis. In addition, there are numerous private huts open only to members of particular SAC sections.

SAC members can reserve bed space in advance and receive priority in the assignment of unreserved spaces. A quarter of the beds in each hut are held open until 8 p.m. each day, when they are assigned on the following basis: SAC members and their families first, then all other visitors. Sick or injured parties always receive top priority.

Most huts have full-time wardens on duty during the summer months. The season for each hut varies, however, and should be checked in advance. All huts have one or more rooms that are left open for use during the off-season.

A small fee is charged for overnight stays in SAC huts. Members receive a 30 to 40 percent discount. The fee is paid directly to the hut warden. If no warden is present, you may leave payment in the hut collection box or mail a postal money order to the warden's home address. In the case of remote mountain bivouacs and refuges, which normally have no warden, you are usually asked to send payment to the warden of a nearby hut.

SAC huts vary greatly both in size and types of facilities available. At one extreme they are tiny bivouacs and refuges stocked with firewood and mattresses. Cooking utensils may or may not be provided, and the stock of firewood may have been depleted. Hence, if you intend to stay in one of these huts, it is advisable to carry your cooking utensils, a stove and sleeping bag in addition to your food. If firewood is provided and you use some, be sure to replace what you use.

At the other extreme are large, fairly elaborate chalets sleeping 50 people or more and providing simple meals as well as cooking space. Some huts even provide full board, if arrangements are made in advance with the wardens. All but the smaller huts serve beverages. Cooking space and utensils are standard in most SAC huts. The use of portable camp stoves, however, is strictly forbidden inside the huts. If you intend to use one, you must go outside.

Hut visitors sleep in dormitories, which range from small rooms with a dozen or fewer beds to larger halls. Pillow and blankets are provided in most huts, but not sheets. A sheet sleeping bag is therefore necessary. Camping near the huts is strictly forbidden.

Walkers planning to stay in SAC huts should purchase the following guide:

- *Clubhütten/Cabanes/Capanne* (in German and French, with some translation into Italian and English), Verlag des SAC. The official guide to SAC huts. Includes a separate map showing their locations, with numbers keyed to descriptions in the book. Each hut description includes a photograph or drawing of the hut; the name and address of the SAC section in charge; the map sheets covering the area; the dates when a warden is present; the hut telephone number (if any); symbols indicating available food and beverages; descriptions of access routes to the hut; and a list of possible ascents in the vicinity. Hut regulations are provided in the introductory section. Available from the Verlag des SAC (see *Address Directory*).

In addition, the huts are listed once a year in the SAC magazine, *Les Alpes*, usually in the spring issue. The list gives the name and phone number (if any) of each hut, as well as its number of beds, the section that owns it, and the name, address and telephone number of the person with whom reservations should be made.

Youth Hostels

There are about 120 youth hostels in Switzerland. They can be found in all major cities, as well as in many towns and villages, including popular mountain resorts and even a few remote locales. Swiss youth hostels are primarily open to people 25 years of age or younger. Hostelers over 25 years old are admitted only if there is room. All users must carry a valid membership card for either the Swiss Youth Hostel Federation or the International Youth Hostel Federation. Advance booking is always advisable, but particularly in the months of February, July and August, as well as during all holidays. Advance booking should be made directly to the youth hostels in which you wish to stay.

Most hostels provide cooking facilities. Some offer meals instead of or in addition to kitchen privileges. Most hostels also provide hot water and showers. Hostelers sleep in dormitories. A sheet sleeping bag—available on the premises from some hostels—is required.

Swiss youth hostels are owned and operated by regional sections of the:

Schweizerischer Bund für Jugendherbergen (SJH)/Fédération Suisse des Auberges de la Jeunesse (ASJ) (see *Address Directory*). Staff speaks German, French, Italian and English. Useful publications include:

- *Die Schweizerischen Jugendherbergen/Guide Suisse des Auberges de la Jeunesse* (in German, French, Italian and English). A map-guide to Swiss youth hostels. Hostel locations are shown on the map by means of reference numbers, which are keyed to a table on the back. The table gives the following information for each hostel: location, postal number, telephone number, the name of the SJH section in charge, dates of operation, total number of beds, number and capacity of dormitories, number of day rooms, cooking facilities, availability of prepared meals, nightly rate and the types of facilities found nearby. The guide also includes a summary of regulations; guide to symbols used in the table; glossary of terms in German, French, English and Italian; and list of addresses and telephone numbers of SJH regional sections. Free from the SJH or Schweizerische Verkehrszentrale (see *Address Directory*).

- *Schweizer Wanderkalender* (in German). A spiral-bound calendar that includes suggested walks in the vicinity of various youth hostels. Also lists the addresses and telephone numbers of SJH sections. Available for a nominal charge.

Friends of Nature Houses

There are some 100 Friends of Nature houses scattered the length and breadth of Switzerland. Typically situated in scenic surroundings, they offer simple, but comfortable accommodation at reasonable prices. Typically, you sleep in dormitories, although smaller rooms are also available in many houses. All provide kitchen facilities and utensils. Many have gas or electric, as well as wood, stoves. Most houses have lounges or common rooms, and feature hot and cold running water, electricity, showers and modern lavatories. Many even have central heating.

Swiss Friends of Nature houses are owned and operated by local sections of the:

Schweizer Touristenverein, "Die Naturfreunde" (TVN)/Union Touristique Suisse, "Amis de la Nature" (AN) (see *Address Directory*). Staff speaks German, French and English. Useful publications include:

- *Häuserverzeichnis/Liste des Maisons AN* (in German and French). The official guide to Friends of Nature houses in Switzerland. Includes a separate map showing their locations, with numbers keyed to descriptions in the book. Each description includes a photograph or drawing of the house; the name of the TVN section in charge; the altitude and map coordinates of the house; its location; access routes; times when a warden is present; house facilities; telephone number (if any); and facilities and attractions in the vicinity. Also describes Friends of Nature houses in Germany, Austria, France, Belgium, Holland, Denmark and California, U.S.A. Available for a nominal charge from the TVN.

Swiss Friends of Nature houses are open only to TVN members. Reservations are recommended. They should be made through the local sections operating the hut in which you wish to stay. The addresses to which you should apply for reservations are listed by hut in the:

- *International House List* (in English, German, French and Dutch). Published annually by Naturfreunde International, Zürich. Lists Friends of Nature houses in Austria, California (U.S.A.), Belgium, Switzerland, Denmark, Germany, France, Holland, Italy and Israel. Gives the address of each house, with a summary of facilities. Also includes maps showing house locations. Contains a list of booking addresses and a sample reservation form. Available for a nominal charge from Naturfreunde International (see *Address Directory*) or from the Naturfreunde groups in other countries.

Hotels, Inns & Guesthouses

Switzerland has some 8,000 hotels, inns and guesthouses ranging from the humble and inexpensive to the elaborate and exceedingly dear. But all are clean and run with characteristic Swiss efficiency. Prices tend to be highest in large cities and popular resorts, but even there a bit of searching can uncover bargains. Local tourist information offices are usually very helpful. Most publish lodging lists for their regions.

The best single guide to hotels, inns and guesthouses in Switzerland is the:

- *Schweizer Hotelführer/Guide Suisse des Hôtels* (in German, French, Italian and English). Published annually by Schweizer Hotelierverein (see *Address Directory*). Lists more than 2,000 establishments, along with the telephone number, name of owner or manager, dates of operation, capacity, winter and summer rates, meal prices and various facilities for each. Prices in the guide are fixed by law. The sports facilities, including marked cross-country ski tracks, are also listed for each community. Free on request from the Schweizer Hotelierverein, tourist information offices and Swiss National Tourist Offices abroad.

In addition, the locations of alpine club huts, youth hostels, Friends of Nature houses, and isolated hotels are shown on the recreational map *Freizeitland Schweiz* (see the section on *Maps*).

Camping

For the most part, camping in Switzerland is restricted to established campgrounds. Open camping, however, is permitted in Alpine regions well away from villages or other settlements. This privilege—for that's what it is—should under no circumstances be abused. Camps should be small and situated well away from lakes, streams and fragile meadows. All trash should be carried out and all human waste buried at least 15 centimeters (6 inches) below ground. Fires should not be lit except in cases of emergency. When you leave, there should be no trace of your stay. Failure to observe such elementary rules of camping etiquette could provoke local authorities to close some or all areas to campers. Moreover, Swiss penalties for littering and defacing the landscape are severe.

Whenever possible you should camp in established campgrounds. And since there are some 450 in Switzerland, you will rarely have to walk far to find one. There are four classes of campgrounds in Switzerland, ranging from primitive types with simple sanitary facilities to fancy establishments with warm showers, modern sanitary facilities and other amenities. Some are open year round, others are closed during the snowy months. Prices vary according to the facilities provided.

The Schweizerische Verkehrszentrale publishes a useful map-guide to campgrounds:

- *Camping Holidays in Switzerland* (in English, French and German). A road map showing the locations of 217 campgrounds. The address, telephone number and facilities of each campground are given by region on a table on the reverse side of the map. Free on request from the Schweizerische Verkehrszentrale (see *Address Directory*).

Information on camping in Switzerland is also available from the following organizations:

Schweizerischer Camping- und Caravanning-Verband (SCCV)/ Fédération Suisse de Camping et de Caravanning (FSCC) (see *Address Directory*). Staff speaks German, French and English. Useful publications include:

- *Swiss Camping and Caravanning List* (in English, French and German). Gives the locations, postal codes, telephone numbers, dates of operation and facilities for approved campgrounds throughout Switzerland. Free from branches of the Swiss National Tourist Office abroad.

Touring-Club der Schweiz/Touring Club Suisse (see *Address Directory*). Staff speaks French, German and English. Useful publications include:

- *Camping and Caravanning Guide* (in French, German and English). A comprehensive guide to the campgrounds throughout Switzerland. Provides full details on each campground. Also includes photographs and maps showing their locations. Available for a nominal charge from branches of the Swiss National Tourist Office abroad.

The locations of Swiss campgrounds are also shown on the recreational map *Freizeitland Schweiz* (see the section on *Maps).*

Water

Tap water is reliable throughout Switzerland. Mountain streams may or may not be potable, depending upon whether livestock frequent them upslope. You can generally trust the water flowing from spouts into wooden troughs, which are a traditional fixture of Swiss farms and villages and are even occasionally found in high alpine pastures. You should only take water from the spouts, however, since you never know what might have fallen into the troughs. Glacial melt water is also okay, despite its milky appearance, although you should allow sediments to settle to the bottom of your cup and warm the water, either by cupping your hands around the cup or by holding the water in your mouth, before drinking. Most high-altitude mountain streams can be trusted if you can see their source. Downslope, it is best to avoid streams and rely on spout and tap water, which is usually readily available throughout Switzerland.

Crowded Trails

Most of Switzerland's footpaths are well used during the summer, both by the Swiss and an international medley of visitors to the country. On any given day during July and August, you may pass a farmer coming down from a high pasture with a scythe draped over his shoulder, an elderly couple out for a morning walk, a young boy herding goats and as many as a hundred other people, each nodding and saying hello in any one of half a dozen different languages.

How many people you encounter will, of course, depend upon where you walk. Perhaps the most heavily used trail in Switzerland is the *Strada alta* in Ticino. It is hiked by as many as 120,000 people between April and October each year—an average of 677 people per day. Trails near popular resorts, such as Arosa, Davos, Grindelwald, St. Moritz and Zermatt, are also heavily traveled during July and August, as are trails near the upper terminals of cable cars, cog railways and chair lifts.

Once you move away from these areas, however, the crowds thin out— sometimes dramatically. There are also numerous side trails to choose from, some of which are practically deserted in comparison to the main route leading up or down to a popular resort.

On no trail are you likely to be completely alone in the summer. But if you avoid the top name resorts and weekends, you can often walk for several hours without seeing more than one or two parties of other hikers. And if you walk during September, you can often have a trail—and once in a while, even a mountain hut—entirely to yourself.

Equipment Notes

Walkers can travel light in Switzerland. Thanks to the extensive network of mountain huts, hostels, guesthouses, inns and hotels, camping is rarely necessary. Since most huts and hostels provide cooking facilities, dishes and cutlery, a camp stove is necessary only if you plan to camp or use primitive bivouacs. If you plan your walks carefully, you won't even need to carry much food—lunch and snacks, plus a few emergency rations. Dinner and breakfast foods must be carried only if you plan to use huts and hostels where meals are not provided.

Respect for the unpredictable Alpine weather requires that wool clothing, including cap and mittens, and raingear be carried at all times. Don't let warm, sunny mornings fool you. By afternoon, the sky may fall, along with the temperature. Alpine summers are notoriously stormy, and under such conditions the danger of hypothermia is great. You should also never venture into the mountains without a map and compass. When mists close in over the peaks and pastures, you may need them to find your way back. You may also want to carry some kind of lightweight shelter, such as a tarpaulin, in case bad weather forces you to hole up for a few hours.

In addition to the usual personal items, you should also carry eating utensils if you plan to walk for more than a day. You may not need them, since most huts supply their own, but such is not always the case. And if you don't take your camera, preferably with a wide-angle lens, you'll kick yourself all the way home.

Walking Tours

No one need walk alone in Switzerland. Dozens of organized walking tours are designed to fit virtually any schedule or budget in all parts of the country. Indeed, judging by the number of tours offered, it seems apparent that the Swiss themselves are especially fond of group excursions, apparently valuing camaraderie over solitude. If you share this taste, Switzerland offers innumerable opportunities for indulging it.

Tours range in length from a few hours to a week or more. They may be devoted to purely walking—anything from easy strolls to difficult Alpine traverses. Or they may combine walking with such activities as climbing, botanizing, observing wildlife, orienteering and the like. Some even feature short daily walks as a part of an overall fitness program that also involves exercise, massage, saunas and hydrotherapy. There are even self-guided tours for people who prefer to walk by themselves or with a few friends. However you like your walking, Switzerland has a tour for you. The best single guide to available walking tours is:

- *Switzerland: 5 Mountaineering Hiking* (in English; also available in French and German). Published annually by the Schweizerische Verkehrszentrale. A directory to mountaineering and walking tours open to the public. Tour descriptions are arranged alphabetically by town or village. The directory gives the itinerary and fee for each tour, as well as any optional costs. It also lists the names, addresses and telephone numbers of organizations sponsoring the tours and includes a directory of mountain guides, mountain guide offices and mountaineering schools. Free from the Schweizerische Verkehrszentrale, local tourist information office and branches of the Swiss National Tourist Office abroad.

Walking tours are briefly listed in two other brochures:
- *Naturkundliche Wanderungen* (in German). Published annually by the Schweizerische Verkehrszentrale. Lists the dates and places of organized nature walks featuring plants, minerals, geology, birds and mushrooms. Gives no details for the walks. Free from Schweizerische Verkehrszentrale.
- *Summer in Switzerland* (in English). Published annually by the Schweizerische Verkehrszentrale. Lists tourist events in Switzerland. Includes a list of dates and places for mountain tours, rambles and excursions. Gives no details for the tours. Free from the Schweizerische Verkehrszentrale and branches of the Swiss National Tourist Office abroad.

Walking, climbing, cross-country skiing and ski mountaineering tours are also offered by Swiss mountain climbing schools (see the section on *Climbing Schools*).

REKA Wanderpass

The REKA Wanderpass is a special holiday ticket for walkers. For a single price it includes transportation, food and lodging in a particular region. When you purchase the Wanderpass, you receive a walking guide listing itineraries in the region, necessary maps and guidebooks, train and bus lines you can use and guesthouses and hotels honoring the pass. The guide also includes a map showing the walking routes and another showing train and bus connections in the region. The tickets can be purchased for 2-, 4-, or 7-day periods. At present, REKA Wanderpässe are available only for Appenzellerland, the Jura, Emmental, Toggenburg and Schwyz—and only for the period from May 1 to October 31.

In effect, the REKA Wanderpass is a package tour for walkers who prefer a greater measure of solitude and degree of freedom than organized walking tours provide. Armed with your Wanderpass and walking guide, you can roam at will through your chosen region, walking when and where you please, traveling on postal buses or train when you like. And wherever you go, there's food and lodging awaiting you.

REKA Wänderpasse are available from information offices and travel agencies of the Swiss Federal Railway (SBB/CFF), at larger train stations in the regions served by the pass and from:

> **Schweizer Reisekasse** (see *Address Directory*). Staff speaks German, French and English.

Walking Club Tours

Sections of the Schweizer Alpen-Club (SAC) and Schweizerische Arbeitge-meinschaft für Wanderwege (SAW) offer a wide variety of walking tours for club members. These range from day walks to week-long excursions and in some cases include trips to foreign countries. It is impractical for most foreign visitors to Switzerland to join the SAC, whose membership requirements tend to be rigorous. Membership in the SAW is more easily obtained, however, and may be worth the effort, if only to be able to participate in the numerous walks hosted by its various sections. These walks are described in the SAW *Wanderprogramm* (see description under *Where to Get Walking Information*. For information on joining a SAW section, see *Switzerland's Walking & Climbing Clubs*). Larger sections, such as the Berner Wanderwege, headquartered in Bern, have extensive walking programs, including foreign excursions. Most sections publish a *Wanderprogramm* listing their offerings. That of the Berner Wanderwege is a sizable booklet. In addition to walks open only to SAW members, many sections also offer occasional *Radiowanderungen*—walks open to the public and announced on the radio.

Other membership organizations, including the Schweizerischer Bund für Jugendherbergen (Swiss Youth Hostel Federation), Schweizer Tour-istenverein, "Die Naturfreunde" and the Schweizerischer Bund für Naturschutz (Swiss League for the Protection of Nature), as well as numerous local groups, also offer walking tours. Mimeographed notices of these walks, with information on train and bus connections, are often posted and made available for the taking in local train stations.

Mountain Guides

If you don't feel up to navigating Alpine routes on your own, yet wish to avoid the regimentation of organized tours, you can arrange your own tailor-made walking program by hiring a mountain guide. They are available year round for summer treks, ski mountaineering trips, glacier crossings and summer and winter climbs. Guide offices are located in most of the major mountaineering centers throughout the Swiss Alps. Most offices are open from March through October, but handle written enquiries year round. Prices vary somewhat from one canton to the next and according to the type of trip undertaken. But in any case, guides do not come cheaply.

Local tourist offices can direct you to the nearest guide office. Or you can obtain a printed list of all offices from:

Schweizerischer Bergführerverband (see *Address Directory*). Staff speaks French, German and English.

Swiss Mountain Guides are certified either by individual cantons or the Schweizer Alpen-Club. They undergo rigorous training programs to obtain their certificate, must take refresher courses and serve a two-year apprenticeship, and are periodically reviewed to assure that their performance and continued training conform to established standards for their profession. Guides who have made something of a reputation for themselves may be booked up a year in advance. Others can sometimes be booked on the spot or with short notice at most. But all are well-trained and reliable.

Climbing Schools

Switzerland, as even most devout lowlanders are aware, is a mountain climber's paradise, offering hundreds of climbs of all degrees of difficulty, over all types of mountain terrain and on rocks of various composition and hardness. An ascent of the Matterhorn, although now a fairly routine affair, remains a classic of its kind. The awesome Eigerwand is perhaps the most notorious mountain wall in the world. The modern sport of mountain climbing was born in Switzerland, which remains a mecca to which serious climbers everywhere must someday return.

Many otherwise normal people, upon exposure to the lofty crags of the Swiss Alps, have been taken by the sudden urge to climb, whereas before they had been content merely to stick to footpaths. Should you be thus overcome, resist the urge until you have obtained proper schooling in mountaineering techniques. Each year, Swiss rescue teams pluck from the peaks dozens of hapless novices whose reach exceeded their grasp. The Alps offer unexcelled climbing to those trained and equipped. They show little mercy, however, to the unschooled or unwary.

Fortunately, excellent training, for both novices and advanced climbers, is available at mountain climbing schools in the Berner Oberland, Central Switzerland, Graubünden, Lake Geneva region, Northeast Switzerland and Valais. These schools offer both courses and individual instruction in rock and ice climbing, general mountaineering, cross-country skiing and ski mountaineering. They also conduct walking, climbing and skiing tours for both beginning and advanced mountaineers.

Information about Swiss mountain climbing schools can be obtained from:

Schweizer Verband der Bergsteigerschulen (see *Address Directory*). Staff speaks German, French and English. Useful publications include:

- *Bergferienangebot für Wanderer, Kletterer, Bergsteiger und Skitouristen* (in German, French, Italian and English). Lists addresses and telephone numbers of Swiss mountain climbing schools. A table lists the types of courses and tours offered by each school, along with the dates for each course. Free on request.

The addresses and telephone numbers of Swiss climbing schools are included in the Schweizerische Verkehrszentrale brochure, *Switzerland: 5 Mountaineering Hiking* (see description under the section on *Walking Tours*). A directory of schools can also be obtained from branches of the Swiss National Tourist Office abroad. For information about specific courses and tours and their costs, it is best to write to the schools in the regions you wish to visit.

Cross-Country Skiing

Switzerland offers superb cross-country skiing and ski touring over more than 2,700 kilometers of well-marked tracks. Whether you prefer the Alps, Mittelland or Jura, you can choose from among innumerable routes of varying lengths and degrees of difficulty. These range from short, gentle tours requiring only a morning or afternoon to longer, more rigorous excursions demanding most of the day. Many areas have lighted tracks for nighttime skiing as well as carefully manicured tracks for competition and practice. In addition, there are more than 1,400 kilometers of marked cross-country routes.

At the beginning of each marked track, or *loipe,* is a sign with a map and profile of the route, indications of skiing distances and times and other pertinent information. Along the way, routes are marked with yellow directional arrows and distance signs. Difficult sections are indicated by triangular hazard signs. In periods of avalanche danger, tracks are posted with circular signs barring the way.

The beginning of each marked cross-country route *(Ski-Wanderweg or itinéraire pour ski de randonnée)* is marked by a large yellow directional arrow bearing the silhouette of a cross-country skier and the legend "Ski-Wanderweg," followed by the name of the route and the distance. Along the way, the routes are marked with smaller directional arrows, poles in the snow, diamond-shaped signs and streamers tied to trees. Warning signs are identical to those used on marked tracks.

The main organization devoted to cross-country skiing in Switzerland is the:

Schweizerischer Ski-Verband (SSV)/Fédération Suisse de Ski (FSS) (see *Address Directory)*. Staff speaks German, French and English. Can provide information on all aspects of cross-country skiing in Switzerland. Organizes ski competitions and proficiency tests. Works in close cooperation with the SAW and cross-country ski schools. Local sections are primarily responsible for marking ski tracks and cross-country routes in their respective regions. Useful publications include:

• *Skiwandern/Ski de randonnée* (in German and French). Published annually. A directory to marked ski tracks and cross-country routes in Switzerland. Tracks are listed by region and town. Information for each track includes its distance, starting point, dates of operation, whether it is open at night, the availability of guided tours and the address and telephone number of the organization able to provide further information. Also given are the names, addresses, telephone numbers and times of operation of cross-country skiing schools in or near the various towns. Marked cross-country ski routes are also described by region. The distance, starting and stopping places and available transportation are given for each route. The booklet also includes: 1) illustrations of signs used to mark both ski tracks and cross-country routes; 2) regulations governing the use of ski tracks and cross-country routes; 3) information on proficiency tests and competitions; 4) a list of competitions, with the date, place, distance, registration address and registration deadline for each; 5) medical recommendations for cross-country skiers; and 6) information about the activities of the Schweizerischer Ski-Verband. Free on request.

The Schweizerische Verkehrszentrale publishes a useful set of six booklets describing winter sports holidays in various regions in Switzerland. These bookets are:

• *Grisons 1;*
• *Eastern Switzerland and Liechtenstein 2, Zürich 3, North-Western Switzerland 5;*
• *Central Switzerland 4;*
• *Berne and Bernese Oberland 6;*
• *Fribourg-Neuchâtel-Jura 7, Lake Geneva Region 8, Ticino 10;* and
• *Valais 9.*

All are available in German, French, Italian and English editions. Each booklet describes all-inclusive winter sports holidays—including cross-country skiing weeks—in a particular region or regions. Listings are arranged by town and include dates, prices and brief descriptions of the activities and services available on each holiday. The booklets also list the addresses and telephone numbers of tourist information offices where holidays can be booked in each town; give the number and kilometers of local ski tracks and cross-country routes, downhill runs, lifts and cleared paths for winter walking; and note the availability of both cross-country and downhill ski instruction for each community. Information on miscellaneous facilities, such as child day-care centers, is also provided. Available from the Schweizerische Verkehrszentrale, local tourist information offices and branches of the Swiss National Tourist Office abroad.

Cross-Country Ski Schools

If you don't know how to cross-country ski, Switzerland is a marvelous place to learn. Cross-country ski schools offering courses for novice, intermediate and advanced skiers are located throughout the country. In addition to providing instruction, most also conduct guided tours. Some, such as the Swiss mountain climbing schools, teach not only cross-country, but ski mountaineering. The booklet *Skiwandern/Ski de randonnée* (see description, above) gives the names, addresses and telephone numbers of cross-country ski schools by region and town. The Schweizer Alpen-Club offers instruction in cross-country skiing and ski mountaineering to its members. You can also obtain the name of reliable schools from local tourist information offices.

Organized Ski Tours

A variety of organized tours are available for cross-country skiers in Switzerland. They range from one-day excursions to week-long holidays, from easy tours over gentle marked tracks to rigorous ski mountaineering treks above timberline. The Schweizerischer Verkehrszentrale's six winter holiday guides (see above) list numerous package tours available in Switzerland's 10 principal tourist regions. But these listings are far from complete. You should also contact the Swiss cross-country ski schools and mountain climbing schools for additional offerings.

Local sections of the Schweizer Alpen-Club and Schweizerischer Arbeitsgemeinschaft für Wanderwege also offer oganized ski tours for members. For information on these tours, you should contact the SAC or SAW section for the area in which you are interested.

Ski Mountaineering

Ski mountaineering combines skiing and climbing. Participants must be physically fit, skilled in both sports, properly equipped and willing to face cold weather and treacherous terrain. But the rewards are enormous—vast fields of untracked snow, solitude in a white wilderness and the challenge of overcoming the obstacles posed by the elements and the terrain. Switzerland is a superb arena for winter mountaineering, not only for its ample snow and magnificent peaks, but because winter is one of the sunniest seasons in the Alps. Between storms, ski mountaineers commonly enjoy long stretches of clear, if cold weather. Ski mountaineers should be accompanied by at least one person with knowledge and experience of winter conditions in the Alps. If you don't have such a companion, you can hire a mountain guide or join one of the many tours offered by Swiss mountain climbing schools. The schools also offer courses in ski mountaineering to students already skilled in skiing and the rudiments of climbing.

Ski Tests & Competitions

In order to promote cross-country skiing among the Swiss and to improve the overall performance level of skiers, the Schweizerischer Ski-Verband sponsors proficiency tests and public competitions.

The Schweizerischer Ski-Verband inaugurated the proficiency tests in the winter of 1975-76. They are conducted by Swiss cross-country skiing schools and are open to anyone 14 years of age or older. There are three levels of tests, one each for beginning, intermediate and advanced skiers. Upon successfully passing the tests, you are awarded a medal of achievement: bronze for the first level test, silver for the second level, gold for the third. Further information on these tests is included in the booklet *Skiwandern/Ski de randonnée*.

More than 80 public cross-country ski competitions are held each year in Switzerland. All are sponsored by the Schweizerischer Ski-Verband. Distances range from under 5 to more than 50 kilometers. There are both junior and senior classes for each race and anyone can participate. The booklet *Skiwandern/Ski de randonnée* provides further information on the competitions, including tips for getting in shape and a calendar of events giving dates, distances and whom to contact for registration.

Guidebooks

- *DSV Langlauf Kompass* (in German), edited by Franz Wöllzen-müller. Published by Südwestdeutscher Verlag in cooperation with the Deutscher Skiverband. Updated annually. A guide to cross-country ski routes in Germany, Austria, Switzerland and Italy. Describes routes at 55 locations in Switzerland. Route descriptions include directions on where to start and how to get there, indications of route length and difficulty, brief itinerary descriptions, information on local ski schools and ski shops, and the addresses and telephone numbers where additional information can be obtained. Each route is shown on a sketch map. Available by mail from Südwestdeutscher Verlag. Also available in many bookstores in Switzerland.

- *Skilanglauf Atlas* (in German), edited by Claus-Peter Berner, Berner-Verlag. Updated annually. Describes more than 1,000 cross-country ski tracks in Europe, including over 120 in Switzerland. Descriptions are arranged alphabetically by canton and community. Each track is described briefly and its distance is given. Lists the addresses and telephone numbers where additional information on each track can be obtained, as well as places where equipment can be rented and which communities have cross-country ski schools. Sketch maps and profiles are included for some of the routes. Available from most bookstores in Switzerland and by mail from Berner-Verlag.

- *Skiwander- und Langlaufführer Schweiz* (in German), Hallwag Verlag. Describes 100 marked ski tracks and cross-country ski routes in Switzerland, with full details on each. Contains 44 route maps. Published in cooperation with the Schweizerischer Ski-Verband and Schweizerische Arbeitsgemeinschaft für Wanderwege. Available in most bookstores and by mail from the SAW.

Special Train & Bus Fares

Switzerland offers a wide choice of special reduced-fare tickets for train and postbus travel throughout the country. These tickets provide the least expensive means—other than walking—of traveling through Switzerland. And because the trains and buses together serve virtually every nook and cranny in the country with both speed and efficiency, they provide hikers with excellent access to and from footpaths.

Holiday Card. For a reduced rate this card allows you to travel freely on Swiss rail, boat and postbus lines for a period of 8 days, 15 days or one month. You also receive reductions of up to 50 percent from mountain railways and aerial tramways. The tickets can be purchased by anyone living outside Switzerland or Liechtenstein. They are available from many travel agencies and from branches of the Swiss National Tourist Office abroad. Outside of Europe, many Swissair offices sell vouchers for the Swiss Holiday Card. If you cannot obtain the card in your country, it can be purchased at railway information offices at Zürich Airport, Geneva Airport and the main train stations in Zürich, Geneva-Cornavin, Basel, Bern, Buchs, Interlaken-West, Lausanne, Lugano città, Luzern, Montreux, St. Margrethen and Schaffhausen.

Holiday Ticket. For a reduced fare you can choose your own route through Switzerland to and from a chosen destination. The route can include stretches by rail, tramway, boat and postbus. You can even walk part of the way, if you like, using public transportation for the rest. The journey, however, must begin and end at a frontier railway station or international airport town. The ticket is good for one month, but for an additional fee can be extended for periods of 10 days up to a total of 30 days. The Holiday Ticket also allows you to purchase up to five half-fare excursion tickets for rail, boat or postbus lines anywhere in Switzerland. The fare reduction is less for excursions over 150 kilometers. If you wish to take more than five excursions, you can purchase supplementary vouchers that entitle you to three additional half-fare excursion tickets. The Holiday Ticket is available from travel agencies outside Switzerland, the Swiss National Tourist Office in London, and all major railway stations and travel agencies in Switzerland.

Half-fare Travel. Half-fare Season Tickets are available for periods of 15 days, 1 month, 3 months or 12 months. They entitle you to purchase either first- or second-class tickets at half-price for rail, boat or postbus lines. Men aged 65 years or older and women 62 and over receive almost an 80 percent discount on the purchase of Half-fare Season Tickets for 12 months. This card also entitles them to reduced rates at participating hotels. Young people aged 16 through 22 can purchase Half-fare Season Tickets at discounts of about 40 percent for one month and 60 percent for one year. In addition, all bearers of Half-fare Season Tickets can purchase at reduced rates General Season Ticket Day Cards entitling them to unlimited travel on the Swiss Federal Railway network, as well as some private railways and boat lines, on freely chosen days. These cards are available covering 3 days, 5 days and 10 days. Half-fare Season Tickets and Day Cards are available at travel agencies and railway stations throughout Switzerland.

Regional Holiday Seasonal Tickets. These tickets permit travel at reduced rates in particular holiday regions. Two-week tickets are available for Montreux/Vevey, Berner Oberland, the Lake Lucerne region and Grau-bünden. The tickets entitle you to 5 days of free unlimited travel and 10 days of half-fare unlimited travel on the trains, boats and postbuses of the respective regions. One-week tickets are available for Locarno/Ascona and Lugano. They entitle you to 7 days of free, unlimited travel in those regions. You can purchase these tickets at train stations in the regions in which they will be used. Exchange vouchers negotiable in Switzerland are available from foreign travel agencies and branches of the Swiss National Tourist Office. Holders of Holiday Tickets receive a 25 percent discount on the purchase of Regional Holiday Season Tickets. Children between the ages of 6 and 16 receive a 50 percent discount.

Postbus Holiday Season Ticket. This ticket entitles you to travel at reduced fares on the Swiss postbus system. Valid for a full month, the ticket provides three days of unlimited free travel and unlimited half-price journeys for the balance of the month. Children and holders of Holiday Tickets receive a 50 percent discount on the purchase of Postbus Holiday Season Tickets. They are available at all major post offices with postbus facilities.

Brochures describing these and other special reduced-fare tickets are available from train stations throughout Switzerland, usually from a display holder near the ticket window or in the train information offices. Notices of walking tours organized by local groups are often to be found in the display holders as well.

Walkers can also purchase a REKA Wanderpass, which covers transportation, room and board for periods of two, four or seven days. For a complete description of the Wanderpass, which is in effect a self-guided tour package, see the section on *Walking Tours*.

Useful Addresses & Telephone Numbers

General Tourist Information

In Switzerland:

Schweizerische Verkehrszentrale (SVZ)/Office National Suisse du Tourisme (see *Address Directory*). Staff speaks German, French, Italian and English. Can provide general tourist information as well as information on Switzerland's long-distance footpaths, suggested walking itineraries, organized walking and cross-country skiing tours, mountaineering and ski schools, mountain guides and guide offices. Useful publications include numerous leaflets and brochures on walking and cross-country skiing, a guide to walking tours (see the section on *Walking Tours*), guides to winter sports holidays (see the section on *Cross-Country Skiing*), a guide to long-distance footpaths (see *Where to Get Walking Information*) and:

• *Schweiz/Suisse/Svizzera/Switzerland* (available in German, French, Italian and English). A general tourist guide containing essays on Switzerland's land and people, a map showing main roads and rail lines, a list of foreign branches of the Swiss National Tourist Office, brief descriptions of Switzerland's 10 principal tourist regions and summary information on lodgings, food, transportation, cultural activities, health resorts and outdoor sports such as walking, climbing and cross-country skiing.

Abroad:

Branch offices of the Swiss National Tourist Office are located in EUROPE: Amsterdam, Brussels, Copenhagen, Frankfurt, Lisbon, London, Madrid, Milan, Nice, Paris, Rome, Stockholm and Vienna; CANADA: Toronto; the U.S.A.: New York and San Francisco; and several other countries.

London: Swiss National Tourist Office, Swiss Centre, 1 New Coventry Street, London W1V 3HG. Tel. (01) 734 1921.

New York: Swiss National Tourist Office, The Swiss Center, 608 Fifth Avenue, New York, New York 10020. Tel. (212) 757-5944.

Sport Shops & Bookstores

Sport shops carrying or specializing in equipment for walking, climbing and cross-country skiing are found throughout Switzerland. The largest shop is Eiselin Sport, with stores in Bienne, Moutier, Luzern, Basel, Bern, Zürich and Emmenbrücke. Correspondence should be directed to:

Eiselin Sport (see *Address Directory*). A free catalog is available on request.

Bookstores carrying walking maps and guidebooks are located throughout Switzerland. Local stores usually carry a full line of walking maps and guides at least for their regions, and sometimes for other areas of Switzerland as well.

Search & Rescue

Search and rescue operations in Switzerland are conducted on the ground by trained Schweizer Alpen-Club rescue teams and in the air by Schweizerische Rettungsflugwacht (SRFW), the Swiss Air Rescue Service. In most search and rescue operations air and ground teams cooperate closely.

In case of emergency: telephone the SRFW's emergency number: Tel. (01) 47 47 47 or (01) 814 14 14.

Often, the nearest telephone will be in an SAC mountain hut or in one of the SAC-staffed rescue posts *(les Stations Secours)* located throughout the country. There are between 150 and 160 in all. In addition to assisting in search and rescue, the personnel can administer on-the-spot first aid and arrange for transportation out of the mountains, if necessary.

Within five minutes of your call, the SRFW will have chosen and dispatched a doctor, notified the nearest SAC ground rescue teams and, if necessary, arranged for search dogs, helicopter assistance and a hospital bed.

The service is efficient but expensive. A single rescue can cost anywhere from 200 to 20,000 Swiss Francs (roughly $150 to $15,000), depending on the time, personnel and equipment required. Rescue costs average about 1,000 Swiss Francs and you must pay, for the SRFW is a private company receiving no government subsidies.

Unless you have insurance covering such costs, you should consider subscribing to SRFW services if you plan to do much mountaineering in Switzerland. For a moderate subscription fee, you are entitled to free search and rescue service. And should you perchance have a mishap anywhere in Europe or North Africa, the SRFW will fly you back to Switzerland for treatment free of charge. All rescue and transport helicopters have full ambulance facilities. For information about subscribing to the SRFW, contact:

Schweizerische Rettungsflugwacht (see *Address Directory*). Staff speaks German, French, Italian and English.

Switzerland's Long-Distance Footpaths

Switzerland has six national long-distance footpaths stretching the length and breadth of the country, with several more in preparation. In addition, sections of European Long-Distance Footpaths E-1, E-2 and E-4 cross the country. The paths allow you to traverse Switzerland from east to west along five different routes, each offering the choice of a distinctive slice of Switzerland to explore enroute: the Jura, the Central Plateau, the Alpine foothills, the crest of the Alps, or the valleys of the Rhône and Rhine. Or you can walk across the country from north to south and sample a bit of all its major geographic regions, plus the Mediterranean flavor of the Italian-speaking canton of Ticino.

All the paths are marked with yellow signposts and a series of arrows, diamonds and horizontal bars located within sight of each other. All lowland paths have yellow markings and all mountain paths white-red-white markings, except those in the Jura, which are indicated with red-yellow markings.

Lodgings are generally located within a day's walk of each other, sometimes requiring less than three hours of walking to reach the next accommodation, and only rarely requiring more than eight hours (not counting stops for lunch, admiring the view, meditating or delays due to bad weather). Signposts along the paths give the walking times to the next mountain hut, trailside chalet or community where you can find lodgings. Nonetheless, it is advisable to obtain a list of the available lodgings (see the section on *Trailside Lodgings*) prior to beginning your walk, particularly in mid-summer, when advance reservations may be required to secure a place to sleep for the night. Mountain huts have a policy of not turning anyone away, even when all beds have been taken, although you might have to take potluck on the floor if you arrive late and the hut has reached capacity. Elsewhere, lodgings often fill up early in the day during July and August and a telephone call ahead each morning—or, at the least, a mid-afternoon arrival—are sensible precautions to assure yourself a place to stay.

The booklet *On Foot Through Switzerland*, available from the Schweizerische Verkehrszentrale and Swiss National Tourist Offices abroad, provides an excellent overview of Switzerland's long-distance footpaths. Further information on walking the long-distance footpaths can be obtained from the Schweizerische Arbeitsgemeinschaft für Wanderwege (see *Address Directory*).

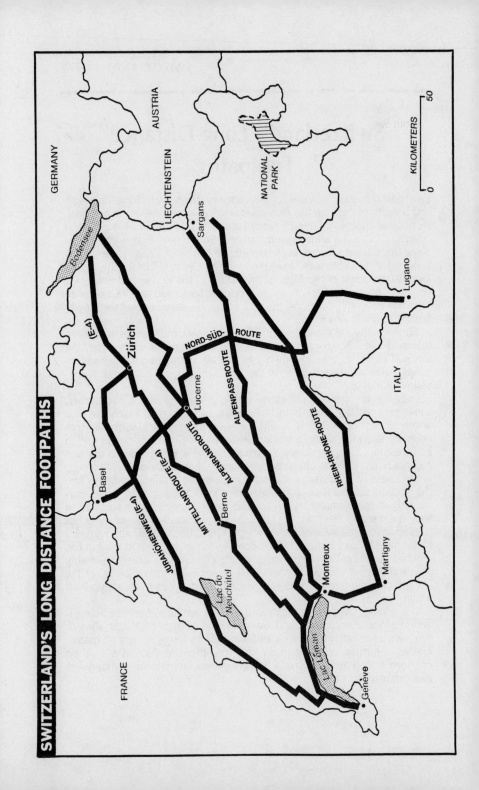

Guidebooks:
- *Wanderbuch Jurahöhenwege* (in German) or *Guide pédestre chemins des crêtes du Jura Suisse* (in French), Kümmerly + Frey, Bern. Available in most bookstores and by mail from the Schweizerischer Juraverein and the SAW.

Mittellandroute

From Romanshorn to Genève. Through Switzerland's gentle heartland from the Bodensee (Lake Constance) to Lac Léman (Lake Geneva). Passes through woods, orchards and thriving farmlands among hills, valleys and plains, with frequent views southward to the Alps. Enroute, small farms and rural villages, castles and monasteries, and the attractions of the cities of Zürich, Bern, Fribourg and Lausanne. **Walking Time:** 17 to 24 days. **Difficulty:** Easy.
Maps:
- Landeskarten der Schweiz 1:50,000, sheets 216 *Frauenfeld,* 217 *Arbon,* 225 *Zürich,* 226 *Rapperswil,* 233 *Solothurn,* 234 *Willisau,* 243 *Bern,* 251 *La Sarraz,* 252 *Bulle,* 260 *St. Cergue,* 261 *Lausanne* and 270 *Genève.*
- Several Wanderkarten also cover portions of the route.
Guidebook:
- *Wanderbuch Mittellandroute* (in German), Kümmerly + Frey, Bern. Available in most bookstores and by mail from the SAW.

Rhein-Rhone-Route

From Chur to Lausanne. Up the Rhine Valley through the Rhaetian Alps to the Gotthard Massif, central knot of the Swiss Alps, then down the Rhône Valley, flanked on one side by the Berner Oberland, on the other by the Valais Alps, the two mightiest ranges in Switzerland. Spectacular Alpine scenery from beginning to end, with chances for numerous side trips into the high country—4,000-meter peaks, glaciers, cliffs, waterfalls, forests, pastures and charming Alpine villages. **Walking Time:** 14 to 18 days. **Difficulty:** Easy to moderately difficult.
Maps:
- Landeskarten der Schweiz 1:50,000, sheets 247 *Sardona,* 248 *Prättigau,* 255 *Sustenpass,* 256 *Disentis,* 257 *Safiental,* 261 *Lausanne,* 262 *Rochers de Naye,* 264 *Jungfrau,* 265 *Nufenenpass,* 272 *St. Maurice,* 273 *Montana,* 274 *Visp* and 282 *Martigny.*
Guidebook:
- *Wanderbuch Rhein-Rhone-Route* (in German), Kümmerly + Frey, Bern. Available from most bookstores and by mail from the SAW.

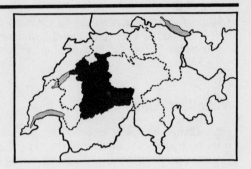

Bernerland

The Bernerland has three distinct personalities: the gentle, pastoral countryside surrounding Bern, the Swiss capital; the jagged, glacier-draped crest of the Berner Oberland, or Bernese Alps; and, dividing the two, the glistening lakeland on either side of the resort town of Interlaken.

Situated on steep bluffs overlooking the Aare River, Bern lies at the base of the Alpine foothills in the west-central Mittelland. Here, footpaths wind among rolling hills, over fertile plains and along river valleys and gorges, passing prosperous farms and villages nestling in a patchwork of pastures, fields, orchards and woods. Emmental—the valley of the Emme River—east of Bern, is particularly lovely with its massive geranium-bedecked and frescoed barns, lush pasturelands and thriving herds. It is also renowned the world over for its Emmentaler cheese, which, to North Americans, is the variety commonly known as Swiss cheese.

To the south, beyond the foothills, lie the twin lakes of Thunersee and Brienzersee. Above the lakes rise the rugged limestone crest of the Berner Oberland, culminating in the 4,000-meter peaks of the Finsteraarhorn group. Among these peaks are the awesome trio of the Eiger, Mönch and Jungfrau (Ogre, Monk and Maiden), as well as the Finsteraarhorn itself, which, at 4,277 meters, is the highest peak in the range.

Glaciers have carved the Berner Oberland into a breathtaking panoply of spires, horns and pinnacles, which rise abruptly from broad amphitheaters and meadowy valley floors. Glaciers and permanent snowfields still mantle the higher slopes, and waterfalls plunge through scree-choked gorges with an awesome, whispering roar. Strewn among the peaks are rocky morraines, cradling tiny, aqua-colored Alpine lakes. Lush valleys, such as the steep-walled Lauterbrunnental with its forested terraces, haystacks and mountainside villages, provide a sharp contrast to the peaks looming on their rims.

Villages and resorts such as Grindelwald—at the foot of the Eiger—Kandersteg, Adelboden and Gstaad, as well as Interlaken, provide excellent starting points for countless walks in the region. Footpaths lead through flowery Alpine pastures and conifer forests; past cliffs, lakes and cascading streams; and into remote, icy basins gouged from the shoulders of the peaks; leading you to high passes and summits, then down again to a deep valley and the comfort of a congenial inn.

In winter, the region is mantled with snow and offers both gentle cross-country ski tours and taxing winter traverses to challenge even the most experienced ski mountaineer.

Useful Addresses

Verkehrsverein Berner Oberland (see *Address Directory*). Provides general tourist information on Bernerland. Also can provide brochures giving information on walking, cross-country skiing and other activities. Staff speaks German, French, Italian and English. Very helpful. Useful publications include:

* *Berner Oberland Schweiz* (in German; also available in French, English, Italian, Dutch and Japanese). A color brochure with a pictorial map of the Brienzersee and Thunersee (the two lakes near Interlaken) and the mountain areas surrounding Grindelwald, Adelboden and Gstaad. Gives a good overview of the area but does not show footpaths. Briefly describes the area and its holiday activities; lists towns, their altitudes and tourist facilities; and lists the footpath guides and walkers' maps covering the area. Also includes a sketch map showing where various discount tickets issued by the Swiss National Railway can be used. Free.

* *Berner Oberland: Winter* (in English, German, French and Italian). A color brochure with a pictorial map of the Berner Oberland in winter, showing ski lifts, cable cars and mountain railways. Includes an index of towns with information on the tourist and sports facilities in each, including cleared winter paths. Gives the lengths of all winter paths and cross-country ski tracks. Free.

* *Berner Oberland: Reserviert für Hobby-Ferien* (in German). Gives information on package arrangements for mountain climbing, walking, mountain photography, horseback riding and other summer activities, along with the price and duration of each. Includes a list of guidebooks and walkers' maps covering the Berner Oberland and a booking form. Free.

* *Berner Oberland: Pauschalangebote* (in German). Gives information on package arrangements for downhill skiing, cross-country skiing, ski touring, winter walking, tobogganing, ice hockey and other winter sports activities. Gives dates and prices and lists the services included for each holiday arrangement. Also includes a calendar of winter events and a booking form. Free.

* *Wandervorschläge: Berner Mittelland, Berner Oberland, Wallis* (in French and German). A booklet published by the Bern-Lötschberg-Simplon Railway (BLS) listing 404 suggested walks; 286 in this region; 118 of them in Wallis/Valais. All the walks begin and end at a railway, bus, boat or cable car terminal. Walking times range from 30 minutes to 10 hours. A small-scale walkers' map showing the

walks—*Karte 1:150,000 Berner Oberland, Wallis*—is available from: Publizitäts-und Reisedienst BLS (see *Address Directory).*

- *Wanderungen Berner Oberland-Zentralalpen* (in German). A booklet published by the Schweizer Reisepost—the Swiss Postal Authority—listing 25 suggested walks in the Berner Oberland and Central Alps. For each walk there is a sketch map, brief route description, and information on how to get to and from the walk on the Swiss Postautos, which *Wanderbillet* to buy, and the name of the 1:50,000 walkers' map covering the area. There is also a map in the center of the brochure showing the location of each walk. Free.

- *Rundfahrt- und Wanderbillette: Bern* (in German). One in a series of booklets published by the Schweizerische Bundesbahn (SBB)—the Swiss Federal Railway. The booklet contains 13 sketch maps, each showing a series of suggested walks. Information on special train fares within the region covered by each map is also given. Free.

- *Wandern im Obersimmental* (in German). A leaflet giving information on walking in the Obersimmen Valley above Lenk. Lists 28 circular walks, has a sketch map showing the location of the walks, lists the dates of annual "walking weeks" organized by a local mountaineer and gives information on weekly nature walks led by a local photographer in the nature preserve of Spillgerten. The leaflet also lists the departure times for the last daily cable cars and buses, shows the most commonly used path markings, and lists the maps and guidebooks covering the area. Free.

- *Ramslauenen (Kiental)—Wyssenmatte-Kandersteg* (in English, German and French). One in a series of leaflets published by the BLS Railway. Has a topographical strip map of the Kander Valley leading up to Kandersteg showing the Höhenweg Nordrampe in red, a brief description of the path, a list of suggested detours and estimated walking times between points. Free.

- *Höhenweg Südrampe BLS/Höhenweg Nordrampe BLS* (in German). A timetable for the BLS trains to the stations from which these two paths can be walked. Includes a price list of fares and gives the times for walking each section of the paths. Free.

- *Kandersteg: Skiwanderkarte* (in German). A 1:10,000 sketch map showing cross-country ski tracks and cleared winter paths in the region surrounding Kandersteg. Each path and ski track is color-coded according to its degree of difficulty. Hotels in Kandersteg are also listed. Easily understood even if you do not speak German. Free.

- *Schynige Platte* (in English, German and French). Gives information on walking excursions in the Schynige Platte area southeast of Interlaken, including a visit to a cheese-making establishment, a moonlight ramble and a night in the Alps followed by an alp breakfast. Free.

- *Wengen Männlichen* (in German). A color brochure with a pictorial map of the Männlichen peak above Wengen and surrounding mountains, including the Eiger, Mönch and Jungfrau. Shows routes of the cable car from Wengen to the Männlichen and the cog wheel railway from Lauterbrunnen to the Jungfraujoch. Also describes 17 suggested walks, along with their estimated walking times. Free.

- *Programme Chemins de Fer Region de la Jungfrau-Interlaken* (in French). A brochure with a pictorial map of the Jungfrau region. Lists guided ski mountaineering tours, glacier tours, moonlight walks and other attractions in the region, including a nocturnal walk to Harder Kulm to hear traditional Swiss folk music. Free.

- *Grindelwald: Winterspazierwege und Skiwanderwege* (in German, French and English). A large-scale sketch map of the area surrounding Grindelwald with exquisite line drawings of each building, fence, cable car—even individual trees. Shows cleared winter paths and both marked and unmarked cross-country ski tracks. Free.

- *Meiringen-Hasliberg: Wandervorschläge* (in German). A leaflet describing five suggested day hikes in the region west of Meiringen. One side of the leaflet has a pictorial map showing the routes of the suggested walks (each letter-coded to the descriptions on the back of the leaflet) as well as other footpaths in the area. Also shows the locations of railways, cable cars and postbus stops. Lists the prices for cable car and chair-lift rides to the starting points of the suggested walks. Also gives the length and walking time for each walk. Free.

- *Hasliberg: Bergbahnen—Postauto—Wanderwochen* (in German). A leaflet giving information on special walking weeks. Package prices include room, breakfast and unlimited use of selected buses, cable cars and railways in the area. Free.

- *Emmental Oberaargau: 30 Wandervorschläge* (in German). A booklet containing 30 cards, each describing a suggested walk in the Emme Valley west of Bern. Each card includes a sketch map, brief route description, the estimated walking time, access information, the name of the appropriate walkers' map and the title of the guidebook covering the route. Available for a nominal charge.

- *Emmental Wanderland-Wunderland im Herzen der Schweiz* (in German). Gives general tourist information on the Emmental, a calendar of events and full details on hotels in the valley. Includes a 1:300,000 map of the Emmental and brief information on guided walks. Free.

- *Berner Oberland Hotelführer* (in English, German, French and Italian). Gives full details on hotels throughout the Berner Oberland, including prices (not guaranteed). Free.

- *Regionales Ferienabonnement* (in English, German, French and Italian). Gives information on special holiday passes that can save you money on public transportation in the Berner Oberland. Includes cable cars, chair lifts and boats. Free.

Brochures showing each of the cross-country ski tracks and ski mountaineering routes near principal villages and towns in the Berner Oberland are also available. To obtain these, simply ask for the *Skiwandern Karte* covering the locality you wish to visit.

Berner Wanderwege (see *Address Directory*). Maintains more than 9,700 kilometers of marked footpaths and 400 kilometers of marked cross-country ski routes. Provides information on walking throughout Bernerland. Also sells maps and guidebooks (listed below). Staff speaks French, German and English. Very helpful.

Maps

Special walkers' maps covering the Bernerland are available from the Schweizerische Arbeitsgemeinschaft für Wanderwege and Berner Wanderwege (see *Address Directory*). They are:

- Wanderkarte 1:10,000, sheet *Interlaken*.
- Wanderkarte 1:12,500, sheet *Gstaad*.
- Wanderkarte 1:20,000, sheet *Brünig-Hasliberg*.
- Wanderkarte 1:25,000, sheets *Bern und Umgebung, Brienz, Bielersee-Chasseral-Seeland* and *Schwarzenburgerland und Ganstrischgebiet*.
- Wanderkarte 1:33,333, sheets *Beatenberg, Kandersteg und Umgebung* and *Lauterbrunnental/Jungfrau Region*.
- Wanderkarte 1:50,000, sheets *Berner Oberland Ost, Berner Oberland West, Emmental-Napf-Entlebuch, Frutigen, Lenk, Niedersimmental-Diemtigtal-Stockhorn-Gantrisch, Oberaargau-Bucheggberg-Weissenstein, Oberhasli, Reichenbach-Keintal-Griesalp, Sensetal* and *Thunersee*.
- Wanderkarte 1:75,000, sheet *Berner Oberland und Oberwallis*.

The Bernerland is also covered by the 1:25,000, 1:50,000 and 1:100,000 maps published by the Eidgenössische Landestopographie (see *Address Directory*).

Guidebooks

All guidebooks are in German unless otherwise noted below.

Available from Bergverlag Rudolf Rother (see *Address Directory*):

- *Berner Alpen Grosser Führer* by Königer and Munter. Covers the entire Berner Oberland.

Available from Groupe Haute Montagne (see *Address Directory*):

- *Selection d'Ascensions en Oberland Bernois: I: Blumisalp-Balmhorn* (in French) by J. M. Pruvost and G. Tassaux.
- *Selection d'Ascensions en Oberland Bernois: II: Bietschhorn-Nesthorn* (in French) by J. M. Pruvost and G. Tassaux.
- *Selection d'Ascensions en Oberland Bernois: III: Letschhorn* (in French) by J. M. Pruvost and J. L. Colas.
- *Selection d'Ascensions en Oberland Bernois: IV: Petersgrat-Jungfrau* (in French) by J. M. Pruvost and J. L. Colas.

Available from the Verlag des SAC (see *Address Directory*):

- *Berner Alpen I:* Diablerets–Gemmi Pass.
- *Berner Alpen II:* Gemmi Pass–Petersgrat.
- *Berner Alpen III:* Bietschhorn–Lötschentaler Breithorn–Nesthorn–Aletschhorn.
- *Berner Alpen IV:* Petersgrat–Finsteraarhorn–Unteres Studerjoch–Galmilücke.
- *Berner Alpen V:* Grindelwald–Meiringen–Grimsel–Münster.

Available from West Col Productions (see *Address Directory*):

- *Bernese Alps:* Lötschenpass–Grimselpass (in English).
- *Bernese Alps West:* Col du Pillon–Lötschenpass (in English).
- *Bernese Alps Central:* Lötschenpass–Jungfraujoch–Aletschgletscher (in English).
- *Bernese Alps East:* Jungfraujoch–Grimselpass (in English).

Available from The Alpine Club, London (see *Address Directory*).

- *Selected Climbs in the Bernese Alps* (in English) by R. G. Collomb.

The following Kümmerly + Frey guidebooks are available from Schweizerische Arbeitsgemeinschaft für Wanderwege, Berner Wanderwege and most bookstores:

- *Wanderbuch 1: Wanderwege im Kanton Bern*
- *Wanderbuch 2: Emmental I*
- *Wanderbuch 3: Passrouten im Berner Oberland*

- *Wanderbuch 4: Emmental Iı*
- *Wanderbuch 6: Lütschinentäler*
- *Wanderbuch 7: Bern-West*
- *Wanderbuch 8: Freiberge*
- *Wanderbuch 9: Brienzersee*
- *Wanderbuch 10: Seeland*
- *Wanderbuch 11: Kandertal*
- *Wanderbuch 13: Niedersimmental-Diemtigtal*
- *Wanderbuch 14: Oberaargau*
- *Wanderbuch 15: Bern-Süd*
- *Wanderbuch 16: Thunersee*
- *Wanderbuch 17: Obersimmental-Saanenland*
- *Wanderbuch 18: Bern-Nord*
- *Wanderbuch 19: Oberhasli*
- *Wanderbuch 20: Bern-Ost*
- *Spazierwege 1: Rund um Bern*
- *Spazierwege 3: Rund um Biel* (also available in French)
- *Rundwanderungen 1: Bern-Mittelland*
- *Rundwanderungen 2: Berner Oberland*

Suggested Walks

Höhenweg Nordrampe BLS: From Ramslauenen to Kandersteg along the north ramp of the Lötschberg Railway, high above the Kander Valley. **Walking Time:** 6 hours. **Difficulty:** Easy to moderately difficult. **Path Markings:** Red and white horizontal bars.
Maps:
- *Ramslauenen (Kiental)–Wyssenmatte–Kandersteg,* a 1:50,000 strip map published by the Bern-Lötschberg-Simplon Railway showing the path in red. Includes a brief route description. Available from the Verkehrsverein Berner Oberland (see *Address Directory).*
- Wanderkarte 1:50,000, *Berner Oberland West.*
Guidebooks:
- *Ramslauenen (Kiental)–Wyssenmatte–Kandersteg* (in French, German and English). Available from Verkehrsverein Berner Oberland.
- *Wanderbuch 11: Kandertal,* Kümmerly + Frey.

From Kirchberg to Utzenstorf: A lovely walk through cornfields and quaint villages along the Emme River. Beautiful castle in Utzenstorf. **Walking Time:** 2¾ hours. **Difficulty:** Easy. **Path Markings:** Yellow triangles, arrows and bars.

Maps:
* Wanderkarte 1:50,000, *Emmental-Napf-Entlebuch.* Or:
* Landeskarte der Schweiz 1:25,000, sheets 1127 and 1147.

Guidebooks:
* *Emmental Oberaargau: 30 Wandervorschläge* (in German). Available from the Verkehrsverein Berner Oberland.
* *Wanderbuch 18: Bern-Nord,* Kümmerly + Frey. Routes 39 and 40.

Rundwanderung Interlaken: A circular walk from Interlaken up to Alp Grön, with a wonderful view over the Thunersee; along the bubbling Grön Brook to Merlingen; onto the Beatushöhlen (a series of subterranean caves); then through a nature preserve on the shores of the Thunersee and back to Interlaken. **Walking Time:** 5½ hours. **Difficulty:** Easy to moderately difficult. **Path Markings:** Yellow triangles, arrows and bars.

Maps:
* Wanderkarte 1:50,000, sheets *Berner Oberland Ost* and *Thunersee.*

Guidebooks:
* *Wanderungen Berner Oberland-Zentralalpen* (in German). Available from Verkehrsverein Berner Oberland.
* *Wanderbuch 16: Thunersee,* Kümmerly + Frey.

Rundwanderung Männlichen-Wengen: From Wengen up to Männlichen, above the village. Sweeping views of the Lauterbrunnen Valley, the Eiger, Mönch and Jungfrau, and to the lakes surrounding Interlaken. Numerous circular routes are possible. You can also start the walk from the cable car terminal at Männlichen, or from the cog railway station at Kleine Scheidegg. **Walking Time:** 2 to 6 hours, depending upon the route chosen. **Difficulty:** Easy to moderately difficult if you utilize the cable car or cog railway; otherwise, moderately difficult. **Path Markings:** Red and white horizontal bars.

Map:
* Wanderkarte 1:50,000, *Berner Oberland Ost.*

Guidebooks:
* *Wengen Männlichen* (in German), available from Verkehrsverein Berner Oberland.
* *Rundwanderungen 2: Berner Oberland,* Kümmerly + Frey.

For longer walks, two possibilities are:

From Meiringen to Gstaad: Over high alpine passes through one of the most spectacular mountain regions in Switzerland. Passes through the towns and villages of Grindelwald, Wengen, Lauterbrunnen, Mürren, Kandersteg, Adelboden and Lenk to Gstaad. Takes you across Grosse Scheidegg below the Wetterhorn and Kleine Scheidegg below the Eiger; down into the steep-sided Lauterbrunnen Valley; over the Sefinenfurgge with its head-on view of the Eiger, Mönch and Jungfrau to the east; down to the small alpine community of Griesalp in the deep Kiental; over

Hohtürli; past the spectacular, cliff-rimmed Öschinensee, a beautiful lake at the foot of the glacier-draped Blümlisalphorn and Doldenhorn; then from Kandersteg, over the Bonderchrinde, Hahnenmoospass, and Reulisenpass to Gstaad. **Walking Time:** 7 to 8 days. **Difficulty:** Moderately difficult; some difficult sections such as on the final ascent of Hohtürli pass. **Path Markings:** Red and white horizontal bars.

Maps:
• Wanderkarte 1:50,000, sheets *Berner Oberland Ost* and *Berner Oberland West.*

Guidebook:
• *Wanderbuch 3: Passrouten im Berner Oberland,* Kümmerly + Frey.

From Rosenlaui to the Grimselsee: A high-alpine walk from the village of Rosenlaui in the Rosenlaui Valley above Meiringen to Grimsel Lake at the top of Grimselpass. This is extremely rugged country, with steep ascents and descents and several glacier crossings. A guide or prior rock and ice climbing experience are required. The route winds from Rosenlaui via Dossenhütte, Rosenlauigletscher, Gaulihütte, Wetterlimmi, Lauteraarhütte and Unteraargletscher to the Grimselsee. Several optional side trips are possible. **Walking Time:** 3 to 5 days. **Difficulty:** For experienced mountain walkers only; should only be walked in good weather. **Path Markings:** Red and white horizontal bars; no markings on the glaciers.

Maps:
• Landeskarte der Schweiz 1:25,000, sheets 1209, 1210, 1229, 1230, 1249 and 1250.

Guidebooks:
• *Berner Alpen V,* Verlag des SAC.
• *Berner Alpen Grosse Führer,* Bergverlag Rudolf Rother, Munich.

Cross-Country Skiing

The Bernerland has nearly 30 ski centers with marked tracks totaling more than 350 kilometers. In addition, there are more than 20 marked cross-country routes. For full details, refer to the annual booklet published by the Schweizerische Arbeitsgemeinschaft für Wanderwege, *Ski Wandern/ Ski de Randonnée* (described in the section on *Cross-Country Skiing*). You can also obtain sketch maps from the SAW showing marked ski tracks described in the booklet.

The *DSV Langlauf Kompass* and *Skilanglauf Atlas* (described under "Guidebooks" in the secton on *Cross-Country Skiing)* list many of the marked cross-country ski tracks in the Bernerla.d. In addition, the Verkehrsverein Berner Oberland can supply sketch maps showing the marked ski tracks near many towns and villages in the region. To obtain these sketch maps, simply ask for the *Skiwandern Karten* covering the town in which you are interested.

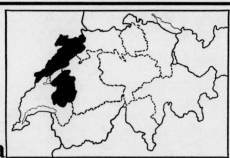

Fribourg-
Neuchâtel-Jura

The hills and valleys of the Mittelland extend across the center of this region, separating the Fribourg Alps on the south from the Jura Mountains on the north. Running along the foot of the Jura is the long, deep Lac de Neuchâtel and its much smaller twin, Bielersee. It is characteristic of this region that one lake should bear a French name and its neighbor a German one, for the dividing line between French- and German-speaking Switzerland runs between them. On this line lie the bilingual cities of Biel/Bienne, in the Bernese Jura, and Fribourg, where the Saane River separates the French and German parts of town.

Walkers who wish to explore the Jura, Mittelland and Alps will find all three close at hand. The Jura, with its cloak of beech forests, meadowy ridge tops, narrow gorges and high plateaus, offers excellent walking and cross-country skiing. In clear weather, the ascents to its summits and ridges are rewarded with sweeping views to France, southern Germany and the string of Alpine peaks from Mont Blanc to the Jungfrau. The panoramas from the twin summits of Chasseron and Chasseral are especially breathtaking, leading your eyes in a 360° arc across the mountains and valleys of three nations.

The nearby Mittelland offers gentle walking across rolling, green hills, through broad valleys, and along winding rivers and large lakes. Most of the land is devoted to agriculture, especially dairy cattle and cheese making, at which its herders excel. The cheese from Gruyères, a village at the base of the Alpine foothills, is world-renowned.

The Fribourg Alps, though only half as high as the Berner Oberland, are scarcely less beautiful. Bold, serrated ridges are surrounded by vast, sloping parklands which are carpeted in early summer with a vibrant display of Alpine flowers. Nestled among the meadows are small, jewel-like lakes reflecting the peaks above, scattered forests and the rustic summer huts of Alpine herdsmen.

More than 4,000 kilometers of marked footpaths wind throughout Fribourg-Neuchâtel-Jura, offering pleasant, seldom difficult rambles through a largely rural countryside. The cities of Fribourg and Neuchâtel are both small and charming, with roots extending back to the Middle Ages. Numerous old churches and castles are found throughout the region, as well as scattered Roman ruins. There is also evidence of much earlier inhabitants. The Jura, which gave its name to the Jurassic Age, is noted for the dinosaur bones preserved in its ancient limestone beds.

Useful Addresses—Fribourg

Union Fribourgeoise du Tourisme (see *Address Directory*). Provides general tourist information on the Pays de Fribourg. Also can provide brochures giving information on walking, cross-country skiing and other activities. Staff speaks French, German and English. Useful publications include:

- *Pays de Fribourg/Freiburgerland* (in French, German, Italian and English). A general tourist brochure, with a color pictorial map of the canton of Fribourg, showing footpaths, railways, postauto routes, castles and numerous other points of interest. Free.

- *Guide touristique/Reiseführer: Pays de Fribourg/Freiburgerland* (in French, German and English). A booklet richly illustrated with color photographs. Provides information on local customs, lodgings, gastronomy, transportation in the Pays de Fribourg. Gives the addresses and telephone numbers of tourist offices and describes each of the principal towns and villages in the region. Available for a nominal charge.

- *Chemins pédestres: Saignelégier* (in French and German). A leaflet describing six walks from Saignelégier to the Gruyère and Royes plateaus, to the Rochers des Sommétres, and to Goumois, Haut-du-Bémont and Muriaux. Includes a sketch map, a symbol showing the path markings used along each route, and their walking times. Free.

- *Pays de Fribourg carte des chemins pédestres/Freiburgerland Wanderkarte* 1:100,000. A five-color 1:100,000 topographical map showing footpaths in red. On the back of the map is a list of more than 100 possible walks, giving the names of localities along each route, its starting and ending points, and the walking time each way. Available for a nominal charge. (Recommended)

- *Châtel St-Denis* (in French, German and English). A color brochure describing the resort of Châtel St-Denis in the prealps. Includes a pictorial map of the region, showing ski lifts and cross-country ski tracks, and a reduction of the 1:50,000 Landestopographie der Schweiz map covering the area, on which more than 100 kilometers of footpaths are shown in red. Free.

- *Pays de Fribourg: Guide des hôtels* (in French, German, Italian and English). Gives full details on lodging possibilities throughout the Pays de Fribourg. Free.

Useful Addresses—Neuchâtel

Office Neuchâtelois du Tourisme (see *Address Directory*). Provides general tourist information on the canton of Neuchâtel. Also can provide brochures giving information on walking, cross-country skiing and other activities. Staff speaks French, German and English. Useful publications include:

• *Country of Neuchâtel Tourist Guide* (in English; also available in French and German). Provides a comprehensive overview of Neuchâtel, with photographs and descriptions of its principal towns and attractions. Includes brief information on walking, cross-country skiing and other activities, along with the addresses and telephone numbers of the associations to write for further information on each activity. Also includes the addresses and telephone numbers of local tourist offices. Free.

• *Pays de Neuchâtel: Quelques buts d'excursions à pied* (in French). Lists 17 possible walks, each of which can be started from any one of several towns. Includes a list of mountain huts, chalets and other lodgings; information on maps and path markings; the walking times between points enroute for each walk; and a list of useful addresses and telephone numbers. Free.

• *Compagnie des chemins de fer des Montagnes neuchâteloises* (in French and German). A timetable for trains and postautos in the southern Jura. Also lists 22 suggested walks. A sketch map shows where each walk goes and how its starting point can be reached by train. Information is also given on lodgings and cross-country skiing. Published by the Compagnie des chemins de fer des Montagnes neuchâteloises (see *Address Directory*). Free.

• *Chemins pédestres Pays de Neuchâtel*, 1:50,000 (with a key to symbols in French and German). A 1:50,000 pictorial map showing marked walking routes, railway lines, postauto routes and the locations of chair lifts and cable cars in Neuchâtel. A series of symbols indicates the locations of mountain huts, youth hostels, isolated hotels and restaurants, castles, nature reserves, notable viewpoints and keep fit trails. The back of the map outlines 17 suggested walks and gives the walking times between points enroute for each; has an index of place names with a key to where they can be found on the map; and includes line drawings of the protected plants in the region. Published by the Association neuchâteloise de tourisme pédestre. Available for a nominal charge.

• *Le Pays de Neuchâtel à la carte* (in French and German). A brochure describing seven-day summer holidays, some of which include walking excursions. Gives full details, including prices. Free.

• *Pays de Neuchâtel en hiver* (in French and German; separate insert in English). A color brochure with a pictorial map showing marked tracks and cross-country ski routes in red. Briefly describes the principal cross-country skiing centers. Free.

- *12 itinéraires de ski de randonnée au Pays de Neuchâtel/12 Skiwanderungen im Neuenburgerland* (in French and German). A brochure describing 12 cross-country skiing routes in the Neuchâtel Jura. For each, there is a list giving the length of the route, its average altitude, the total altitude gain and loss enroute, and the sheet numbers of the 1:25,000 Landeskarten der Schweiz covering the route; a chart showing an elevational profile of the route; and a sketch map showing the locations of lodgings, restaurants, viewpoints, tourist information offices and other facilities on and near the route. A pictorial map showing all the marked ski tracks and cross-country routes in the region in red is also included. Free. (Recommended)
- *Paradis du ski de randonnées* (in French and German). A leaflet describing seven-day cross-country skiing holidays. Free.
- *Langläufer Leben Länger: Tête de Ran sur les Hauts-Geneveys* (in German). One in a series of postcard-size sketch maps showing marked cross-country ski tracks and ski touring routes. This one covers the Tête de Ran ski area. The locations of ski lifts, chalets, mountain refuges, roads and railway lines are also shown. On the back is a key to symbols used on the sketch map, a list of useful addresses and telephone numbers, and space for addressing the postcard. Published by Maurice Villemin (see *Address Directory*). Free on request.
- *Pays de Neuchâtel: Guide des hôtels et restaurants* (in French and German). Gives full details on hotels and restaurants throughout Neuchâtel. Free.

Association Neuchâteloise de Tourisme Pédestre (see *Address Directory*). Provides information on walking in the canton of Neuchâtel. Also sells a 1:50,000 five-color walkers' map showing marked footpaths in the canton:

- *Chemins et sentiers balisés au Pays de Neuchâtel,* 1:50,000.

Association Neuchâteloise des Skieurs de Fond et de Randonnée (see *Address Directory*). Provides information on cross-country skiing in the canton of Neuchâtel. Staff speaks French, German and English.

Useful Addresses—Jura

Office Jurassien du Tourisme (see *Address Directory*). Provides general tourist information on the Jura. Also can provide numerous brochures giving information on walking, cross-country skiing and other activities. Staff speaks French, German and English. Useful publications include:

- *Jura Schweiz: à vol d'oiseau* (in French and German). A color pictorial map of the Jura. On the back is a list of nearly 75 suggested walks, giving the names of the towns and villages through which each walk passes and the walking times between points enroute.

- *Schweizer Wanderbuch Nr. 16/Guide pédestre no. 16a—Jura: Verzeichnis der Verpflegungs- und Unterkunftsmöglichkeiten längs der Jurahöhenwege/Liste des possibilités de ravitaillement et de logement le long des chemins de crêtes* (in German and French). Published by the Association du Jura Suisse. A comprehensive list of lodgings and restaurants on and near footpaths in the Jura Mountains. The lodgings and restaurants are listed alphabetically by town, along with the postal code of the town. The telephone number is given for each, as well as information on its type and number of sleeping facilities. Designed as a companion to the Kümmerly + Frey walkers' guide to the Jurahöhenwege. Available for a nominal charge. (Recommended)

- *Jura à la carte; Jura les spécialités;* and *Jura à discrétion* (in French and German). A series of three brochures, plus a postauto timetable published by the Schweizer Reisepost. The brochures describe several suggested excursions by postauto within the Jura, each highlighting a different aspect of the region. Two of the brochures, *Jura à discrétion* and *Jura à la carte,* include suggestions for several walks which can be combined with the bus trips. Sketch maps showing the walks and linking postauto routes are included along with brief route descriptions and information on special walkers' tickets. Free.

- *Wanderungen im Jura* (in German). Another brochure published by the Schweizer Reisepost, this one describing 16 suggested walks. For each, there is a sketch map, brief route description, information on how to get to and from the walk on the Swiss Postautos, which *Wanderbillet* to buy, and the name of the 1:50,000 topographical map covering the area. A map in the center of the brochure shows the location of each walk. Free.

- *Chemins de fer du Jura* (in French). A timetable for trains and postautos in the Jura. Also lists 40 suggested walks. A sketch map shows where each walk goes and how its starting point can be reached by train. Information is also given on special fares, lodgings and cross-country skiing. Published by the Chemins de fer du Jura, (see *Address Directory).* Free.

- *Rundfahrt- und Wanderbillette/Billets circulaires: Biel/Bienne* (in French and German). One in a series of booklets published by the Schweizerische Bundesbahn (SBB)—the Swiss National Railway. The booklet contains four sketch maps, each showing a series of suggested walks in the region around Biel. Information on special train fares within the region covered by each map is also given. Free.

- *Billets circulaires (avec ou sans parcours pédestre): La Chaux-de-Fonds/Le Locle* (in French). Another booklet published by the Schweizerische Bundesbahn, this one containing six sketch maps showing suggested walks that can be reached by train in the region around La Chaux-de-Fonds. Free.

- *Laufen* (in German). A color brochure giving tourist information on the town of Laufen. Includes several maps, including a reduction of the 1:50,000 Landeskarte der Schweiz showing nine walks in red in the vicinity of the town.

- *Tramelan* (in French and German). Another general information color brochure. Includes a separate leaflet with municipal information—altitude, number of inhabitants, telephone numbers of police and doctors, for instance—a lodging list, a list of suggested walks, and a sketch map showing footpaths, ski lifts, railway lines and postauto routes.

- *Vallon de Saint-Imier* (in French, German and English). Similar to the brochure to Tramelan. Also has a separate leaflet giving municipal information, a list of lodgings and information on cross-country skiing.

- *Jura Suisse: randonnées à ski* (in French and German). A color brochure showing the locations of cross-country and ski touring centers in the Jura. Gives the lengths of marked ski tracks near each locality and the telephone number to call for additional information. Also tells how to get to the tracks. Free.

- *Pro Jura: randonnées à ski* (in French and German). A series of 25 postcard-size sketch maps showing marked cross-country ski tracks and ski touring routes throughout the Jura. Each card covers a single locality and shows the locations of ski lifts, chalets, mountain refuges, roads and railway lines, postauto stops and the lengths of each cross-country track and ski touring route. On the back is a key to symbols used on the sketch map, a brief description of the ski tracks and ski touring routes, a list of useful addresses and telephone numbers and space for a control stamp. Each person who completes six of the routes indicated on the cards receives a bronze medal when the stamped cards are returned to the Office Jurassien du Tourisme. Available for a nominal charge.

- *Jura Suisse: Séjours forfaitaires "à la carte"* (in French and German). A brochure giving information on package arrangements for ski touring holidays at 16 localities in the Jura. Information on prices and a booking form are included. Free.

- *Piste nordique de tourisme: Franches Montagnes* (in French and German). A color brochure describing ski touring opportunites in the Franches Montagnes. Includes a sketch map showing a 20-kilometer ski touring route from La Ferriere to Les Reussilles. Free.

- *Ski de Fond: du Mollendruz à la Givrine* (in French). A brochure giving information on lodgings, ski equipment rental, ski instruction and the emergency telephone number for the village of Mollendruz on the crest of the Jura. Includes a sketch map showing nine marked cross-country ski tracks along the crest of a mountain ridge stretching from the Col du Mollendruz to the Col de la Givrine. Free.

- *Ecole Suisse de ski de randonnée: Vallée de Joux* (in French). A sketch map showing five ski touring routes in the vicinity of the village of Le Brassus, as well as the locations of lodgings, ski lifts and other facilities. Free.

- *Jura: Guide des hôtels et restaurants* (in French and German). Gives full details on hotels and restaurants throughout the Jura. Free.

Schweizerisher Juraverein/Association du Jura Suisse (see *Address Directory*). Maintains more than 600 kilometers of marked footpaths. Provides information on walking throughout the Jura. Also sells maps, guidebooks and a walkers' lodging list. Staff speaks French and German. Very helpful.

Maps

Special walkers' maps covering the cantons of Fribourg, Neuchâtel and the Jura are available from the Schweizerische Arbeitsgemeinschaft für Wanderwege (see *Address Directory*). They are:

- Carte d'excursion/Wanderkarte 1:25,000, sheet *Bielersee-Chasseral-Seeland*.

- Carte d'excursion 1:50,000, sheet *Gruyère*.

- *Chemins et sentiers balisés au Pays de Neuchâtel*, 1:50,000.

- *Pays de Fribourg carte des chemins pédestres/Freiburgerland Wanderkarte*, 1:100,000.

- Carte speciale du Jura 1:50,000, sheets 3, 4 and 5.

The three cantons are also covered by the 1:25,000, 1:50,000 and 1:100,000 maps published by the Eidgenössische Landestopographie (see *Address Directory*).

Guidebooks

Available from the Verlag des SAC (see *Address Directory*):

- *Escalades dans le Jura I: Ste-Croix–Val de Travers–Bienne* (in French).

- *Escalades dans le Jura II: Moutier–Raimeux–Bâle–Olten* (in French).
- *Prealpes fribourgeoises* (in French). Covers Moléson, Vanil Noir, Gastlosen, Chemiflue, Gantrisch and the Stockhorn.

The following Kümmerly + Frey guidebooks are available from Schweizerische Arbeitsgemeinschaft für Wanderwege (see *Address Directory)* and most bookstores:

- *Wanderbuch Gelbe 5: Chasseral* (in German).
- *Wanderbuch Gelbe 8: Freiberge* (in German).
- *Guide pédestre jaune 8a: Franches-Montagnes* (in French).
- *Wanderbuch Gelbe 12: Delsberg-Laufen* (in German).
- *Wanderbuch Grüne 16: Jurahöhenwege* (in German).
- *Guide pédestre vert 16a: Chemins des crêtes du Jura Suisse* (in French).
- *Wanderbuch Gelbe 21: Moutier und Umgebung* (in German).
- *Guide pédestre jaune 21a: Région de Moutier* (in French).
- *Spazierwege 3: Rund um Biel* (in German; also available in French).
- *Rundwanderungen 3: Freiburgerland* (in German).
- *Itinéraires circulaires 3a: Région de Fribourg* (in French).

Suggested Walks

Portions of three of Switzerland's long-distance footpaths cross Fribourg-Neuchâtel-Jura—one leading along the crest of the Jura, another crossing the Mittelland, and the third leading through the Fribourg Alps. Each offers an unequaled opportunity to explore these three regions.

Jurahöhenweg. From Frinvillier (outside Biel/Bienne) to Sainte-Croix. Leads from the Schüss Valley across the Chasseral, one of the most prominent viewpoints in the whole Jura; dips down to the lakeside town of Neuchâtel, with its imposing castle; climbs through vineyards and woods to a high plateau overlooking the Creux-du-Van, an impressive rocky promontory 280 meters high; and crosses high fields to the peak of Chasseron, with its extensive views. Passes numerous small dairy farms enroute. **Walking Time:** 4 to 5 days. **Difficulty:** Easy to moderately difficult. **Path Markings:** Red and yellow horizontal bars.
Maps:
- Cartes spéciales du Jura 1:50,000, sheets 4 *Neuchâtel-Chasseral-Bienne* and 5 *Yverdon-Ste Croix-Val de Travers.*
Guidebooks:
- *Wanderbuch 16: Jurahöhenwege* (in German) or *Guide pédestre 16a: Chemins des crêtes du Jura Suisse* (in French), both Kümmerly + Frey.

Mittellandroute. From Bern to Lausanne. Leads through the Chünizberg Forest, passing the country villages of Herzwil, Liebewil and Thörishaus, with superb examples of Bernese farmhouses; across the deep gorge of the Sense River; and through richly cultivated, hilly country to Fribourg, a charming city with old houses and medieval city walls, gates and churches. Crosses the central lowlands, leading through Romont, a picturesque medieval town built prominently on an isolated hill. Winds along a rocky ridge above Broye Castle, with distant views toward Lac Léman, the Alps and Jura. Crosses the Broye Valley, then leads across the wooded hills of the Jorat down to Lausanne. Numerous attractive villages enroute. **Walking Time:** 4 to 5 days. **Difficulty:** Easy. **Path Markings:** Yellow arrows, diamonds and bars.
Maps:
• Landeskarten der Schweiz 1:50,000, sheets 243, 251, 252 and 261.
Guidebook:
• *Wanderbuch Mittellandroute* (in German), Kümmerly + Frey.

Alpenrandroute. From Thun on the Thunersee to Vevey on the shores of Lac Léman. Passes through the magnificent Greyerzer region in the Fribourg Alps. Winds through wooded country up to the Gurnigel Mountain hut; across Alpine meadowland with wide views to the Mittelland and Jura; past the Schwarzee, a lake often mentioned in legends; across the Monts-de-Corsier to Jongny; and through terraced vineyards down to Vevey. Leads through Charmey, a holiday center surrounded by mountains; Bulle; and Châtel-Saint-Denis, with its 14th century castle. **Walking Time:** 3 to 4 days. **Difficulty:** Easy to moderately difficult; some steep sections. **Path Markings:** Yellow arrows, triangles and bars in the lowlands; red and white horizontal bars in the mountains.
Maps:
• Landeskarten der Schweiz 1:50,000, sheets 252, 253 and 262.
Guidebook:
• *Wanderbuch Alpenrandroute* (in German), Kümmerly + Frey.

Cross-Country Skiing

Fribourg-Neuchâtel-Jura has more than 30 ski centers with marked tracks totaling more than 350 kilometers. In addition, there are over 20 marked cross-country routes, including the 63-kilometer Piste du Haut-Plateau, in the Bernese Jura. For full details, see the booklet published by the Schweizerische Arbeitsgemeinschaft für Wanderwege, *Ski Wandern/Ski de Randonnée*. You can also obtain sketch maps from the SAW showing marked ski tracks described in the booklet. In addition, the *Skilanglauf Atlas* describes several marked cross-country tracks in the Bernese Jura and the brochure, *12 itinéraires de ski de randonnée au Pays de Neuchâtel* (described under "Useful Addresses—Neuchâtel," above), gives details on ski touring routes in the Neuchâtel Jura. Finally, the Union Fribourgeoise du Tourisme, Office Neuchâtelois du Tourisme and Office Jurassien du Tourisme can supply sketch maps showing marked ski tracks near many towns and villages in their respective regions.

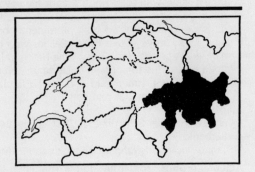

Graubünden (Grisons)

The canton of Graubünden, or Grisons, is the largest and least populated in Switzerland. And it's all mountains: dozens of ranges and some 700 major peaks, of which more than 300 rise above 3,000 meters. Between the mountains lie more than 150 valleys, including those of the Rhine and Inn rivers. The Inn Valley, known as the Engadine, is one of the loveliest in Switzerland and is the home of the jet-set resort of St. Moritz. Yet by and large, Graubünden is less tourist-ridden than such popular areas as Luzern, the Berner Oberland and the Valais Alps. Its 11,500 kilometers of marked footpaths offer some of the loneliest walking through some of the wildest mountains in Switzerland.

The walking opportunities are so vast that even a brief summary is hardly possible. Whatever you seek in the mountains—snowy crags, glaciers, granite walls, vast parklands, forests, streams, lakes, waterfalls, wilderness, wildlife or comfortable resorts—can be found somewhere in Graubünden. The major ranges include the Bündner Oberland, north of the Rhine Valley; the Rhätikon, Silvretta and Samnaun ranges, along the Austrian frontier; the lofty Bernina Massif, culminating in 4,049-meter Piz Bernina, the highest peak in eastern Switzerland; the Bergell Alps, with their imposing granite pyramids; the Albula Alps, running along the north side of the Engadine; and the ranges of the Unterengadin and Val Mustair, near the Italian border. In addition, there are numerous ranges occupying the center of the canton, between the Rhine Valley on the north and the Engadine on the south.

The Alps of Graubünden have been subjected less to human pressures than others in Switzerland. Consequently, they boast of some of the finest remaining stands of native forest as well as the greatest concentrations of wildlife, including animals such as steinbock and ibex, which are either rare or absent elsewhere in Switzerland. The best place to observe wildlife in the entire country is the Swiss National Park, located in the Alps of

Unterengadin. This 169-square-kilometer preserve has numerous marked footpaths winding through what is perhaps the least disturbed landscape in Switzerland.

Graubünden is also notable for its cultural diversity. Here, you encounter speakers not only of German and Italian, but of Romansh, the Latinate tongue of the Rhaetian peoples. This distinct language dates from Roman times, when imperial legions conquered the Rhaetian tribes. That the language still survives is a tribute to the independence and inherent conservatism of the Rhaetian Graubündner. These qualities also account for the persistence in the canton of numerous folk customs. Modern life has had less of an impact here than elsewhere in Switzerland. And this quality, as well as the mountains, makes walking in Graubünden a special experience.

Useful Addresses

Verkehrsverein für Graubünden (see *Address Directory*). Provides general tourist information on Graubünden. Also can provide brochures giving information on walking, cross-country skiing and other activities. Staff speaks German, French, Italian and English. Useful publications include:

- *Graubünden/Grisons* (in German; also available in French, English and Italian). A general information tourist brochure containing no specific information on footpaths, but useful for its overview of the region. Includes a map showing roads, railway lines and tourist facilities, including the locations of SAC mountain huts. Free.

- *Wandern in Graubünden* (in German). A detailed guidebook to walking routes throughout Graubünden. Includes maps. Available for a nominal charge.

- *Wanderungen in Graubünden* (in German). A brochure published by the Schweizer Reisepost—the Swiss Postal Authority—listing 32 suggested walks. For each walk there is a sketch map, brief route description, and information on how to get to and from the walk on the Swiss postautos, which *Wanderbillet* to buy, and the name of the 1:50,000 walkers' map covering the area. There is also a map in the center of the brochure showing the location of each walk. Free.

- *Via Engiadina* (in German). A leaflet published by the Schweizer Reisepost describing a six-hour walk along the Via Engiadina (Oberengadiner Höhenweg), from Signal to Maloja, on the south side of the upper Engadine Valley. Contains a route description, sketch map showing the path and its variants, and information on path markings, walking times, postauto connections and which *Wanderbillette* to buy. Also includes a postauto timetable for the area. Free.

- *Kleiner Wanderführer der Engadiner Bergbahnen* (in German). A brochure describing eight walks in the mountains around St. Moritz, in the upper Engadine Valley. For each walk there is a sketch map and brief route description. Also includes a color panorama of the area showing footpaths, rail and postauto routes and other facilities; information on special rail and postauto tickets; a brief note on winter sports; and a mini-guide to 14 local wildflowers—a nice touch. Free.

- *Klosters, Sommer-Vogelschaukarte* (in German, French, Italian and English). A color brochure with a pictorial map of the mountains around Klosters, showing footpaths, rail and postauto routes and other facilities. Lists 44 suggested walks, with the distances and walking times to and elevations of points enroute. Also includes two black and white panoramic views of the surrounding mountain ranges, showing the principal peaks and their elevations. Free.

- *Skilanglauf + Skiwandern, Kurski und Miniski* (in German). A chart listing cross-country skiing opportunities throughout Graubünden. For each town, the chart gives the length of cross-country ski tracks, their operating times, starting points, and the telephone numbers to call for information on the tracks, sport shops and cross-country ski schools. Free.

- *Schweizerischer Nationalpark/Parc National Suisse* (in German and French). A brochure listing guided nature walks in the national park. For each walk there is a brief route description and summary of the flora and fauna to be encountered, as well as information on walking time, amount of climbing required and where and when to meet. A schedule lists the days, times and meeting places for the walks. Free.

- *Laax/Falera* (in German). A brochure featuring a color pictorial map showing footpaths in blue (easy strolls) and red (longer, more difficult walks). Identified by number, each path is listed below and its walking time is given. Also included is a calendar of events and information on hotels and local cable car service. Free.

- *Madrisa Rundtour* (in German; also available in English and French). A leaflet describing a three-day walk around the Madrisa Massif. Includes a daily route description, with walking times, advice on weather and equipment, information on lodgings and the sheet numbers of necessary walking maps. Free.

- *Münstertal/Val Müstair* (in German, French and English). A brochure describing walking and cross-country skiing opportunities in the Münster Valley, the easternmost in Switzerland. Lists 14 day walks in the area and two longer excursions through the Swiss National Park. Walking times are given for each walk. Also gives information on cross-country skiing, local villages, the Swiss National Park and summer skiing. Features a color panorama showing footpaths. Free.

- *Pontresina* (in German). A brochure listing 80 walks, and the times required for each, near Pontresina, in the upper Engadine. A color panorama of the area shows each walk. Free.

* *Pontresina* (in German, French, Italian and English). A leaflet describing tourist facilities, including footpaths, walking tours, mountain guide service, SAC mountain huts, climbing schools, climbing excursions and campsites. Free.
* *Pontresina Hotel-Liste, Liste des hôtels* (in German, French and English). A guide to hotels and pensions. Free.
* *Surselva* (introduction in German, French and English; descriptions in German only). A brochure describing facilities near Surselva, in the Bündner Oberland of northwest Graubünden. Summarizes walking and cross-country skiing opportunities. Includes several color panoramas. Free.

Bündner Arbeitsgemeinschaft für Wanderwege (BAW) (see *Address Directory*). Provides information on walking throughout Graubünden. Also publishes several guidebooks (see below). Staff speaks German.

Maps

Special walkers' maps covering Graubünden are available from the Schweizerische Arbeitsgemeinschaft für Wanderwege (see *Address Directory*). They are:

* Wanderkarte 1:25,000, sheet *Valsertal-Bad Vals.*
* Wanderkarte 1:50,000, sheets *Albula-Landwasser, Arosa-Schanfigg, Davos, Disentis-Tavetsch, Flims-Laax, Lenzerheide-Thusis, Nationalpark-Münstertal, Oberengadin-Oberhalbstein, Poschiavo, Prättigau, St. Moritz, Splügen-San Bernadino, Unterengadin* and *Valsertal-Bad Vals.*
* *Reisekarte Graubünden* 1:250,000 mit Wanderwegen. A good map for planning walks.

Available from Bergverlag Rudolf Rother (see *Address Directory*):

* BV–Tourenblätter: Mappe 10 (Bernina, Engadin).

Graubünden is also covered by the 1:25,000, 1:50,000 and 1:100,000 Landeskarten published by the Eidgenössische Landestopographie (see *Address Directory*).

Guidebooks

All guidebooks are in German.

Available from Bergverlag Rudolf Rother (see *Address Directory)*:

- *Graubünden* by Condrau. Covers the entire canton.
- *Bernina* by Flaig. Covers the Engadin and Bernina-Gruppe.

Available from the Verlag des SAC (see *Address Directory)*:

- *Bündner Alpen I:* Tamina- und Plessurgebiet
- *Bündner Alpen II:* Oberland-Rheinwald
- *Bündner Alpen IV:* Bergeller Berge und Monte Disgrazia
- *Bündner Alpen V:* Berninagruppe
- *Bündner Alpen VI:* Albula (Septimer-Flüela)
- *Bündner Alpen VII:* Rhätikon
- *Bündner Alpen VIII:* Silvretta und Samnaun
- *Bündner Alpen IX:* Unterengadin, Münstertal, Nationalpark
- *Bündner Alpen X:* Mittleres Engadin und Puschlav (Spöl-Bernina-pass-Puschlav)

Available from the Schweizerische Arbeitsgemeinschaft für Wanderwege (see *Address Directory)* and most bookstores:

- *Wandern in Graubünden* (also available from Verkehrsverein für Graubünden).
- *Mit dem Auto zum Wanderwege: Rundwanderungen in Graubünden,* Verlag TCS, Chur.
- *Wanderbuch 3: Oberengadin,* Kümmerly + Frey.
- *Wanderbuch 4: Unterengadin,* Kümmerly + Frey.
- *Wanderbuch 11: Davos,* Kümmerly + Frey.
- *Wanderbuch 24: Prättigau,* Kümmerly + Frey.
- *Wanderbuch 26: Valsertal,* Kümmerly + Frey.
- *Wanderbuch 28: Bergell,* Kümmerly + Frey.
- *Wanderbuch 30: Schanfigg-Arosa,* Kümmerly + Frey.
- *Wanderbuch 32: Puschlav,* Kümmerly + Frey.
- *Wanderbuch 35: Misox,* Kümmerly + Frey.
- *Wanderführer Albula,* Bündner Arbeitsgemeinschaft für Wanderwege (BAW), Chur.
- *Wanderführer Disentis,* BAW.

- *Wanderführer Flims-Laax,* BAW.
- *Wanderführer Herrschaft-Fünf Dörfer,* BAW.
- *Wanderführer Lenzerheide,* BAW.
- *Wanderführer Oberhalbstein,* BAW.
- *Wanderführer Rheinwald,* BAW.
- *Wanderführer Schams-Avers,* BAW.
- *Wanderführer Sedrun,* BAW.

Suggested Walks

Madrisa Rundtour: A spectacular circular walk from Klosters to Saaseralp and around the Madrisa Massif. A section of the walk passes through Austria (passports required). Visits several remote, largely unspoiled valleys and crosses three high passes. Offers sweeping views of countless distant ranges as well as close-up looks at the gneiss and limestone peaks of the Madrisa Massif. **Walking Time:** 3 days. **Difficulty:** Easy to moderately difficult (several steep ascents). **Path Markings:** Red and white horizontal bars.
Maps:
- Wanderkarte 1:50,000, sheet *Prättigau.* Or:
- Landeskarte der Schweiz, 1:25,000, sheet 1177.
Guidebooks:
- *Madrisa Rundtour* (in German, English or French versions). Available from Verkehrsverein für Graubünden (see *Address Directory).*
- *Wanderbuch Grüne 24: Prättigau,* Kümmerly + Frey.

Via Engiadina (Oberengadiner Höhenweg): From Signal to Maloja, along the three large lakes at the head of the Engadine Valley. Through forest and meadows, with views across the valley to the glacier-clad Bernina peaks. **Walking Time:** 3 to 4 hours. **Difficulty:** Easy. **Path Markings:** Yellow and blue signs.
Maps:
- Wanderkarte 1:50,000, sheet *Oberengadin-Oberhalbstein.* Or:
- Landeskarte der Schweiz, 1:50,000, sheet 268.
Guidebooks:
- *Via Engiadina* (in German). Available from Verkehrsverein für Graubünden.

Wieseneralpen Rundtour: A circular walk through the mountains near Wiesen, a village in the beautiful Landwassertal. Through forest and flowery meadows with views of the valley and the craggy peaks of the Wieseneralp. **Walking Time:** 5 hours. **Difficulty:** Easy to moderately difficult. **Path Markings:** Red and white horizontal bars.
Maps:
- Wanderkarte 1:50,000, sheet *Albula-Landwasser.* Or:
- Landeskarte der Schweiz 1:50,000, sheet 258.

Guidebook:
* *Wanderführer Albula* (in German), Bündner Arbeitsgemeinschaft für Wanderwege (BAW).

From Chur to Andermatt. Up the beautiful valley of the Rhine, with its castles, monasteries, charming villages, meadows and forests to Oberalppass and down to Andermatt, in Uri canton. Numerous side trips possible into the Bündner Oberland. **Walking Time:** 4 to 6 days. **Difficulty:** Easy to moderately difficult. **Path Markings:** Yellow arrows, bars and diamonds.

Maps:
* Wanderkarten 1:50,000, sheets *Disentis-Tavetsch* and *Flims-Laax*. Or:
* Landeskarte der Schweiz, 1:50,000, sheets 247, 248, 255, 256, and 257.

Guidebook:
* *On Foot Through Switzerland* (in English), Schweizerische Verkehrszentrale.

Cross-Country Skiing

Graubünden has more than 30 ski centers with marked tracks totaling more than 600 kilometers. In addition, there are over 20 marked cross-country routes. For full details, see the booklet published by the Schweizerische Arbeitsgemeinschaft für Wanderwege, *Ski Wandern/Ski de Randonnée* (described in the section on *Cross-Country Skiing*). You can also obtain sketch maps from the SAW showing marked ski tracks described in the booklet. In addition, the *DSV Langlauf Kompass* and *Skilanglauf Atlas* (described under "Guidebooks" in the section on *Cross-Country Skiing)* list many marked cross-country tracks in Graubünden. Finally, the Verkehrsverein für Graubünden can supply sketch maps showing marked ski tracks near many towns and villages in the canton.

Nordwestschweiz (Northwest Switzerland)

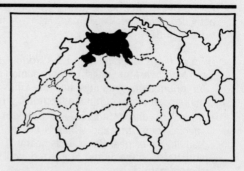

Nordwestschweiz, which includes the cantons of Solothurn, Basel, Baselland, and Aargau, is unlike the Switzerland of storybooks and travel brochures. No Alps, no chalets, no alpenhorns, no Wilhelm Tell. A visitor is more likely to be reminded of neighboring Germany and Alsace, with which Nordwestschweiz has close historical and cultural ties. The medieval towns along the Rhine, the region's more than 50 castles and chateaus—including the family seat of the Habsburgs—the churches and sandstone townhouses of Basel: these and other, subtler touches lend to Nordwestschweiz a distinctly Northern European flavor.

The region's economic and cultural center is the city of Basel, Switzerland's second largest, which straddles the Rhine where Switzerland, France and Germany meet. Founded in Roman times, Basel, home of Erasmus and the Holbeins, was for centuries one of the most important cities in Europe. It remains a lively center of learning and commerce and, owing to its location on the Rhine, is Switzerland's only major port. Its museum is one of the finest in Europe.

Southeast of Basel rise the tablelands of the Jura, from which you can see the Vosges Mountains of Alsace, the Schwarzwald of southern Germany and across the Mittelland, the snowy summits of the Alps from Uri to Mont Blanc. Covering most of Nordwestschweiz, the Jura offers excellent walking and cross-country skiing among beechwoods, meadowy glens, idyllic farms, ridge-top pasturelands, fertile river valleys and narrow gorges ringing with the music of cascades and waterfalls. At 1,445 meters elevation, Hasenmatt, in the canton of Solothurn, is the highest summit in the Jura of Nordwestschweiz.

The region includes, in addition to the Jura and Rhine Valley, the gentle hills and valleys of the Mittelland. Here, you can walk among tidy farmlands, follow the winding courses of the Aare and Reuss rivers and visit picturesque rural villages and lovely old towns such as Solothurn, Olten and Aarau. Here too is the region's largest lake, the Hallwilersee.

Useful Addresses

Nordwestschweizerische Verkehrsvereinigung (see *Address Directory*). Provides general tourist information on Nordwestschweiz. Also can provide brochures giving information on walking and other activities. Staff speaks German, French, and English. Useful publications include:

- *For Millions, Switzerland in the Northwest; For You, Switzerland in the Northwest* (in English). A tourist map of Nordwestschweiz useful for orientation. Includes line drawings and brief descriptions of major scenic and cultural attractions. Free.
- *Rundfahrt- und Wanderbillette: Basel* (in German). Lists the fares of special round-trip and walker's tickets on the SBB (Swiss Federal Railway) lines near Basel. Lists nearly 50 walks, with walking times and train connections. Suggested walking routes are shown on sketch maps. Free.
- *Treffpunkt Postauto* (in German). Lists 15 strolls and longer walks between postbus stops in the region surrounding Basel. Each walk description includes a sketch map showing the route and connecting bus lines, as well as information about bus connections, ticket prices, route itinerary and walking time. Includes a map showing postauto lines in Nordwestschweiz. Also lists walkers' maps for the region and provides information on the REKA Wanderpass (see the section on *Walking Tours* earlier in this chapter). Free.
- *Geführte Wanderungen* (in German). Lists 32 walking tours conducted by the SBB (Swiss Federal Railway) tour office in Basel. Gives the date, price, itinerary and walking time of each tour. Free.
- *Diese Woche in Basel* (in German, French and English). Lists tourist attractions and events in Basel. Includes descriptions of two circular walks in the city. Also gives the addresses and telephone numbers of local tourist information offices. Free.
- *Hotelliste/Guide des Hotels/List of Hotels* (in German). A guide to hotels in Nordwestschweiz. Includes youth hostels. Free.
- *Baselland* (in German). A general tourist brochure. Summarizes walking and cross-country skiing possibilities and lists the starting points for several excursions. Includes a pictorial map of the Basel region, with major footpaths shown in red. Free.

Waldenburgerbahn AG (see *Address Directory*). One of the many privately owned small railways in Switzerland. Provides information on walking in the area serviced by the Waldenburgerbahn. As a nostalgic feature, the railway also offers trips by steam railway every third Sunday from May to October. Staff speaks French and German. Useful publications include:

- *Wandervorschläge der Waldenburgerbahn* (in German). A booklet containing 12 cards, each with a sketch map and brief description of a suggested walk in the area serviced by the Waldenburgerbahn. Lists the walkers' maps needed for each walk. Free.

- *Vorschläge für lohnende Wanderungen* (in German). A leaflet with a sketch map of the area serviced by the Waldenburgerbahn. Lists 50 suggested walks from various stops along its routes. Gives brief information on each town; estimated walking times are also given. Free.
- *Die Waldenburgerbahn* (in German). A booklet describing the past and present of the railway. Free.

Aargauische Verkehrsvereinigung (see *Address Directory*). Provides walking information for all of Aargau. Also sells maps and guidebooks. Staff speaks German and French.

Wanderwege beider Basel (see *Address Directory*). Provides walking information for all of Basel. Also sells maps and guidebooks and conducts walking tours. Staff speaks German and French.

Solothurner Wanderwege (see *Address Directory*). Provides walking information for all of Solothurn. Also sells maps and guidebooks. Staff speaks German and French.

Maps

Special walkers' maps covering Nordwestschweiz are available from the Schweizerische Arbeitsgemeinschaft für Wanderwege (see *Address Directory*). They are:

- Wanderkarte 1:50,000, sheets *Kanton Aargau, Basel und Umgebung* and *Solothurn und Umgebung.*
- Spezialkarte des Jura, 1:50,000, sheets 1 *Aargau–Lägeren–Bözberg,* 2 *Basel–Baselland–Olten* and 3 *Solothurn–Delémont–Porrentruy.*

All the Wanderkarten are published by Kümmerly + Frey.
  Nordwestschweiz is also covered by the 1:25,000, 1:50,000 and 1:100,000 Landeskarten published by the Schweiz Eidgenössiche Landestopographie (see *Address Directory*).

Guidebooks

All guidebooks are in German unless otherwise noted below.

Available from the Verlag des SAC (see *Address Directory):*

- *Escalades dans le Jura:* Vol. II, Moutier-Raimeux-Bâle-Olten (in French).

Available from the SAW (see *Address Directory*) and most bookstores:
- *Wanderbuch 1: Basel I,* Kümmerly + Frey.

- *Wanderbuch 2: Basel II,* Kümmerly + Frey.
- *Wanderbuch 5: Olten und Umgebung,* Kümmerly + Frey.
- *Wanderbuch 6: Solothurn Umgebung,* Kümmerly + Frey.
- *Wanderbuch 14: Baden,* Kümmerly + Frey.
- *Wanderbuch 16: Jurahöhenwege,* Kümmerly + Frey.
- *Guide pédestre vert 16a: Chemins des Crêtes du Jura Suisse* (in French), Kümmerly + Frey.
- *Wanderbuch 18: Seetal-Freiamt, Wynetal,* Kümmerly + Frey.
- *Wanderbuch Blau 2: Spazierwege Rund um Basel,* Kümmerly + Frey.
- *Rundtourenbände: Rundwanderungen Aargau,* Kümmerly + Frey.
- *Wanderungen in der Regio Basiliensis,* Verlag TCS, Basel.

Suggested Walks

From Grellingen to Hohe Winde. Through the Kaltbrunnen Valley, with its cliffs, Stone Age caves, woods, pastures and rural villages, to a panoramic viewpoint from the summit of Hohe Winde. **Walking Time:** 5 hours. **Difficulty:** Easy to moderate. **Path Markings:** Yellow and red horizontal bars.
Maps:
- Spezialkarte des Jura, 1:50,000, sheet 2 *Basel-Baselland-Olten*. Or:
- Landeskarte der Schweiz, 1:50,000, sheets 213, 214 and 223.
Guidebook:
- *Wanderbuch Grüne 1: Basel I,* Kümmerly + Frey.

From Baden to Grenchenberge. Through Nordwestschweiz along the crest of the Jura, with views southward across the Mittelland to the Alps and northward to the Vosges and Schwarzwald. Follows the Jurahöhenwege (European Long-Distance Footpath E-4). **Walking Time:** 4 to 5 days. **Difficulty:** Easy to moderately difficult. **Path Markings:** Yellow and red horizontal bars.
Maps:
- Spezialkarte des Jura 1:50,000, sheets 1 *Aargau-Lägaren-Bözberg,* 2 *Basel-Baselland-Olten* and 3 *Solothurn-Delémont-Porrentruy.*
Guidebooks:
- *Wanderbuch 16: Jurahöhenwege* (in German) or *Guide pédestre 16a: Chemins des crêtes du Jura Suisse* (in French), Kümmerly + Frey.

From Talhaus to Waldenburg. Takes you past a lovely castle at Wildenstein, through groves of old oak trees and past ancient farming communities. From Wil, there is a beautiful view of the surrounding countryside. Steep descent into Waldenburg. **Walking Time:** 4½ hours. **Difficulty:** Easy to moderately difficult. **Path Markings:** Yellow triangles and horizontal bars

Maps:
- Spezialkarte de Jura 1:50,000, sheet 2 *Basel-Baselland-Olten*. Or:
- Landeskarte der Schweiz 1:25,000, sheets 1068 and 1088.

Guidebook:
- *Wandervorschläge der Waldenburgerbahn* (in German). Available from the Waldenburgurbahn (see *Address Directory*).

Cross-Country Skiing

Nordwestschweiz has five ski centers with marked tracks totaling more than 50 kilometers. In addition, there is one marked cross-country route near Grenchenberge. For full details, see the booklet published by the Schweizerische Arbeitsgemeinschaft für Wanderwege, *Ski Wandern/Ski de Randonnée*. You can also obtain sketch maps from the SAW showing marked ski tracks described in the booklet. Finally, the Nordwestschweizerische Verkehrsvereinigung can supply sketch maps showing marked ski tracks near many towns and villages in the region.

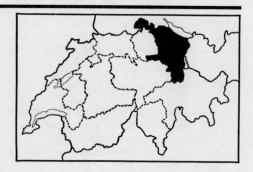

Ostschweiz (East Switzerland)

Ostschweiz, which includes the cantons of St. Gallen, Appenzell, Glarus, Thurgau and Schaffhausen, occupies Switzerland's northeast corner. The Rhine Valley borders the region on the east, separating it from Austria and the principality of Liechtenstein. The river flows north to empty into the Bodensee (Lake Constance), Switzerland's second largest lake, then west into smaller Untersee and across the lowlands of Thurgau and Schaffhausen. At Neuhausen, the river plunges 21 meters at the Falls of the Rhine. Ostschweiz is bordered on the west by Zürich and Zentralschweiz and on the south by Graubünden.

The region offers a cross-section of Swiss landscapes—hills, mountains and valleys, large lakes and small, Alpine torrents and the mighty Rhine. The northern half of the region, including Schaffhausen, Thurgau and part of St. Gallen, presents a typical Mittelland landscape of wooded hills, broad, open plains and meandering rivers. This lowland is bordered on the south by the Alpine foothills, which culminate in Appenzell in the spectacular limestone crescent of the Alpstein Massif.

Appenzell is one of the most idyllic places in all of Switzerland. The town nestles among rolling green hills, accented here and there with wooded crests—all within view of the Alpstein peaks. Scattered over the countryside are the lovely Appenzeller farmhouses, which combine house, barn and shed under a single gabled and shingled roof. Appenzell is one of the few cantons in Switzerland where citizens of each community still gather in traditional democratic assemblies, or *Landsgemeinden*. Here, too, people still wear traditional costumes and practice such time-honored crafts as embroidery.

South of the Alpstein lies the equally beautiful Toggenburg Valley, a great trough of rolling meadows bounded on either side by rugged peaks. Scattered villages command views of the Alpstein to the north and the equally rugged, though somewhat lower Churfirsten Alps on the south. Beyond this range, lies the long, deep Walensee and yet farther south, the awesome peaks of the Glarner Alps.

The canton of Glarus, or Glarnerland, is a great maze of ranges separated by broad, deep valleys. Dozens of lakes nestle among the peaks, and glaciers mantle the higher crests. Presiding over the region is Tödi (3,623 meters), the highest peak in Ostschweiz. The entire canton is dotted with tiny villages, whose citizens, like those of Appenzell, still gather once a year in the traditional *Landsgemeinden*.

Useful Addresses

Nordostschweizerische Verkehrsvereinigung (see *Address Directory*). Provides general tourist information for Ostschweiz. Also can provide brochures giving information on walking, cross-country skiing and other activities. Staff ·speaks German, French and English. Useful publications include:

- *Ostschweiz* (in German, French, Italian and English). A color pictorial map of the entire region. Shows some major footpaths. Useful for general orientation. Free.

- *Ostschweiz: Winterparadies Ostschweiz und Fürstentum Liechtenstein* (in German). A color pictorial map of Ostschweiz in winter. On the reverse side, it lists winter sports facilities, including resorts with cross-country ski schools and the locations and distances of marked ski tracks and cross-country routes. Free.

- *Appenzell Innerrhoden* (in German, French and English). A leaflet providing general tourist information for Appenzell. Includes the addresses and telephone numbers of local tourist information offices, youth hostel, campgrounds and mountain climbing school. Also lists walkers' maps for the region. Free.

- *Appenzell Innerrhoden: Wandervorschläge* (in German). A leaflet listing nearly 50 walks in Appenzell. Provides a route summary and gives walking times for each. Also lists six marked ski tracks (with telephone numbers for further information) and two marked cross-country ski routes. Includes a sketch map showing footpaths, with walking times from point to point. Also lists walkers' maps and guidebooks. Free.

- *Appenzell Innerrhoden:* Winterinformation (in German). Describes winter sports facilities. Includes a list of six marked ski tracks and three marked cross-country ski routes, which are shown on sketch maps. Also gives the addresses and telephone numbers of local cross-country skiing schools. Free.

- *Bad Ragaz* (in German, French, Italian and English). A general information tourist brochure. Includes a leaflet listing hotels and guest houses. A second leaflet, *Wanderprogramm Sommer,* contains a color sketch map showing 21 footpaths on nearby Pizol peak and gives the walking time for each. Free.

- *Beim Wandern Mehr Erleben* (in German). A leaflet describing a 300-kilometer circuit around Bodensee and Untersee. Includes a sketch map showing the route and graphs giving distances between points along the route. Free.

- *Braunwald* (in German). A general information tourist brochure about Braunwald, in the Glarner Alps. Includes a pictorial map of the district, showing cross-country ski tracks and footpaths. Free.

- *Sportbahnen Elm* (in German). A general information tourist brochure on Elm, in the Glarner Alps. Includes a pictorial map of the district, showing footpaths and indicating areas where wildlife is likely to be seen. Lists seven footpaths (each numbered on the map) and gives their walking times. Free.

- *Erholung im Toggenburg* (in German, French and English). A lodging list for the Toggenburg Valley. Gives addresses, rates and facilities for each establishment. Also includes the addresses and telephone numbers of local tourist information offices. Free.

- *Flumserberge* (in German, French and English). A pictorial map showing marked cross-country tracks, cleared winter paths and other winter facilities at Flumserberge, in the Glarner Alps overlooking Walensee. A supplementary leaflet, *Flumserberge: Information, Winter,* describes winter sports facilities, including two marked ski tracks and one cross-country route. A second leaflet, *Hotelliste: Winter in den Flumserbergen,* lists lodgings and their facilities and includes a sketch map showing, among other things, marked ski tracks and cleared winter paths. Free.

- *Ihr Wanderweg nach Teufen* (in German). A leaflet listing 30 short walks near Teufen, in Appenzellerland. Gives walking times and points enroute for each walk. Includes a black-and-white reproduction of a Landeskarte showing the routes. Free.

- *Komm ins Glarnerland: ins Wander-Paradies* (in German). Pamphlet describing four walking routes in Glarus. A sketch map showing the route in red accompanies each description. Free.
- *Pizol* (in German). A brochure describing walking and downhill skiing routes on Pizol peak, in southern St. Gallen. Includes two color sketch maps of the peak, one showing ski facilities; the other, 10 walking routes. Gives walking times for 10 short routes and for the 5 Seen Wanderung (5 Lakes Route). Free.
- *Rundfahrt- und Wanderbillette: St. Gallen* (in German). One in a series of booklets published by the Schweizerischen Bundesbahnen (SBB)—the Swiss Federal Railway. Contains five sketch maps, each showing a series of suggested walks. Information on special train fares within the region covered by each map is also given. Free.
- *Rundfahrt- und Wanderbillette: Schaffhausen* (in German). Similar to the above booklet. Contains four sketch maps showing suggested walks. Free.
- *St. Gallen* (in German). Leaflet showing 10 walks near the city of St. Gallen. Each is illustrated on a sketch map. Brief route descriptions and walking times are included. Bus and rail lines are shown on a color map of St. Gallen and its environs. Free.
- *Sernftal* (in German). A lodgings list for Sernftal, a valley in Glarus. Includes a list of mountain huts and telephone numbers to call for information on marked ski tracks. Free.
- *Sie möchten wandern oder einen schönen Spaziergang unternehmen—und Sie wissen nicht wohin? Da können wir Ihnen helfen!* (in German). A leaflet listing 30 walks served by the Bodensee-Toggenburg railway. Free.
- *30 Wandervorschläge in der Nordost- und Zentralschweiz* (in German). A booklet describing 30 walks served by the Bodensee-Toggenburg railway. Includes sketch maps, train connections and walking times.
- *Wanderkarte des Oberen Neckertals* (in German). A color sketch map showing footpaths near St. Peterzell and Schönengrund, in the Neckertal region of St. Gallen. Free.
- *Wandern im Sommer und Herbst* (in German). A leaflet describing six walks near Reitbach-Wolzenalp-Speer. Free.
- *Wanderungen Zwischen Bodensee und Klausenpass* (in German). A booklet published by the Schweizer Reisepost—the Swiss Postal Authority—listing 28 walks in Ostschweiz. For each walk there is a sketch map, brief route description and information on how to get to and from the walk on the Swiss Postautos, which *Wanderbillet* to buy, and the name of the 1:50,000 walkers' map covering the area. There is also a map in the center of the booklet showing the location of each walk. Free.

- *Wildhaus, Unterwasser, Alt St. Johann* (in German, French and English). A leaflet describing winter sports facilities near Wildhaus, Unterwasser and Alt St. Johann, in the upper Toggenburg. Includes a color pictorial map showing marked ski tracks and other facilities.
- *Wildhaus, Unterwasser, Alt St. Johann: Wintersport Obertoggenburg, Information Hotelliste* (in German and French, with some English translation). Lodging list for the upper Toggenburg Valley and nearby mountains. Gives the addresses and telephone numbers of two local cross-country ski schools.

Verband Appenzell Ausserrhoden Verkehrsvereine (see *Address Directory*). Provides walking information for Appenzell Ausserrhoden (Outer Appenzel). Staff speaks German.

Kur- und Verkehrsverein Appenzell Innerrhoden (see *Address Directory*). Provides walking information for Appenzell Innerrhoden (Inner Appenzell). Staff speaks German.

Verkehrsverein Glarnerland und Walensee (see *Address Directory*). Provides walking information for Glarnerland. Staff speaks German. Useful publications include:

- *Komm ins Glarnerland: ins Wander-Paradies* (in German). A book-let describing five walks in Glarnerland. Includes sketch maps. Free.

Kantonal St.-Gallische Wanderwege (see *Address Directory*). Provides walking information for all of St. Gallen. Publishes three walking guides (see below). Staff speaks German.

Schaffhauser Arbeitsgemeinschaft für Wanderwege (see *Address Directory*). Provides walking information for Schaffhausen. Staff speaks German.

Wanderwegkommission des Kantons Thurgau (see *Address Directory*). Provides walking information for Thurgau. Staff speaks German.

Maps

Special walkers' maps covering Ostschweiz are available from the Schweizerische Arbeitsgemeinschaft für Wanderwege (see *Address Directory*). They are:

- Wanderkarte 1:25,000, sheets *Flumserberge-Walensee, Niederurnen, Obertoggenburg* and *Schaffhausen*.
- Wander- und Skitourenkarte, 1:25,000, sheet *Obertoggenburg*.
- Wanderkarte 1:50,000, sheets *Bodensee/Walensee, Liechtenstein/ St. Galler Rheintal, St. Gallen-Appenzell, Thurgauer Wanderkarte,*

Toggenburg/St. Galler Oberland, Untersee und Rhein and *Zürich-Schaffhausen.*

• Wanderkarte 1:75,000, sheets *Bodensee-Gesamtgebiet* and *Schwarzwald* (Nr. 11 *Nordblatt,* Nr. 12 *Mittelblatt* and Nr. 13 *Südblatt).*

• Wanderkarte 1:100,000, sheet *Bodensee.*

Ostschweiz is also covered by the 1:25,000, 1:50,000 and 1:100,000 Landeskarten published by the Eidgenössiche Landestopographie (see *Address Directory).*

Guidebooks

All the guides listed below are in German.

Available from the Verlag des SAC (see *Address Directory):*

• *Glarner Alpen* (mit Skiführer). Includes information on ski touring.

Available from Bergverlag Rudolf Rother (see *Address Directory):*

• *Allgäuer Bergland* by Kornacher.

Available from the SAW (see *Address Directory)* and most bookstores:

• *Wanderbuch 7: St. Gallen-Appenzell,* Kümmerly + Frey.
• *Wanderbuch 34: Glarnerland,* Kümmerly + Frey.
• *Wanderbuch 38: Schaffhausen,* Kümmerly + Frey.
• *Wanderbuch Rot 2: Bodensee,* Kümmerly + Frey.
• *Bodensee-Rundwanderweg,* Kümmerly + Frey.
• *Wanderbücher St. Gallen: Buch 1) St. Gallen-Fürstenland-Rheintal-Appenzellerland; Buch 2) Toggenburg;* and *Buch 3) St. Galler Oberland-Werdenberg-See und Gaster,* Kantonal St. Gallische Wanderwege.
• *Heimat- und Wanderführer Reiat* (Schaffhausen), Verlag P. Meili.
• *Mit dem Auto zum Wanderweg Thurgau,* Verlag Huber & Co.
• *Thurgauer Wanderbuch,* Verlag Huber & Co.
• *Wandervorschläge Appenzellerland,* Verlag Trogenerbahn.

Suggested Walks

Wasserauen to Säntis. Up a broad, meadowy valley flanked by crags, past beautiful Seealp Lake, to the summit of Säntis, monarch of the Alpstein.

From the top, panoramic views of Appenzell, the St. Gallen lowlands, Bodensee, the Toggenburg and the Glarner Alps. **Walking Time:** 5 hours. **Difficulty:** Easy to moderately difficult, with a steep ascent of Säntis. **Path Markings:** Yellow arrows, bars and diamonds.
Maps:
• Wanderkarte 1:50,000, sheet *St. Gallen-Appenzell.* Or:
• Landeskarte der Schweiz 1:25,000, special sheet 2506.
Guidebooks:
• *Wanderbuch 7: St. Gallen-Appenzell,* Kümmerly + Frey. Or:
• *Wanderbücher St. Gallen: Buch 1) St. Gallen-Fürstenland-Rheintal-Appenzellerland,* Kantonal St. Gallische Wanderwege. Or:
• *Wandervorschläge Appenzellerland,* Verlag Trogenerbahn.

Wanderwege rund um den Bodensee. A circular walk around Bodensee and nearby Untersee. Carry a passport because part of the route is through Germany. May be taken from any point along the route, but Konstanz, between the two lakes, is the usual place to start. Along the gentle lakeshores with views toward the distant Alps. **Length:** 250 kilometers. **Walking Time:** 12 to 16 days. **Difficulty:** Easy. **Path Markings:** Yellow arrows, bars and triangles in Switzerland; vary in Germany.
Maps:
• Wanderkarte 1:75,000, sheet *Bodensee-Gesamtgebiet.*
Guidebook:
• *Wanderbuch Rot 2: Bodensee,* Kümmerly + Frey.

Toggenburg Circuit. From Alt. St. Johann over the gentle, wooded Mittelberg ridge to Gräppelensee, a secluded lake at the base of Säntis. Then up the valley to Alpli and back over the ridge to Unterwasser. Glorious views of Säntis and the Churfirsten Range across the Toggenburg Valley. From Unterwasser, east along the road to Lisighaus, then up to Schwendi Lake in the Churfirsten foothills. Finally, a long, easy foothill traverse to Alp Sellamatt and back down to Alt. St. Johann. Glorious views throughout of Säntis, the Toggenburg and the Churfirsten Range. **Walking Time:** 6 to 7 hours. **Difficulty:** Easy to moderate. **Path Markings:** Yellow arrows, bars and diamonds.
Maps:
• Wanderkarte 1:50,000, sheet *Toggenburg/St. Galler Oberland.* Or:
• Landeskarte der Schweiz, 1:50,000, sheets 227 and 237.
Guidebooks:
• *Wanderbücher St. Gallen: Buch 2) Toggenburg,* Kantonal St. Gallische Wanderwege. Or:
• *Wanderungen Zwischen Bodensee und Klausenpass* (in German), walks 15 and 16. Available from Nordostschweizerische Verkehrsvereinigung.

From Tierfehd village to the Grünhornhütte. A high trip through the Glarner Alps, with overnight stays at the Planura, Fridolin and Grünhorn mountain huts. Close-up views of Glarner peaks, including Claridenstock,

Piz Cazarauls, Bifertenstock and Tödi. Glacier crossing optional. If you plan to do so, a guide is necessary. **Walking Time:** 3 days. **Difficulty:** Moderately difficult to difficult. **Path Markings:** Red and white horizontal bars.
Maps:
• Landeskarte der Schweiz, 1:25,000, sheet 1193. Or:
• Landeskarte der Schweiz, 1:50,000, sheet 246.
Guidebook:
• *Glarner Alpen,* Verlag des SAC.

Cross-Country Skiing

Ostschweiz has some 50 ski centers with marked tracks totaling more than 465 kilometers. In addition, there are 27 marked cross-country routes. For full details, see the booklet published by the Schweizerische Arbeitsgemeinschaft für Wanderwege, *Skiwandern/Ski de Randonnée.* You can also obtain sketch maps from the SAW showing marked ski tracks described in the booklet. In addition, the *DSV Langlauf Kompass* and *Skilanglauf Atlas* (described under "Guidebooks" in the section on *Cross-Country Skiing)* describe many marked cross-country tracks in Ostschweiz. Finally, the Nordostschweizerische Verkehrsvereinigung can supply sketch maps showing marked ski tracks near many towns and villages in the region.

Région du Léman (Lake Geneva Region)

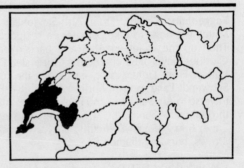

The Région du Léman lies in extreme southwestern Switzerland, encompassing the cantons of Vaud and Genève. It forms a broad, irregular crescent around the northern shore of Lac Léman (Lake Geneva) and includes portions of the Jura, Mittelland and Alps. The lakeshore is heavily populated, but the rest of the region is given over to farmlands, terraced vineyards, rolling hills and rugged mountains, where scattered villages and small towns nestle in verdant valleys.

Lac Léman occupies a deep, broad basin along the valley of the Rhône, which enters the lake on the east and leaves it at the westernmost end on its way toward France and the Mediterranean. The lake is Switzerland's largest: 72 kilometers long, 13 kilometers across at its widest point and about 300 meters deep. On its shores sit the cities of Genève and Lausanne, Switzerland's third and fifth largest, as well as numerous villages and resorts, including fashionable Montreux, whose grand old hotels and Mediterranean-style villas front on a magnolia-lined promenade, with a lake-edge view of the Mont Blanc Massif on the French side of the lake. There are also several castles near the lake, including the former home of Madame de Stael and the wildly romantic Château du Chillon, which sits on a small island in the lake near Montreux and was immortalized in poetry by Lord Byron.

Rising above the western end of the lake are the parallel ridges of the Jura Mountains, with their open, sometimes rocky crests, wooded slopes and lush, pastoral valleys. Some regard the Vallée de Joux, with its large lake, as the most beautiful in all the Jura. Nearby rise the sharp crest of Dent de Vaulion and the gentle summit of Mont Tendre, from which you have a breathtaking view of Lac Léman and the Alps from Jüngfrau to Mont Blanc.

Between the Jura and the lake lies the gentle Mittelland, with its vineyards, farms, small villages and scattered medieval castles. The Vaudois Mittelland extends north to the southern end of Lac de Neuchâtel. It is bordered on the south by the Alpine foothills, which rise in terraced steps from the shores of Lac Léman.

The Vaudois Alps rise above the lake near Vevey and Montreux and extend eastward to merge imperceptibly with the Berner Oberland. They are characterized by ragged sawtooth crests flanked by sprawling parklands and broad, green valleys. Numerous steeply gabled and ornately decorated chalets are scattered over the high pasturelands, where cattle graze through the summer. The most prominent peaks are the bold Rochers de Naye, which rise abruptly above Montreux, and Les Diablerets, a ridge of limestone pinnacles on the Valais border.

Useful Addresses

Office du Tourisme du Canton de Vaud (see *Address Directory*). Provides general tourist information for Région du Léman. Also can provide brochures giving information on walking, cross-country skiing and other activities. Staff speaks French, German and English. Useful publications include:

- *Région du Léman* (in French, German and English). A general tourist brochure. Includes a list of recreational facilities, including campgrounds, at various places in the region. Free.

- *Canton de Vaud* (in French, German and English). A general tourist guidebook to the region. Describes various attractions and activities, mentions places where you can walk or cross-country ski.

Lists the address and telephone numbers of local tourist offices and lodgings, including guesthouses and youth hostels.

- *Lake of Geneva Official Guide Book* (in English). Published annually by the Compagnie Générale de Navigation du Lac Léman (C.G.N.), operator of the lake steamships. A general tourist guidebook. Free.

- *Nord Vaudois* (in French, German and English). A collection of leaflets describing tourist attractions near the Lac de Neuchâtel. Includes leaflets on camping and lodgings. Indicates places with cross-country ski tracks. Free.

- *Plan de Situation: Chesières-Villars-Arveyes* (in French). A map of the district around the resort of Villars, in the Vaudois Alps. Shows footpaths. Free.

- *Hauts de Montreux: Itinéraires pédestres* (in French). An excellent color walkers' map of the mountains above Montreux, including the Rochers de Naye. Footpaths and cross-country routes are shown in red; marked ski tracks in blue. The map is a reproduction of a 1:25,000 Landeskarte der Schweiz and therefore is extremely detailed. Walks shown on the map are listed on the reverse side. The basic itinerary and walking time is given for each walk. Also lists hotels and restaurants, points of interest and tourist information offices. Available for a nominal charge.

- *Promenades: Région du Mt. Pelerin* (in French). A leaflet with three panoramic photographs on which 23 walks are shown in green. Parking places and railways are also indicated. Includes a brief route outline and gives the walking times for each walk. Also lists restaurants and lodgings in the district. Free.

- *Promenades dans la Région de Vevey* (in French). A collection of 10 leaflets describing walks in the region around Vevey and Montreux. Each leaflet describes a walk in detail and includes brief notes on route difficulty, equipment, means of transportation to and from the walk, walking time and sundry other information. Also includes a separate map on which all the walks are shown. Free.

- *Glion sur Montreux* (in French, German, Italian and English). General tourist brochure with a color pictorial map showing the mountains above Montreux and the roads and footpaths winding up and among them. Includes a separate hotel list. Free.

- *Les Diablerets* (in French, German and English). A brochure describing holiday facilities at the resort of Les Diablerets, below the peaks of the same name in the Vaudois Alps. Includes a color pictorial map of the area in winter. Free.

- *Chemin de Fer Montreux-Oberland Bernois* (in French, German, Italian and English). An advertisement brochure for the MOB railway. Includes a color pictorial map of the Vaudois Alps, through which the line passes.

- *MOB* (in French and German). Schedule for the Montreux-Oberland Bernois (MOB) railway. Includes schedules for buses, aerial tramways and ski lifts in the Vaudois Alps and western Berner Oberland. Also contains a color pictorial map of the region in winter. Free.
- *Vallée de Joux* (in French, German and English). General tourist brochure. Includes a color pictorial map of the area. Free.
- *Possibilités d'Hébergement Avantageu pour Groupes, Jeunes, Individuels dans le Canton de Vaud* (in French). A lodging list for Vaud. Includes youth hostels, chalets and mountain refuges. Gives telephone number, capacity, rates, operation dates and other information for each. Free.

Association Genevoise de Tourisme Pédestre (see *Address Directory*). Provides walking information for the canton of Genève. Staff speaks French and German.

Association Vaudoise de Tourisme Pédestre (see *Address Directory*). Provides walking information for Vaud. Staff speaks French and German.

Maps

Special walkers' maps covering the Région du Léman are available from the Schweizerische Arbeitsgemeinschaft für Wanderwege (see *Address Directory*). They are:

- Wanderkarte 1:25,000, sheets *Lausanne et Environs, Est Vaudois* and *Les Diablerets*.
- Carte Speciale du Jura 1:50,000, sheets 5 *Yverdon-Ste Croix-Val de Travers* and 6 *Lausanne-La Côte-St Cergue-Vallée de Joux*.

Special walkers' maps are also available for Saint-Cergue, Montreux, Château d'Oex et Environs and Leysin.

The Région du Léman is also covered by the 1:25,000, 1:50,000 and 1:100,000 Landeskarten published by the Eidgenössiche Landestopographie (see *Address Directory*).

Guidebooks

Available from the Verlag des SAC (see *Address Directory*):

- *Alpes Vaudoises* (in French), Dents de Morcles-Sanetsch.

Available from the Schweizerische Arbeitsgemeinschaft für Wanderwege and most bookstores:

- *Wanderbuch 16: Jurahöhenwege* (in German), Kümmerly + Frey.

- *Guide pédestre 16a: Chemins des crêtes du Jura Suisse* (in French), Kümmerly + Frey.
- *Guide pédestre 27: La Côte et Jura Sud-Ouest* (in French), Kümmerly + Frey.
- *Circuits Pédestres Vaudois* (in French), Editions Payot, Lausanne.
- *Préalpes et Alpes Vaudoises* (in French), Editions Payot, Lausanne.

Suggested Walks

Rochers de Naye Circuit. From Veytaux, on Lac Léman, the route climbs steeply through forest to the parklands of Sonchaud, then upwards along the ridge top to Sautodo, with a final traverse around the south side of Rochers de Naye to the summit. Spectacular views of the Vaudois Alps, Berner Oberland, Fribourg Alps, Valais Alps, Mont Blanc and Lac Léman. From the summit, the route continues through meadowlands and rock fields to Jardin Alpin, then follows an open ridge crest down to Col de Chaude, with breathtaking views the whole way. From Col de Chaude, the path switchbacks steadily downhill through forest and meadow back to Veytaux. **Walking Time:** 8 to 9 hours. **Difficulty:** Moderately difficult to difficult; long, steep ascents and descents, plus a short cross-country ramble from the summit to Jardin Alpin. **Path Markings:** Red and white horizontal bars.
Map:
- *Hauts de Montreux, Itinéraires pédestres,* 1:25,000. Available from Office du Tourisme du Canton de Vaud.
Guidebook:
- *Préalpes et Alpes Vaudoises* (in French), Editions Payot.

Sainte Croix to Crassier. Along the Jurahöhenweg through the Vaudois Jura. Open ridge crests with panoramic views of the Alps and Lac Léman; forests and meadows, lakes and streams, gentle summits and rocky peaks. Highlights include the Vallée de Joux, Lac de Joux, Mont Tendre and La Dôle. **Walking Time:** 5 to 6 days. **Difficulty:** Easy to moderately difficult. **Path Markings:** Yellow and red horizontal bars.
Maps:
- Spezialkarte des Jura 1:50,000, sheets 5 *Yverdon-Ste Croix-Val de Travers* and 6 *Lausanne-La Côte-St Cergue-Vallée de Joux.*
Guidebook:
- *Wanderbuch 16: Jurahöhenwege* (in German) or *Guide pédestre 16a: Chemins des crêtes du Jura Suisse* (in French), Kümmerly + Frey.

Cross-Country Skiing

The Région du Léman has 15 ski centers with marked tracks totaling more than 150 kilometers. In addition, there are nearly a dozen cross-country routes. For full details, see the booklet published by the Schweizerische

Arbeitsgemeinschaft für Wanderwege, *Skiwandern/Ski de Randonnée* (described in the section on *Cross-Country Skiing* earlier in this chapter). You can also obtain sketch maps from the SAW showing marked ski tracks described in the booklet. Finally, the Office du Tourisme du Canton de Vaud can supply sketch maps showing marked ski tracks near many towns and villages in the region.

Ticino (Tessin)

Ticino, the southernmost canton in Switzerland, lies on the southern side of the Alps, exposed to the moderating influence of the Mediterranean. Its summers are warmer and its winters milder than anywhere else in Switzerland. Palm trees line the shores of the Lago di Maggiore and Lago di Lugano, within sight of the snowy summits of the Lepontine Alps. The woodlands on the surrounding foothills are quite unlike those on the north side of the Alps. Beech and pine are gone, replaced by such Mediterranean species as Spanish chestnut and pseudo-acacia. Here and there, silvery patches among the darker green signal the presence of olive groves.

Italian is the principal language of Ticino. And in customs, native dress and architecture, the canton has much in common with neighboring Lombardy, in northern Italy. The chalets of central Switzerland are gone, replaced in the high mountain valleys by stone houses with wooden galleries, outside stairways and, sometimes, open gables. The red tile roofs, iron balconies, pastel facades and liberal use of arches and towers so characteristic of buildings in the larger towns are also distinctly Italian in flavor.

Most of Ticino is mountainous, with the highest peaks in the north. Although craggy summits abound, they are less prominent than in the northern Alps. Glaciers and snowfields are also less extensive and widely developed. Snow arrives later and melts earlier than in the cooler northern ranges, providing a longer walking season. This is particularly true of the lower ranges of southern Ticino.

Numerous long, deep valleys, with grassy floors and mountainous flanks, penetrate the Alps of Ticino. Among the loveliest—and busiest—is the Valle Leventina, the main highway corridor to the north. Others include the Val Blenio, Val Calanca, Val di Bosco and Valle Maggia. The largest valleys wind through southern Ticino, cradling the Lago Maggiore and Lago di Lugano. The warm Mediterranean climate of these southern valleys, combined with the presence of these two large lakes, have made them popular—and expensive—resort areas. But from the outskirts of Locarno, on Lago Maggiore, and Lugano, on the Lago di Lugano, you can within a few minutes walk into the mountains, leaving the crowds behind.

Useful Addresses

Ente Ticinese per il Turismo (see *Address Directory*). Provides general tourist information for Ticino. Also can provide brochures giving information on walking, cross-country skiing and other activities. Staff speaks Italian, French, German and English. Useful publications include:

- *Ticino: Southern Switzerland* (in English; also available in French, German and Italian). A general tourist brochure featuring three color pictorial maps. Free.
- *Itinéraires artistiques au Tessin* (in French and German). A booklet describing 16 walks featuring artistic and historic monuments in Ticino. A sketch map for each walk shows its route and the locations of attractions described in the accompanying text. Free.
- *Hotels Motels: Tessin* (in Italian, French, German and English). A guide to lodgings in Ticino. Includes the addresses and telephone numbers of local tourist information offices. Free.
- *Mini-Holiday, Maxi-Holiday in the Tessin* (in English). Describes 16 organized holiday tours in Ticino, most of which include short walks as part of the package. Free.
- *Randonnées au Tessin* (in French and German). A brochure describing 15 walks in Ticino. A sketch map for each walk shows the route and variants, refuges, bus and rail lines, villages and other features. Also includes walking times and full route descriptions. Free.
- *Wanderungen im Tessin* (in German). A booklet published by the Schweizer Reisepost—the Swiss Postal Authority—listing 21 walks in Tessin. For each walk there is a sketch map, brief route description and information on how to get to and from the walk on the Swiss Postautos, which *Wanderbillette* to buy, and the name of the 1:50,000 walkers' map covering the area. There is also a map in the center of the booklet showing the location of each walk. Free.

Maps

Special walkers' maps covering Ticino are available from the Schweizerische Arbeitsgemeinschaft für Wanderwege (see *Address Directory*). They are:

- Wanderkarte 1:25,000, sheet *Gambarogno.*
- Wanderkarte 1:50,000, sheets *Blenio, Strada alta (Airolo-Biasca), Strada alta Valle Bedretto (Airolo-Ronco)* and *Valle Maggia.*
- Wanderkarte 1:60,000, sheet *Lugano und Sottoceneri.*

Ticino is also covered by the 1:25,000, 1:50,000 and 1:100,000 Landeskarten published by the Eidgenössiche Landestopographie (see *Address Directory).*

Guidebooks

Available from West Col Productions (see *Address Directory):*

- *Mittel Switzerland* (in English)

Available from the Verlag des SAC (see *Address Directory):*

- *Alpi Ticinesi e Mesolcinesi* (in Italian)
- *Tessiner Alpen* (in German)

Available from the Schweizerische Arbeitsgemeinschaft für Wanderwege (see *Address Directory)* and most bookstores:

- *Wanderbuch 22: Lugano* (in German), Kümmerly + Frey.
- *Wanderbuch 23: Locarno* (in German), Kümmerly + Frey.
- *Wanderbuch 33: Tessin* (in German), Kümmerly + Frey.
- *50 Tourenvorschläge Locarno und Umgebung* (in German), Verkehrsverein Locarno.
- *100 Tourenvorschläge im Bereich des Sottoceneri* (in German), Verkehrsverein Lugano.
- *Kreuz und Quer durch den Gambarogno* (in German), Verkehrsverein in Vira.
- *Rund um das Mendrisiotto und den Basso Ceresio* (in German), Verkehrsverein Mendrisio.
- *Sentiero alpino Blenio* (in German), Schweizerische Bundesbahnen (SBB).
- *Strada alta: Wanderung Airolo-Biasca* (in German), SBB.
- *Strada alta Valle Bedretto: Wanderung Airolo-Ronco* (in German), SBB.
- *Auf Wanderwegen im Tessin* (in German), Verlag NZZ.
- *Wanderwege im Malcantone* (in German), Rengger Verlag.

Suggested Walks

Strada alta. From Biasca to Ronco. Up the Valle Leventina to Airolo, then onward through the Valle Bedretto to Ronco. This spectacular walk winds through forest and meadows, with constant views of the rugged peaks lining the valleys. One of the most popular, and therefore crowded, routes in Switzerland. May be extended from Ronco to the head of the Valle Bedretto and beyond to Griessee, Griesgletscher and Nufenenpass. **Length:** 58 kilometers. **Walking Time:** 2 to 4 days. **Difficulty:** Easy to moderately difficult. **Path Markings:** Red and white horizontal bars. **Maps:**
- Wanderkarte 1:50,000, sheets *Strada alta (Airolo-Biasca)* and *Strada alta Valle Bedretto (Airolo-Ronco).*

Note: The guidebooks listed below contain strip maps suitable for walking the Strada alta. No other maps are necessary.

Guidebooks:
- *Strada alta: Wanderung Airolo-Biasca* and *Strada alta Valle Bedretto: Wanderung Airolo-Ronco* (in German), both published by Schweizerische Bundesbahnen.

Sentiero Alpino Blenio. From Biasca to Airolo via the spectacular Blenio Valley. Two routes are possible. The *Alto,* or high route, traverses the range on the west side of the valley. The *Basso,* or low route, winds up the valley floor. Both meet near Olivone and strike westward across the mountains to Airolo, where you can return to Biasca via the Strada alta (see above) or continue northward on the Strada alta to Ronco. Or, the *Alto* and *Basso* routes can be combined for a loop trip from Biasca. Beautiful forests and Alpine parklands, lakes and streams, close-up views of craggy peaks and charming Ticino stone villages enroute. **Walking Time:** Sentiero Alto—Biasca to Airolo: 2 to 3 days; Sentiero Basso—Biasca to Campiero, where it meets the Sentiero Alto: 1 to 2 days. **Difficulty:** Easy to moderately difficult. **Path Markings:** (Sentiero Alto) Red and white horizontal bars; (Sentiero Basso) yellow arrows, bars and diamonds. **Maps:**
- Wanderkarte 1:50,000, sheet *Blenio.* Or:
- Landeskarte der Schweiz 1:25,000, sheets 1252, 1253 and 1273.

Guidebook:
- *Sentiero Alpino Blenio* (in German), SSB.

From Miglieglia to Rivera. Along the summit of the Malcantone Range between Lago Maggiore and Lago di Lugano. Through woodlands, forest and high pasturelands to the summit ridge, with its breathtaking views of the lakes and surrounding mountains. The route begins with an aerial tramway ride to the top of Monte Lema, then north to the summits of Zoltone, Monte Magno, Monte Gradiccioli and Monte Tamaro. Then north to Corte di Sopra and the aerial tramway back down to Rivera. **Walking Time:** 4 hours. **Difficulty:** Easy to moderate. **Path Markings:** Red and white horizontal bars.

Maps:
• Landeskarte der Schweiz 1:50,000, sheet 286 or special sheet 5007.
Guidebook:
• *Randonnées au Tessin* (in French). Available from Ente Ticinese per il Turismo.

Cross-Country Skiing

Ticino has 10 ski centers with marked tracks totaling more than 65 kilometers. For full details, see the booklet published by the Schweizerische Arbeitsgemeinschaft für Wanderwege, *Skiwandern/Ski de Randonnée*. You can also obtain sketch maps from the SAW showing marked ski tracks described in the booklet. Finally, the Ente Ticinese per il Turismo can supply sketch maps showing marked ski tracks near many towns and villages in the region.

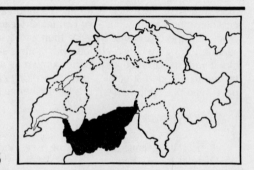

Valais/Wallis

The Swiss Alps reach their grand climax in the Valais. Here rise the highest, snowiest, most famous summits, arrayed on either side of the Valleé du Rhône, which runs east-west the length of the canton. On the north rise the great peaks of the Berner Oberland—Jungfrau, Eiger, Mönch and Finsteraarhorn, all topping 4,000 meters. On the south side of the valley, strung out along the Italian frontier, rise the even higher summits of Dom Mischabel, Grand Combin, the Matterhorn and Monte Rosa, the highest peak in Switzerland. Both ranges are capped with perennial snow and ice and bear the most extensive glacier systems in Switzerland. The Aletschgletscher, which originates in a large ice field at the foot of Jungfrau, flows 25 kilometers southward toward the Rhône.

Former glaciers carved not only the broad Vallée du Rhône, but also the numerous side-valleys, which extend upward into the mountain on either side. The valleys are deep-cut and cradle small villages, such as Arolla, where cattle are still driven up to summer pastures on time-worn paths; Zermatt, the famous resort at the foot of the Matterhorn; Saas Fee, as beautiful as Zermatt, but much less visited; Champex, where French Jews were led into neutral Switzerland during World War II; and Fafleralp, nestled beneath the awesome snows of Jungfrau.

More than 3,200 kilometers of marked footpaths wind throughout the Valais, some following the valley floors, others climbing into the high country through forests and sprawling pastures to the lower limits of perennial snow. More difficult, unmarked routes lead across glaciers and snowfields (guides recommended) or into high, remote areas rarely visited by the average walker. The famed *Haute Route,* a difficult ski traverse leading from Zermatt to Chamonix, France, also crosses Valais. And everywhere, the great peaks—among the most boldly sculpted in the world—march across the horizons.

Valais is bilingual. French is the principal language in Lower (western) Valais; German in Upper (eastern) Valais. As you journey up the Rhône Valley, you cross from French to German Valais just beyond the town of Sierre.

Almost entirely bordered by mountains, Valais is the most remote of the Swiss cantons. Long shut off from outside influences, traditional ways of life have hung on longer here than in most other parts of Switzerland. In many remote valleys tucked among the mountains Valaisian peasants still carry on much as they have for centuries, wearing their traditional dress, practicing the old crafts, herding their cattle to the high pastures each summer. Rough wooden chalets with stone slab roofs dot the parklands, along with the distinctive graneries known as *raccards,* or *mazots.* These ingenious wooded structures perch on pilings around which stone discs have been placed to prevent rats from pilfering the grain.

Useful Addresses

Union Valaisanne du Tourisme (see *Address Directory).* Provides general tourist information on Valais. Also can provide brochures giving information on walking, cross-country skiing and other activities. Staff speaks French, German, Italian and English. Useful publications include:

- *Valais: Switzerland* (in English; also available in French and German). General tourist brochure that includes a color pictorial map of Valais, a list of places with youth hostels, a road map, a list of communities with marked cross-country ski tracks, campgrounds and other facilities, and general comments about walking in the canton. Free.

- *Valais: Winter* (in English; also available in French and German). A booklet describing facilities, including marked ski tracks, at winter sports centers in the Valais. Lists telephone numbers for obtaining further information. Free.

- *Valais/Wallis* (in French, German and English). A directory of winter sports centers in the Valais. For each center there is a color pictorial map showing ski facilities, including marked tracks. Each center is also briefly described, with a note indicating the marked ski tracks nearby. Free.

- *Hohtenn-Ausserberg-Eggerberg-Lalden-Brigerbad-Brig* (in German, French and English). One of a series of leaflets published by the BLS railway. Has a topographical strip map of the Rhône Valley showing the Höhenweg Südrampe in red. Also includes a brief description of the path, a list of suggested detours and walking times between points, and a route profile showing distances and elevations. Free.

- *A pied à travers le Valais* (in French). Contains four color relief maps showing footpaths in red. Tables accompanying the maps list points enroute, the walking times between them and the facilities— including lodgings, post offices and train and bus stations—at each. Free.

- *Sonnige Halden am Lötschberg* (in German, French and English). A brochure listing 23 walks, with walking times, along the Höhenweg Südrampe, in the Rhône Valley. Includes a sketch map showing footpaths in red. Free.

- *Stock-Gemmi/Gemmi-Torrent* (in German and French). A leaflet summarizing a walking route from Kandersteg to the village of Leukebad and over the Torrentalp to Ferden. Includes a color pictorial map of the area and the addresses and telephone numbers of local public transportation lines, hotels and restaurants. Free.

- *Gommer Höhenweg/Rottenweg* (in German). A topographical strip map showing the Gommer Höhenweg and Rottenweg in Red. On the reverse there is a brief description of each part and route profiles giving elevations, distances and walking times. Both paths parallel the FOB railway in Upper Valais. Available for a nominal charge.

- *Tour des Dents-du-Midi* (in French). A leaflet describing a circular walk around the Dent-du-Midi crags in Lower Valais. Divides the walk into five sections, describing and giving the walking time for each. Includes a sketch map of the route. Free.

- *Wanderungen im Wallis* (in German). A booklet published by the Schweizer Reisepost—the Swiss Bus Authority—listing 30 walks in the Valais. For each walk there is a sketch map, brief route description and information on how to get to and from the walk on the Swiss Postautos, which *Wanderbillette* to buy, and the name of the 1:50,000 walkers' map covering the area. There is also a map in the center of the booklet showing the location of each walk. Free.

Association Valaisanne de Tourisme Pédestre (see *Address Directory*). Maintains more than 3,000 kilometers of footpaths. Provides walking information for Valais. Also sells maps and guidebooks. Staff speaks French, German and English.

Maps

Special walkers' maps covering the Valais are available from the Schweizerische Arbeitsgemeinschaft für Wanderwege (see *Address Directory*). They are:

- Wanderkarte 1:25,000, sheets *Anzère, Bürchen und Zeneggen, Crans-Montana, Grächen, Haute Nendaz, Isérables, Nax, Ovronnaz, Saas Fee, St. Martin* and *Val des Dix.*
- Wanderkarte 1:40,000, sheets *Champex Lac, Evolène und Umgebung, Val d'Anniviers* and *Vallée du Trient.*
- Wanderkarte 1:50,000, sheets *Aletsch, Binntal und Umgebung, Du Lac Léman aux Dents-du-Midi, Entremont, Fiesch-Fieschertal, Leukerbad, Lötschental, Obergoms, Unteres Goms Riederalp-Bettmeralp-Eggishorn* and *Zermatt.*

Walkers' maps are also available for *Loye-Grône* and *Les Marécottes.* Valais is also covered by the 1:25,000, 1:50,000 and 1:100,000 Landeskarten published by the Eidgenössiche Landestopographie (see *Address Directory*).

Guidebooks

Available from West Col Productions (see *Address Directory*):

- *Mountains of the Alps: Zermatt and District* (in English)
- *High Level Route* (in English). Chamonix-Zermatt ski traverse

Available from Bergverlag Rudolf Rother (see *Address Directory*):

- *Walliser Alpen* (in German)
- *Haute Route* (in German)

The following guides are in French. They are also available in German-language editions under the title *Walliser Alpen.* Available from the Verlag des SAC (see *Address Directory*):

- *Chaîne Frontière Valais–Haute-Savoie:* Préalpes Franco-Suisses
- *Alpes Valaisannes I:* Col Ferret–Col Collon
- *Alpes Valaisannes II:* Col Collon–Col du Théodule
- *Alpes Valaisannes III:* Col du Théodule–Monte Moro
- *Alpes Valaisannes IV:* Strahlhorn–Simplon
- *Alpes Valaisannes V:* Simplon–Furka

SWITZERLAND   189

Available from the Schweizerische Arbeitsgemeinschaft für Wanderwege (see *Address Directory*) and most bookstores:

- *Wanderbuch 8: Vispertäler* (in German), Kümmerly + Frey.
- *Guide pédestre 8a: Zermatt, Saas Fee, Grächen* (in French), Kümmerly + Frey.
- *Guide pédestre 12: Val d'Anniviers, Val d'Hérens* (in French), Kümmerly + Frey.
- *Wanderbuch 12a: Val d'Anniviers, Val d'Hérens* (in German), Kümmerly + Frey.
- *Guide pédestre 13: Bas-Valais* (in French), Kümmerly + Frey.
- *Wanderbuch 13a: Monthey, Val d'Illiez, Dents-du-Midi* (in German), Kümmerly + Frey.
- *Wanderbuch 15: Lötschberg* (in German), Kümmerly + Frey.
- *Guide pédestre 17: Val de Bagnes et d'Entremont* (in French), Kümmerly + Frey.
- *Wanderbuch 17a: Martigny, Bagnes, Entremont* (in German), Kümmerly + Frey.
- *Wanderbuch 19: Brig–Simplon–Goms* (in German), Kümmerly + Frey.
- *Guide pédestre 21: Valais Central* (in French), Kümmerly + Frey.
- *Wanderbuch 21a: Sitten, Siders, Montana* (in German), Kümmerly + Frey.
- *Broschüre Walliser Wanderwege* (in German and French), Verkehrsverein Sion.

Available from Hallwag Verlag (see *Address Directory*):

- *Zermatt im Sommer und Winter* (in German)
- *Komm mit mir ins Wallis* (in German).

Suggested Walks

From Kandersteg (Berner Oberland) to Ferden. From Kandersteg the route climbs through forest to Stock, emerging into open pasturelands at Sunnbühl. Then, a long, easy, cross-country ramble leads across the meadowy plateau beneath the spire of Rinderhorn to the remote Daubensee and onward to Gemmipass, providing views across the Rhône Valley to Monte Rosa and the Matterhorn. From here a series of steep switchbacks leads down a near-vertical cliff face to the village of Leukerbad (you can also take an aerial tramway down). The route then climbs back out of the valley to Rinderhütte, on the great sloping pastures

of Torrenthorn, and turns up to Restipass, with marvelous views of Eiger, Mönch and Jungfrau. From the pass the route steeply descends the mountainside to tiny Ferden village. **Walking Time:** 1 to 2 days. **Difficulty:** Easy to moderately difficult. **Path Markings:** Red and white horizontal bars.
Maps:
• Wanderkarte 1:33,333, sheet *Kandersteg,* and Wanderkarten 1:50,000, sheets *Leukerbad* and *Lötschental.*
Guidebooks:
• *Stock-Gemmi/Gemmi-Torrent* (in German and French). Available from Union Valaisanne du Tourisme.

Tour des Dents-du-Midi. A circular walk around the lofty sawtooth ridge of the Dents-du-Midi, traversing forest and meadows, crossing high passes and skirting a large lake cupped in a high cirque. As you walk around the peaks exquisite views unfold of Lac Léman, the Rhône Valley, Les Diablerets, the Matterhorn, Mont Blanc and dozens of other peaks. **Walking Time:** 2 to 3 days. **Difficulty:** Moderately difficult to difficult. **Path Markings:** Red and white horizontal bars.
Maps:
• Wanderkarte 1:50,000, sheet *Du Lac Léman aux Dents-du-Midi.* Or:
• Landeskarte der Schweiz, 1:50,000, sheet 272.
Guidebooks:
• *Guide pédestre 13: Bas-Valais* (in French) or *Wanderbuch 13a: Monthey, Val d'Illiez, Dents-du-Midi* (in German), Kümmerly + Frey. Also:
• *Tour des Dents-du-Midi* (in French). Available from Union Valaisanne du Tourisme.

From Le Chargeur to Arolla. Beginning at the dam of Lac des Dix, the path climbs along the lake, up the Val des Dix to the Col de Riedmatten, with close-up views of Mont Blanc de Cheilon and its great snow and ice fields. From the pass, the route snakes down the mountainside to the village of Arolla. **Walking Time:** 4 to 5 hours. **Difficulty:** Moderately difficult. **Path Markings:** Red and white horizontal bars.
Maps:
• Wanderkarte 1:25,000, *Val des Dix.* Or:
• Landeskarte der Schweiz 1:50,000, sheet 283.
Guidebooks:
• *Alpes Valaisannes I* (Includes maps available in French or German), Verlag des SAC. Also:
• *A pied à travers le Valais* (in French). Available from Union Valaisanne du Tourisme.

Saas Fee to Grächen. A relatively easy traverse along the precipitous slopes of lofty Dom Mischabel, high above the Saas Valley. The path winds through forest, with heart-stopping views of the valley far below and

fine panoramas of the peaks across the gulf. The last segment of the route is over gentle parklands to Grächen. **Walking Time:** 6 hours. **Difficulty:** Easy to moderately difficult. **Path Markings:** Red and white horizontal bars.
Maps:
• Landeskarte der Schweiz, 1:50,000, sheets 274 and 284.
Guidebook:
• *Wanderungen im Wallis* (in German). Available from Union Valaisanne du Tourisme.

Cross-Country Skiing

The Valais has more than 25 ski centers with marked tracks. In addition, there are more than a dozen marked cross-country ski routes totaling some 150 kilometers. For full details, see the booklet published by the Schweizerische Arbeitsgemeinschaft für Wanderwege, *Skiwandern/Ski de Randonnée*. You can also obtain sketch maps from the SAW showing marked ski tracks described in the booklet. In addition, the *DSV Langlauf Kompass* and *Skilanglauf Atlas* (see descriptions under "Guidebooks" in the section on *Cross-Country Skiing*) list many cross-country tracks in Valais. Finally, the Union Valaisanne du Tourisme can supply sketch maps showing marked ski tracks near many towns and villages in the canton.

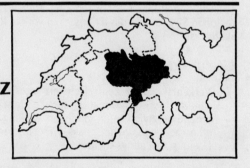

Zentralschweiz (Central Switzerland)

As its name implies, this region is the geographical center of Switzerland. It is also its historical center, or source. For it was the cantons of Uri, Schwyz (which gave the country its name) and Unterwalden that during the 13th century formed the "Everlasting League" that became the modern Swiss Confederation. Zentralschweiz includes these three original cantons, plus Luzern and Zug, which joined the league shortly following its founding.

Although Zentralschweiz includes a small portion of the Mittelland in the north, it is mostly mountainous, encompassing the Urner, Unterwaldner and the Schwyzer Alps, along with their rugged foothill ranges.

Even by Swiss standards, which are high, the mountains and valleys of Zentralschweiz are extraordinarily beautiful, the villages exceptionally charming and picturesque. With its broad green valleys, vast pastures and snowy peaks, its large lakes winding among the mountains, its gaily decorated villages and handsome steep-gabled chalets, its historic chapels and feudal castles, Zentralschweiz fulfills one's fondest expectations of what Switzerland should be.

At the very center of the region sprawls the large, many-armed Vierwaldstättersee (Lake Lucerne), the centerpiece of the Alpine Lake District. Around it are arrayed several other large lakes—the Zugersee, Sempachersee, Sihlsee and others—all of which lie in broad valleys gouged through the Alpine foothills by ancient glaciers. Their shores are typically lined with steep-walled belvederes such as Mt. Pilatus and Rigi-Kulm, whose gentle, open summits offer panoramic views of the central Alps and the vast green pastures that seem to go on forever in Zentral-schweiz. The beautiful city of Luzern, its red roofs boldly set off from the surrounding forest and pastureland, sits on the northwestern arm of the Vierwaldstättersee, in the shadow of the steep east wall of Pilatus.

The mountains of Zentralschweiz are separated by a maze of broad, deep valleys, each seemingly more beautiful than the last. Snow-capped peaks rise abruptly from broad, grassy floors, where nestle villages such as Engelberg, Andermatt and Melchtal. And while the mountains of Zentralschweiz are as bold and craggy as one could wish, they are also very accessible, marked by high plateaus and rolling uplands that offer endless opportunities for wandering and cross-country skiing. And no region in Switzerland has a denser network of footpaths and cross-country ski tracks.

Useful Addresses

Verkehrsverband Zentralschweiz (see *Address Directory*). Provides general tourist information for Zentralschweiz. Also can provide brochures giving information on walking, cross-country skiing and other activities. Staff speaks German, French, Italian and English. Useful publications include:

• *Zentralschweiz* (in German, French, Italian, English, Dutch, Span-ish and Japanese). General tourist brochure. Lists holiday facilities, including marked ski tracks, cleared winter paths, campgrounds and mountain guide services, for each town in the region. Includes a 1:300,000 map. Free.

• *Zentralschweiz* (in German, French, Italian and English). A direc-tory of winter resorts. Tells which have marked ski tracks and cross-country ski schools. Free.

• *Wanderungen Zwischen Bodensee und Klausenpass* (in German). A booklet published by the Schweizer Reisepost—the Swiss Postal

Authority—listing 23 walks in Ostschweiz and 5 walks in the Urner Alps of Zentralschweiz. Free.

- *Wanderungen Rund um den Vierwaldstättersee* (in German). A booklet describing 20 walks around the Vierwaldstättersee. For each walk there is a sketch map, brief route description and indication of walking time. Free.
- *Engelberg Landlauf-Wochen* (in German, Dutch and English). A leaflet describing skiing holidays in Engelberg. Includes a pictorial map showing marked ski tracks. Free.
- *Skiwanderparadies Stalden OW: Langis–Schwendi–Kaltbad* (in German, Dutch and English). A leaflet describing cross-country ski holidays in Obwalden. Includes a schematic map of marked ski tracks in the region. Free.
- *Ski-Region Mythen* (in German). A brochure describing winter sports facilities near the Mythen peaks, in Schwyz. Includes a color pictorial map showing marked ski tracks. Free.
- *Schwedentritt Loipe Gross* (in German). A postcard showing two marked ski tracks and one marked cross-country route near Gross, in Schwyz. Gives telephone numbers for further information. Free.

Kurverein Gersau (see *Address Directory*). Provides general information on Gersau, on the Vierwaldstättersee. Staff speaks German, French and English. Useful publications include:

- *Enjoyable Roundtrip on the Rigi-Mountain* (in English). A mimeographed description, including a sketch map, of a short walk on Rigi. Free.
- *Gersau Pauschal-Arrangements* (in German). A leaflet containing a lodgings list, calendar of events and six suggested walks. Free.

Luftseilbahn Beckenried-Klewenalp (see *Address Directory*). Operates the LBK aerial tramway and can provide walking information for the mountains served by the line. Staff speaks German, French and English. Useful publications include:

- *Wanderkarte Dallenwil, Niederrickenbach, Haldigrat-Brisen* (in German, French and English). A color pictorial map of the Brisen Massif of Nidwalden and Uri, showing 42 walking routes in black. Gives the basic itinerary and walking time for each walk. Free.

Pilatus-Bahnen (see *Address Directory*). Provides information on Mt. Pilatus, in particular on the hotel on its summit and the cog railway and aerial tramway taking tourists to the top. Staff speaks German, French and English. Useful publications include:

- *Mt. Pilatus* (in German, French, Italian and English). A lavish tourist brochure describing holiday facilities on Pilatus. Includes a sketch map of footpaths and brief descriptions of four suggested walks. Free.

Rigibahn-Gesellschaft (see *Address Directory*). Operates a cog railway and aerial tramway on Mt. Rigi. Can provide walking and cross-country skiing information for the mountain. Staff speaks German, French, Italian and English. Useful publications include:

- *Rigi Wanderungen* (in German). A leaflet describing seven walks on Rigi. For each walk there is a brief description, indication of walking time and a note on transportation connections. Also lists the guidebook and walkers' map for the area. Free.
- *Panorama-Langlaufloipe Rigi Kaltbad/First-Rigi Scheidegg* (in German). A mimeographed description of marked ski tracks from Rigi Kaltbad to Rigi Scheidegg. Includes information on skier discounts for the cog railway and aerial tramway. Free.
- *Skiwandern im Rigigebiet* (in German). A postcard showing a marked ski track and a marked cross-country route between Rigi-Kaltbad and Rigi-Scheidegg. Free.
- *Winterwanderung in Rigi-Kaltbad* (in German). A mimeographed description of a winter walk on cleared paths from the upper terminal of the Vitznau-Rigi-Kaltbad railway. Free.

Verkehrsverein Alpnach (see *Address Directory*). Provides tourist information for the village of Alpnach. Staff speaks German, French and English. Useful publications include:

- *Wanderkarte Alpnach* (in German). Includes a topographical map showing footpaths near Alpnach. Lists 20 walks in the vicinity. Free.

Verkehrsbüro Brunnen (see *Address Directory*). Provides general tourist information on the town of Brunnen, in Schwyz. Staff speaks German, French, Italian and English. Useful publications include:

- *Brunnen Programm* (in German, with some French and English). A general tourist pamphlet published weekly. Lists guided walking tours and walking weeks. Also suggests eight walks. Free.
- *Kanton Schwyz: Wolkig bis Heiter* (in German), published by Fremdenverkehrsverband Kanton Schwyz (see *Address Directory*). A general tourist guidebook to Schwyz. Includes lists of walking maps and guidebooks and suggests 40 walks in the region. Free.
- *Verzeichnis der uns Bekannten Wanderkarten und Wanderbücher* (in German). A sheet listing walkers' maps and guidebooks for Schwyz. Free.

• *Wandern* (in German). A sheet listing walking tours in Schwyz and the price of each. Includes nature walks, walking weeks and the like. Free.

Verkehrsverein Buochs (see *Address Directory*). Provides general information on Buochs and vicinity. Staff speaks German, French and English. Useful publications include:

• *Buochs* (in German, French and English). A tourist brochure containing several useful leaflets, including:
—*Buochs: Camping & Caravaning* (in German). A sketch map showing campgrounds in the area. Lists facilities and prices for each.
—*Buochs: Spaziergänge, Wanderungen Ausflüge Car-Fahrten* (in German). Gives the itineraries and walking times for 18 walks in the area.
—*Buochs Vierwaldstättersee: Zentralschweiz-Jederzeit Ferienzeit* (in German). A lodging list. Includes a sketch map showing lodging locations as well as the local fitness path.
• *Parcours Buochs* (in German). Sketch map of the fitness path in Buochs. Includes a chart for recording performance data. Free.

Verkehrsbüro Einsiedeln (see *Address Directory*). Provides tourist information for the village of Einsiedeln, in Schwyz. Staff speaks German, French, Italian and English. Useful publications include:

• *Einsiedeln Hoch-Ybrig* (in German, French, Italian and English). A general tourist brochure. Lists places with walking and cross-country skiing facilities. Free.
• *Einsiedler 30 km Volksskilauf* (in German). A brochure providing information on the annual cross-country ski marathon held in Einsiedeln. Includes a sketch map showing the route and information on entrance fees, dates and other details pertaining to the race. Free.
• *Alois Kälin: Langlauf-Schule Einsiedeln* (in German). A brochure giving information on programs offered by the Alois Kälin cross-country ski school. Free.
• *Parcours Einsiedeln* (in German). A sketch map of the fitness path in Einsiedeln. Includes a chart for recording performance data. Free.
• *Schwedentritt Einsiedeln* (in German). A black and white aerial photo of Einsiedeln in winter, showing a 22-kilometer marked ski track in blue. Also shows three short secondary tracks. A description of the tracks is on the back. Free.

Verkehrsverein Engelberg (see *Address Directory*). Provides tourist information for Engelberg and vicinity. Staff speaks German, French and English. Useful publications include:

- *Engelberg* (in German, French, English and Japanese). A general tourist brochure. Includes pictorial maps showing the area in summer and winter. The latter map shows marked ski tracks and cleared winter paths, as well as other facilities. The winter map is also available separately. Free.
- *Engelberg: Vogelschaukarte mit Wandervorschlägen* (in German, French and English). A color pictorial map of Engelberg showing 35 walking routes. The walks are briefly described on the reverse in German, French and English. The walking time is given for each. Free.
- *Welcome at the Summer- and Winter-Resort Engelberg* (in English). A general tourist brochure, including a summary of walking opportunities. Free.

Verkehrsverein Ennetbürgen (see *Address Directory*). Provides tourist information on Ennetbürgen and vicinity. Staff speaks German, French and English. Useful publications include:

- *Ennetbürgen am Bürgenstock* (in German, French and English). A general tourist brochure with a color pictorial map and general information on walking. Free.
- *Ennetbürgen Ferienwohnungen* (in German). A lodging list with a color sketch map showing nine suggested walks. Gives the basic itinerary and walking time for each walk. Free.

Verkehrsverein Melchtal (see *Address Directory*). Provides tourist information on Melchtal. Useful publications include:

- *Melchtal* (in German, French and English). A general tourist brochure. Includes a separate lodging list and prospectus on winter package holidays, including one featuring cross-country skiing. Free.

Verkehrsverein Sarnen am See (see *Address Directory*). Provides tourist information for Sarnen, in Obwalden. Staff speaks German, French, Italian and English. Useful publications include:

- *Ferien in Obwalden* (in German, French and Dutch). A general tourist guide to Obwalden. Lists 34 suggested walks, giving the basic itinerary and walking time for each. Free.
- *Sarnen am See: Aktive Familienferien* (in German, French and English). A brochure containing leaflets describing family holidays, including some that feature walking and cross-country skiing. Free.

Verkehrsverein Schwyz (see *Address Directory*). Provides tourist information on the canton of Schwyz. Useful publications include:

- *Inneres Land Schwyz* (in German, French and English). A general tourist booklet for Schwyz. Includes a list of suggested walks; a list of marked ski tracks, with the location and length of each; a sketch map showing campgrounds, cross-country ski areas and other facilities; and the addresses and telephone numbers of tourist information offices, railways, bus lines and other facilities. Free.
- *Kanton Schwyz: Information* (in German). For each community in the canton this brochure provides information on facilities, such as footpaths, marked ski tracks and public transportation, and lists the address and telephone number of the local tourist information office. Also gives the addresses and telephone numbers of campgrounds and includes a lodging list. Free.
- *Schwyz: Brunnen/Stoos* (in German, French and English). A walking brochure with a 1:50,000 topographical map showing footpaths in red and a color pictorial map of the region. The basic itinerary and walking time for 74 suggested walks are listed below the topographical map. Free.
- *Stoos Wanderpass* (in German). A sketch map showing seven walks near Stoos. Briefly describes and gives the walking time for each walk. Lists sheet numbers of the 1:25,000 Landeskarte covering the area. Free.
- *Stoos Winter* (in German). A brochure describing winter sports facilities at Stoos. Describes marked ski tracks in the area and gives the dates for local cross-country performance tests (see the section on *Cross-Country Skiing* earlier in this chapter). Also includes a lodging list and useful addresses and telephone numbers. Free.

Luzerner Wanderwege (see *Address Directory*). Provides walking information for Luzern. Also sells mps and guidebooks. Staff speaks German, French and English.

Nidwaldner Wanderwege (see *Address Directory*). Provides walking information for Nidwalden. Staff speaks German.

Obwaldner Wanderwege (see *Address Directory*). Provides walking information for Obwalden. Staff speaks German.

Schwyzer Wanderwege (see *Address Directory*). Provides walking information for Schwyz. Staff speaks German.

Arbeitsgemeinschaft Urner Wanderwege (see *Address Directory*). Provides walking information for Uri. Staff speaks German.

Wanderweg-Kommission des VKZ (see *Address Directory*). Provides walking information for Zug. Staff speaks German.

Maps

Special walkers' maps covering Zentralschweiz are available from the Schweizerische Arbeitsgemeinschaft für Wanderwege (see *Address Directory*). They are:

- Wanderkarte 1:25,000, sheets *Escholzmatt–Marbach, Hoch–Ybrig, Luzern und Umgebung, Rigi Schüpfheim* and *Waldemmental*.
- Wanderkarte 1:33,333, sheets *Engelberger Ortswanderkarte* and *Lungern*.
- Wanderkarte 1:50,000, sheets *Kanton Uri, Muotathal, Nidwalden und Engelberg, Obwalden* and *Schwyz*.
- Wanderkarte 1:75,000, sheet *Schweiz Südostbahn*.

Zentralschweiz is also covered by the 1:25,000, 1:50,000 and 1:100,000 Landeskarten published by the Eidgenössiche Landestopographie (see *Address Directory*).

Guidebooks

Available from West Col Productions (see *Address Directory*):

- *Central Switzerland:* Susten–Furka–Grimsel (in English).

All the following guidebooks are in German:

Available from the Verlag des SAC (see *Address Directory*):

- *Kletterführer: Klausen–Urnersee*
- *Urner Alpen Ost:* Band I) Kaiserstock–Oberalpstock
- *Urner Alpen West:* Band II) Gotthard–Dammastock–Titlis–Urirotstock
- *Zentralschweizerische Voralpen:* Zürichsee—Vierwaldstättersee—Brünigpass.

Available from the SAW (see *Address Directory*) and most bookstores:

- *Wanderbuch 10: Zugerland,* Kümmerly + Frey.
- *Wanderbuch 18: Seetal-Freiamt-Wynental,* Kümmerly + Frey.
- *Wanderbuch 25: Rigigebiet,* Kümmerly + Frey.
- *Wanderbuch 29: Uri,* Kümmerly + Frey.
- *Wanderbuch 31: Engelberg,* Kümmerly + Frey.
- *Wanderbuch 36: Nidwalden,* Kümmerly + Frey.

- *Wanderbuch 37: Obwalden,* Kümmerly + Frey.
- *Der Aegerisee und seine Umgebung,* Verlag Orell Füssli AG.
- *Im Wanderschritt durch das Muotathal,* Verkehrsverein Muotathal.
- *Passwanderungen Zentralschweiz,* Murbacher-Verlag.
- *Spaziergänge und Wanderungen in Luzern und Umgebung,* Murbacher Verlag.
- *Wanderbücher Schwyz,* I and II, Murbacher-Verlag.
- *Wander- und Tourenführer Pilatus,* Murbacher-Verlag.
- *Zentralschweiz im Auto und zu Fuss,* I and II, Murbacher-Verlag.

Suggested Walks

Engelberg to Tannen. From Engelberg, the route crosses the valley to climb steeply through forest to the open pasturelands of the Gerschnialp Plateau, then upward even more steeply, ascending the precipitous Pfaffenwand to a second plateau and the meadow-bordered Trüb Lake. Excellent views of Titlis peak from the lake. From here you can walk back to Engelberg via the Trüben River valley and Untertrübsee. Or you can continue onward, climbing steeply to Jochpass, with great views of the Berner Oberland, descending to Engstlen Lake and climbing finally to the village of Tannen. **Walking Time:** 7 hours, one way; Engelberg-Trübsee-Untertrübsee-Engelberg: 5 to 6 hours. **Difficulty:** Moderately difficult. **Path Markings:** Red and white horizontal bars.
Maps:
- Wanderkarte 1:33,333, sheet *Engelberger Ortswanderkarte.* Or:
- Wanderkarte 1:50,000, sheet *Nidwalden und Engelberg.* Or:
- Landeskarte der Schweiz, 1:50,000, sheet 255.
Guidebooks:
- *Wanderbuch 31: Engelberg,* Kümmerly + Frey. Or:
- *Engelberg: Vogelschaukarte mit Wandervorschlägen* (in German). Available from Verkehrsverein Engelberg.

Urner Alps Tour. From Gadmen, on the Sustenpass road, to Göschenen, on the St. Gotthard pass road, north of Andermatt. An often steep and strenuous, high Alpine route for experienced mountaineers only. Includes a brief glacier crossing. Passes through the highest, wildest part of the Urner Alps, with close-up views of the Steingletscher and the peaks of Gwächtenhorn, Sustenhorn and Dammastock which, at 3,629 meters, is the highest peak in Zentralschweiz. Overnight stays in the Tierberglihütte and Kehlenaphütte. **Walking Time:** 3 days. **Path Markings:** Red and white horizontal bars.
Maps:
- Landeskarte der Schweiz 1:25,000, sheets 1211 *Meiental* and 1231 *Urseren.* Or:

• Landeskarte der Schweiz 1:50,000, sheet 255 *Sustenpass.*
Guidebook:
• *Urner Alpen: Band II,* Verlag des SAC.

From Goldau to Rigi-Kulm. Through forest and meadow up the east slope of Rigi to Klösterli, then up the sloping summit platform to the sheer north wall and along the cliff's edge to the top of the peak. Spectacular views in all directions. Directly below lie the Zugersee on the east and the Vierwaldstättersee on the west. Across the Vierwaldstättersee lies the city of Luzern and rising directly above it, the heights of Pilatus. To the south, the lake pushes into the mountains, which are arrayed across the entire southern horizon. Breathtaking views of the snowy summits of the Urner and Waldner Alps and in the background, the Berner Oberland. **Walking Time:** 3½ to 5½ hours, one way. **Difficulty:** Easy to moderately difficult. **Path Markings:** Red and white horizontal bars.
Map:
• Wanderkarte 1:25,000, sheet *Rigi.*
Guidebook:
• *Wanderbuch 25: Rigigebiet,* Kümmerly + Frey.

From Ennetbürgen to Kehrsiten. Across flowery meadows to the summit of Burgenstock, which plunges steeply into Vierwaldstättersee. Spectacular views of Rigi on the east, Luzern and Pilatus to the north and Urirotstock on the south. **Walking Time:** 3½ to 4 hours. **Difficulty:** Easy. **Path Markings:** Yellow arrows, bars and diamonds.
Maps:
• Wanderkarte 1:50,000, sheet *Nidwalden und Engelberg.* Or:
• Landeskarte der Schweiz, 1:25,000, sheets 1151 and 1171.
Guidebook:
• *Wanderungen rund um den Vierwaldstättersee* (in German). Available from Verkehrsverband Zentralschweiz.

Cross-Country Skiing

Zentralschweiz has more than 25 ski centers with marked tracks totaling more than 280 kilometers. In addition, there are more than 20 marked cross-country ski routes. For full details, see the booklet published by the Schweizerische Arbeitsgemeinschaft für Wanderwege, *Skiwandern/Ski de Randonnée.* You can also obtain sketch maps from the SAW showing marked ski tracks described in the booklet. In addition, the *DSV Langlauf Kompass* and *Skilanglauf Atlas* (see the section on *Cross-Country Skiing* earlier in this chapter) list many cross-country tracks in Zentralschweiz. Finally, the tourist information offices in Zentralschweiz can supply sketch maps showing marked ski tracks in their districts.

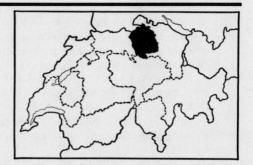

Zürich

Zürich, Switzerland's largest city and one of the financial capitals of the world, sits at the northern end of the long, deep Zürichsee. Hills border the lake on either side, offering easy rambles through forest and pasture-lands. South of the crescent-shaped lake, a broad valley extends south-ward into the St. Gallen and Glarner Alps, which are visible in the distance. The canton of Zürich lies in the northeastern Mittelland, extending northward to the valley of the Rhine and the German frontier.

Zürich is ideally suited to gentle country rambles. Footpaths lead among orchards, grain fields and pastures, past old castles and churches, and through villages with half-timbered houses reminiscent of Northern Europe. Broad river valleys wind through the pastoral patchwork, which here and there, especially on the sides of the steeper hills, are accented with patches of forest. From the tops of such hills, the gentle, lake-strewn landscape spreads in every direction. And on the southern horizon the snow-clad Alps crown the scene.

Useful Addresses

Verkehrsverein der Stadt Zürich und Umgebung (see *Address Directory*). Provides general tourist information for the city and canton of Zürich. Also can provide brochures giving information on walking and other activities. Staff speaks German, French and English. Useful publications include:

- *Ausflüge, Aussichtspunkte, Wanderungen und Erholung in Zürichs nächster Umgebung* (in German). A booklet published by the SZU/LAF railway. Describes six walks in areas served by the line. For each walk there is a brief route description, information on train connections, a note on its walking time and a sketch map showing the route, as well as rail and bus lines. Free.

- *Schnell: Bequem ins Schönste Wandergebiet!* (in German). A booklet published by Forchbahn, a local railway line. Gives information on special round-trip tickets and includes four sketch maps showing walking routes between train stations. Gives brief itineraries and walking times for 19 additional walks. Free.

- *Rundfahrt- und Wanderbillette, Winterthur* (in German). One in a series of booklets published by the Schweizerische Bundesbahn (SBB)—the Swiss Federal Railway. Contains seven sketch maps, each showing a series of suggested walks. Information on special train fares within the region covered by each map is also given. Free.

- *Rundfahrt- und Wanderbillette, Zürich* (in German). Similar to the above booklet. Contains 19 sketch maps showing suggested walks. Free.

- *Wald- und Wiesenwandern Wonnen auf dem Uetliberg* (in German, French and English). A leaflet describing three woodland walks in the Uetliberg, near Zürich. Includes a sketch map showing the routes in orange. Free.

- *Zürich für Fussgänger* (in German). A series of leaflets describing walks in and around Zürich. Each includes a sketch map on which routes are shown in orange. Free.

- *Zürich: Unterkunftsverzeichnis* (in German, French and English). A lodging list for the canton of Zürich. Includes a 1:20,000 map of Zürich and a 1:20,000 map of the surrounding district on which the locations of lodgings and campgrounds are shown. Free.

- *Zürichberg: Wandern ohne Auto* (in German). A leaflet issued by the Swiss Auto Club suggesting three short walks in the woods of Zürichberg. Includes a sketch map showing the walks, plus drawings and descriptions of 16 trees found in the forest. Free.

Züricherische Arbeitsgemeinschaft für Wanderwege (see *Address Directory*). Provides walking information for Zürich. Staff speaks German and French.

Maps

Special walkers' maps covering Zürich are available from the Schweizerische Arbeitsgemeinschaft für Wanderwege (see *Address Directory*). They are:

- Wanderkarte 1:25,000, sheets *Tösstal/Zürcher Oberland* and *Limmattae*.
- Wanderkarte 1:50,000, sheet *Kanton Zürich*.

Zürich is also covered by the 1:25,000, 1:50,000 and 1:100,000 Landeskarten published by the Eidgenössiche Landestopographie (see *Address Directory*).

Guidebooks

Available from the Schweizerische Arbeitsgemeinschaft für Wanderwege (see *Address Directory*) and most bookstores:

- *Im Auto zum Wanderweg: 24 Rundwanderungen im Kanton Zürich*, Verlag TCS
- *Auf Wanderwegen im Sihltal und Knonaueramt*, Verlag NZZ
- *Auf Wanderwegen im Zürcher Oberland und Tösstal*, Verlag NZZ
- *Auf Wanderwegen im Zürcher Unterland, Rafzerfeld und Weinland*, Verlag NZZ
- *Auf Wanderwegen Rund im Winterthur*, Verlag Orell Füssli AG
- *Auf Wanderwegen Rund um Zürich*, Verlag Orell Füssli AG

Suggested Walks

Albishorn Tour. From Uetliberg to Sihlbrugg. Through forest and meadows along the crest of the Albishorn ridge southwest of Zürich. Bird's-eye views of the Sihltal, Zürichsee and the city of Zürich directly below and of the broad Mittelland and snowy Alps in the distance. **Walking Time:** 5 to 6 hours. **Difficulty:** Easy. **Path Markings:** Yellow arrows, bars and diamonds.
Maps:
- Wanderkarte 1:50,000, sheet *Kanton Zürich*.
Guidebook:
- *Ausflüge, Aussichtspunkte, Wanderungen und Erholung in Zürichs Nächster Umgebung* (in German). Available from Verkehrsverein der Stadt Zürich und Umgebung.

From Frauenfeld to Muri. Through the rolling Zürich countryside on the Mittelland Route. Pastoral valleys, tidy farmlands, old castles and churches, half-timbered houses and the city of Zürich itself. **Walking Time:** 4 days. **Difficulty:** Easy. **Path Markings:** Yellow arrows, bars and diamonds.
Maps:
- Landeskarte der Schweiz 1:50,000, sheets 216, 225 and 226.
Guidebook:
- *Wanderbuch Mittellandroute* (in German), Kümmerly + Frey.

Cross-Country Skiing

The canton of Zürich has more than 10 ski centers with marked tracks totaling about 100 kilometers. In addition, there is a 10-kilometer marked cross-country ski route at Albiskamm, near the city of Zürich. For full details, see the booklet published by the Schweizerische Arbeitsgemeinschaft für Wanderwege, *Skiwandern/Ski de Randonnée.* You can also obtain sketch maps from the SAW showing marked ski tracks described in the booklet. Finally, the Verkehrsverein der Stadt Zürich und Umgebung can supply sketch maps showing marked ski tracks near many towns in the canton.

Address Directory

A

- *Aargauische Verkehrsvereiningung,* Wanderwege Aarau, Buchenhof, CH-5001 Aarau.
- *The Alpine Club,* 74 South Audley Street, London W1Y 5FF England.
- *Arbeitsgemeinschaft Urner Wanderwege,* Pfisterweg 9, CH-6460 Altdorf. Tel. (044) 2 18 70.
- *Association du Jura Suisse,* see *Schweizerischer Juraverein.*
- *Association Genevoise de Tourisme Pédestre,* Section Genevoise du TCS, Quai G. Ador 2, CH-1211 Genève 3. Tel. (022) 36 58 67.
- *Association Neuchâteloise de Tourisme Pédestre,* rue de Trésor 9, Case postale 812, CH-2001, Neuchâtel. Tel. (038) 25 17 89.
- *Association Neuchatêloise des Skieurs de Fond et de Randonnée,* rue du Tresor 9 (Place des Halles), Case postale 812, CH-2001 Neuchâtel. Tel. (038) 25 17 89.
- *Association Suisse des Stations Climatiques/Schweizerische Vereinigung der Klimakurorte,* rue de la Gare 2, CH-1820 Montreux. Tel. (021) 62 32 20.
- *Association Valaisane de Tourisme Pédestre,* Union Valaisane du Tourisme, CH-1951 Sion. Tel. (027) 22 21 02.
- *Association Vaudoise de Tourisme Pédestre,* Grand rue 100, CH-1110 Morges. Tel. (012) 71 11 62.
- *Au Vieux Campeur,* 2 rue de Latran, F-75005 Paris, France. Tel. (1) 329 12 32.

B

- *BLV Verlagsgesellschaft,* Lothstrasse 29, Postfach 40 03 20, D-8000 Munich 40, Germany.
- *Bergverlag Rudolf Rother,* Landshuter Allee 49, Postfach 67, D-8000 Munich 19, Germany.

• *Berner-Verlag,* D-8311 Velden, Germany.

• *Berner Wanderwege,* Sekretariat, Nordring 10a, Postfach 263, CH-3000 Bern 25. Tel. (031) 42 37 66.

• *Bundner Arbeitsgemeinschaft für Wanderwege (BAW),* Geschäftsstelle, Dreibündenstrasse 35, CH-7000 Chur.

C

• *Chemins de fer du Jura,* rue General-Voirol 1, CH-2710 Tavannes. Tel. (032) 92 27 45.

• *Compagnie des chemins de fer des Montagnes neuchâteloises,* avenue Léopold-Robert 77, CH-2301 La Chaux-de-Fonds. Tel. (039) 22 58 31.

E

• *Eidgenössische Landestopographie/Service Topographique Fédéral,* Seftigenstrasse 264, CH-3084 Wabern. Tel. (031) 54 13 31.

• *Eiselin Sport,* Gerliswilstrasse 26/28, CH-6020 Emmenbrücke. Tel. (041) 55 88 55. Tel. (01) 47 47 47 or (01) 814 14 14.

• *Ente Ticinese per il Turismo,* Piazza Nosetto, CH-6501 Bellinzona. Tel. (092) 25 70 56.

F

• *Fremdenverkehrsverband Kanton Schwyz,* Bahnhofstrasse 63, CH-6430 Schwyz.

G

• *George G. Harrap & Company, Ltd.,* 182-184 High Holborn, London WC1V 7AX, England.

• *Groupe Haute Montagne,* 7 rue la Boétie, F-75008 Paris, France.

H

• *Hallwag Verlag,* Nordring 4, CH-3001 Bern.

• *Hans Huber,* Marktgasse 9, CH-3000 Bern 9.

K

• *Kontanal St.-Gallische Wanderwege,* Kronbergstrasse 17, CH-9000 St. Gallen. Tel. (071) 22 72 83.

• *Kümmerly + Frey,* Hallerstrasse 10, Postfach, CH-3001 Bern. Tel. (031) 23 51 11.

- *Kur- und Verkehrsverein Appenzell Innerrhoden,* Footpath Chairman, Sonnhalde, CH-9050 Appenzell. Tel. (071) 86 10 56.
- *Kurverein Gersau,* CH-6442 Gersau. Tel. (041) 84 12 20.

L

- *Luftseilbahn Beckenried-Klewenalp,* CH-6375 Beckenried. Tel. (041) 64 12 64.
- *Luzerner Wanderwege,* W. Imbach, Weggisgasse 1, CH-6000 Luzern 5. Tel. (041) 22 80 03.

M

- *Maurice Villemin,* République 14, CH-2208 Les Hauts-Geneveys.
- *The Mountaineers Books,* 719 Pike Street, Seattle, Washington 98101, U.S.A.

N

- *Naturfreunde International,* Kurfirstenstrasse 70, CH-8002 Zürich.
- *Nidwaldner Wanderwege,* Stansstad, Buochserstrasse 10, CH-6370 Stans.
- *Nordostschweizerische Verkehrsvereinigung,* Bahnhofplatz 1a, CH-9001 St. Gallen. Tel. (071) 22 62 62.
- *Nordwestschweizerische Verkehrsvereinigung,* Verkehrsverein der Stadt Basel, Blumenrain 2, CH-4000 Basel. Tel. (061) 25 38 11.

O

- *Obwaldner Wanderwege,* Dorfstrasse 6, CH-6072 Sachseln. Tel. (071) 22 72 83.
- *Office du Tourisme du Canton de Vaud,* 10 avenue de la Gare, CH-1002 Lausanne. Tel. (021) 22 77 82.
- *Office Jurassien du Tourisme,* rue de l'Hôtel de Ville 16, Case postale 338, CH-2740 Moutier. Tel. (032) 93 18 24.
- *Office National Suisse du Tourisme,* see *Schweizerische Verkehrszentrale.*
- *Office Neuchâtelois du Tourisme,* rue du Trésor 9 (Place des Halles), Case postale 812, CH-2001 Neuchâtel. Tel. (038) 25 17 89.

P

- *Pilatus-Bahnen,* Grendelstrasse 2, CH-6002 Luzern. Tel. (041) 23 00 66.

- *Publizitäts- und Reisedienst Bern-Lötschberg-Simplon Railway (BLS),* Genfergasse 10, CH-3001 Bern.

R

- *Rigibahn-Gesellschaft,* CH-6354 Vitznau. Tel. (041) 83 11 18.

S

- *SAC,* see *Schweizer Alpen-Club.*
- *SAW,* see *Schweizerische Arbeitsgemeinschaft für Wanderwege.*
- *SJH,* see *Schweizerischer Bund für Jugendherbergen.*
- *Schâffhäuser Arbeitsgemeinschaft für Wanderwege,* Hegaustrasse 7, CH-8200 Schaffhausen. Tel. (053) 4 75 79.
- *Schweizer Alpen-Club (SAC)/Club Alpin Suisse (CAS),* Helvetiaplatz 4, CH-3005 Bern. Tel. (031) 43 36 11.
- *Schweizer Hotelierverein,* Monbijoustrasse 31, Postfach 2657, CH-3001 Bern.
- *Schweizer Reisekasse,* Neuengasse 15, CH-3001 Bern. Tel. (031) 22 66 33.
- *Schweizer Reisepost,* Viktoriastrasse 72, CH-3030 Bern. Tel. (031) 62 38 33.
- *Schweizer Touristenverein, "Die Naturfreunde" (TVN)/Union Touristique Suisse, "Amis de la Nature" (AN),* Birmensdorferstrasse 67, CH-8036 Zürich. Tel. (01) 23 99 83.
- *Schweizer Verband der Bergsteigerschulen,* Promenade 129, CH-7260 Davos-Dorf. Tel. (083) 33 7 24.
- *Schweizerische Arbeitsgemeinschaft für Wanderwege (SAW)/Association Suisse de Tourisme Pédestre (ASTP),* Im Hirshalm 49, CH-4125 Riehen. Tel. (061) 49 15 35.
- *Schweizerische Bundesbahnen (SBB),* Reisedienst SBB, CH-3030 Bern. Tel. (031) 60 28 24.
- *Schweizerische Klimakurorte,* see *Association Suisse des Stations Climatiques.*
- *Schweizerische Rettungsflugwacht,* Dufourstrasse 43, CH-8008 Zürich. Tel. (01) 69 22 11.
- *Schweizerische Verkehrszentrale/Office National Suisse du Tourisme,* Bellariastrasse 38, CH-8027 Zürich. Tel. (01) 202 37 37.
- *Schweizerischer Bergführerverband,* rue des Vergers 4, CH-1950 Sion.
- *Schweizerischer Bund für Jugendherbergen (SJH)/Fédération Suisse des Auberges de la Jeunesse (ASJH),* Postfach 132, Hochhaus 9, CH-8958 Spreitenbach. Tel. (056) 71 40 46.

- *Schweizerischer Bund für Naturschutz*, Sekretariat, Wartenbergstrasse 22, CH-4052 Basel. Tel. (061) 42 74 42.
- *Schweizerischer Camping- und Caravanning-Verband (SCCV)/ Fédération Suisse de Camping et de Caravanning (FSCC)*, Habsburgerstrasse 35, CH-6000 Luzern. Tel. (041) 23 48 22.
- *Schweizerischer Juraverein/Association du Jura Suisse*, Sekretariat, CH-4600 Olten.
- *Schweizerischer Ski-Verband (SSV)/Fédération Suisse de Ski (FSS)*, Haus des Skisportes, Schlosshaldenstrasse 32, CH-3000 Bern 32. Tel. (031) 43 44 44.
- *Schwyzer Wanderwege*, Waldweg 14, CH-6410 Goldau. Tel. (041) 82 22 33.
- *Service Topographique Fédéral*, see *Eidgenössische Landestopographie*.
- *Sierra Club Books*, 530 Bush Street, San Francisco, California 94108, U.S.A.
- *Solothurner Wanderwege*, CH-4500 Solothurn.
- *Südwestdeutscher Verlag*, Postfach 5760, D-6800 Mannheim 1, Germany.
- *Swiss National Tourist Office, London:* Swiss Centre, 1 New Coventry Street, London W1V 3HG, England. Tel. (01) 734 1921.
- *Swiss National Tourist Office, New York:* The Swiss Center, 608 Fifth Avenue, New York, New York 10020. Tel. (212) 757-5944.

T

- *Touring-Club der Schweiz/Touring Club Suisse*, 9 rue Pierr-Fatio, CH-1200 Genève. Tel. (022) 36 60 00.

U

- *Union Fribourgeoise du Tourisme*, Route Neuve 8, Case postale 901, CH-1700 Fribourg. Tel. (037) 23 33 63.
- *Union Valaisanne du Tourisme*, CH-1951 Sion 1. Tel. (027) 22 21 02.

V

- *Verband Appenzell Ausserrhoden Verkehrsvereine*, K. Fässler, CH-9038 Rehetobel. Tel. (071) 95 18 09.
- *Verkehrsbüro Brunnen*, Bahnhofstrasse 32, CH-6440 Brunnen. Tel. (043) 31 17 77.
- *Verkehrsbüro Einsiedeln*, CH-8840 Einsiedeln. Tel. (055) 53 25 10.

- *Verkehrsverband Zentralschweiz,* Pilatusstrasse 14, CH-6002 Luzern 2. Tel. (041) 22 70 55.
- *Verkehrsverein Alpnach,* Société de Dévelopement, Vierwaldstattersee, Alpnach. Tel. (041) 76 12 04 or 76 12 44.
- *Verkehrsverein Berner Oberland,* Jungfraustrasse 36, CH-3800 Interlaken. Tel. (036) 22 26 21.
- *Verkehrsverein Buochs,* Beckenriederstrasse 8, CH-6374 Buochs. Tel. (041) 64 20 64.
- *Verkehrsverein der Stadt Zürich und Umgebung,* Bahnhofbrücke 1, CH-8023 Zürich. Tel. (01) 211 12 56.
- *Verkehrsverein Engelberg,* CH-6390 Engelberg. Tel. (041) 94 11 61.
- *Verkehrsverein Ennetbürgen,* CH-6373 Ennetbürgen. Tel. (041) 64 33 84.
- *Verkehrsverein für Graubünden,* Ottostrasse 6, Postfach, CH-7001 Chur. Tel. (081) 22 13 60.
- *Verkehrsverein Glarnerland und Walensee,* Footpath Chairman, CH-8755 Ennenda. Tel. (058) 61 15 52.
- *Verkehrsverein Melchtal,* CH-6067 Melchtal. Tel. (041) 67 12 37.
- *Verkehrsverein Sarnen am See,* CH-6060 Sarnen. Tel. (041) 66 40 55.
- *Verkehrsverein Schwyz,* Ob der Kirche, CH-6430 Schwyz. Tel. (043) 21 34 46.
- *Verlag des SAC/Editions du CAS,* Postfach, CH-8304 Wallisellen.

W

- *Waldenburgerbahn AG,* CH-4437 Waldenburg. Tel. (061) 84 71 09.
- *Wanderwege beider Basel,* Basel Sekretariat, Vrenelisgärtli 6, CH-4102 Binningen. Tel. (061) 38 96 73.
- *Wanderwegkommission des Kantons Thurgau,* Schlosshaldenstrasse 4, 8570 Weinfelden. Tel. (072) 5 02 23.
- *Wanderweg-Kommission des VKZ,* Kantonsforstamt Zug, P. Güttinger, CH-6300 Zug. Tel. (042) 23 12 33.
- *Weather Forecasts* (Wetterbericht/Prévisions météorologique): Tel. 162.
- *West Col Productions,* 1 Meadow Close, Goring-on-Thames, Reading, Berkshire RG8 9AA, England.

Z

- *Züricherische Arbeitsgemeinschaft für Wanderwege,* Eggweg 5, CH-8620 Wetzikon. Tel. (01) 930 20 36.

A Quick Reference

In a hurry? Turn to the pages listed below. They will give you the most important information on walking in Switzerland.

Search & Rescue, page 133.

Weather Forecasts, page 100.

Associations to Contact for Information:
On Walking, page 100.
On Switzerland's Principal Footpaths, page 135.
Tourist Information, page 132.

Maps, page 106.

Guidebooks, page 108.

Equipment, page 122.

Address Directory, page 204.

About the Author

CRAIG EVANS is an avid walker, winter mountaineer, writer, editor and photographer. He worked his way through college as a reporter for the *San Jose Mercury-News* in San Jose, California, and wrote an award-winning student travel publication, *Tripping*, which was distributed through West Coast student travel offices from 1973 to 1975. Mr. Evans then spent a year as editor of BACKPACKER Magazine and was project editor for the revised edition of BACKPACKER's *Backpacking Equipment Buyer's Guide* (a comprehensive, 285-page book that includes articles on how virtually every type of hiking equipment is made, as well as individual product reports on more than 1,000 pieces of gear). He has written articles on walking and traveling in Europe, and compiled reports on lightweight stoves, binoculars, winter tents and winter footwear for the equipment sections in BACKPACKER Magazine.

Mr. Evans visited Europe for the first time in 1971, and during the next two years traveled and walked in virtually every one of the Western European countries. He has since returned to Europe six times.

In 1973, he spent six months in the Alps, walking more than 2,000 kilometers (1,300 miles) from Menton, France, to Trieste, Italy. He has also led walking tours in the Alps.

For the *On Foot Through Europe* series, Mr. Evans worked for three years compiling information, checking facts and writing. He visited virtually every one of Europe's major walking organizations and alpine clubs, taking time to accompany members on the trails they know best. In the end, he had collected more than 450 kilos (half a ton) of information in 12 languages—the information from which this book was distilled.

To this, he added the experience gained backpacking in the East and West coast mountains of the United States, the Arizona desert and the Canadian Rockies.

Born in Klamath Falls, Oregon, in 1949, he holds a Bachelor of Arts degree in English from the California State University, San Jose. He now lives in Washington, D.C.